The Raven's Feather

by

Tamalyn Nicholas

E-Book ISBN: 1-892745-15-1
Handcrafted Print Book ISBN: 1-892745-14-3

For information on Petals of Life, please contact the publisher at:

http://www.petalsoflife.com

MDJ, Inc.
Petals of Life
231 Oil Well Road, Suite C
Jackson, TN 38305
(901) 668-6622
(901) 664-2743 Fax
petals@petalsoflife.com
http://www.petalsoflife.com/

D1378302

Dedication

For Diane~

Thank you for your love, laughter & encouragement.
Save me a seat in God's library.

~Tamalyn~

PROLOGUE

How manifold and strong a bond
The child was bound to the father.
-King Lear

The unwanted sounds drifted from the nursery, echoing through the hallway, seemingly magnifying as they reached his ears. The father stirred from his deep slumber, pushing away dreams of sailing through the clear blue Caribbean. The gentle bobbing of the waves tempted him back to sleep.

The cries, insistent and penetrating, came even louder now. His wife groaned and buried her head beneath her pillow.

"Not again," she moaned. "It's only been fifteen minutes."

Her husband reached over, patting her hip. "I'll take a turn. Go back to sleep."

He swung his feet out of the bed, pushed his slippers aside and padded down the hallway in bare feet. The baby's cries were now at full roar.

The smiling father entered the room. "Hello there, little one. Don't you know it's time for you to be asleep?"

He reached into the crib, lifting the baby with a strong, sure grip.

"Ah, yes, I forgot. You're right. Your days and nights are supposed to be flip-flopped now. But why don't we give your mom a break?"

He checked the baby's backside. "Your diaper's dry. I know you just ate. The room is warm. Do you just need a little tender, loving care?"

He carried the baby to the rocking chair near the window and sat down, gently stroking the baby's cheek with his fingertips. He lowered his head to kiss the tiny nose. "Okay, sweet stuff. Let's just rock for a while. Daddy will stay with you as long as you like."

As he rocked, he began to hum. The baby, sucking on two fingers, settled in. The father leaned his head against the back of the chair, still humming. Within minutes, father and child slept.

Through the father's dreams came memories of another child. A perfect, golden-haired boy with dimples and wide set blue eyes. A boy who had slept in a room just like this. A boy who had tragically lost his life when his tiny head had slipped between the bars of his crib, his fragile neck twisting until he could no longer breathe.

3

That crib. That beautiful Wyndham's Deluxe crib that his wife had insisted they buy for their firstborn. The crib with the intricate detailing of gently curving flowers and balloons painted at each end. The crib that had bars spaced too far apart. The crib that he'd smashed in his anger and his grief. The crib that he had cursed as he watched the flames in the fireplace consume it.

The man jerked in his sleep, as if the flames still scorched his face. The baby in his arms stirred and began to cry again. The father leaned over and kissed the fluttering eyelids, the wriggling fingers, and the tear-streaked cheeks.

"Hush, little one. Daddy will always take care of you. Sleep now. Everything's all right. Daddy's right here."

CHAPTER ONE

With cunning hast thou filch'd my daughter's heart.
-Midsummer Night's Dream

"Jordan, what time are you girls..." The question was cut off mid-stream by the slamming of the front door. Emerson Blake looked skyward, asking the good Lord for patience. His wife slipped up behind him and wrapped her arms around his waist. Her chuckle was familiar and warm.

"Leaving?" she finished for him.

"I guess the slamming of the door answers my question."

As the two parents watched through the windows at either side of the door, their daughter's best friend, Paige Kendell, ran across the street, beach towel wrapped around her waist, her bag of surf and sand necessities thrown over her shoulder. They lost sight of her as she ran into the garage.

Squealing tires announced their departure. The two girls waved from the small silver convertible as Jordan pulled swiftly out of the driveway. "Bye, Moms and Dads," they hollered, first to the Kendell home, then to the Blake. Impish grins on their faces, they knew they had achieved success...a trip to the beach, while they were both grounded. It was a good day's work!

"We did it," Paige shouted gleefully.

"Did you doubt it for a minute?" Jordan asked, skillfully maneuvering her car into the next lane. She waved at the trucker who had slowed to let them over. "After all, they got their way. They want us to call when we're going to be late, and now we will. And they want us to be more careful about who we ride with. So, we'll do that, too. Besides, we kissed up pretty good." She wrinkled her nose and gave a small laugh. "We're pretty lucky to have the folks we've got, you know that?"

Paige lifted her ponytail over the back of the seat, leaned her head back and closed her eyes. "Yeah, we are. I guess I'm just not done giving them grief. We're supposed to, you know. It's our job as teenagers."

Jordan smiled. "Then we haven't done our job very well. We're way too goody-two-shoes. Maybe we should get tattoos and pierce our noses."

"I think we have to be drunk sailors to do that. Besides, I'm not into pain."

"And you want to be a doctor? You don't think all of those shots you'll give those poor, innocent children will cause pain?"

"That's what nurses are for," Paige sighed. "I'm there to stop the pain. I keep telling you that. Now, be quiet.

I'm going to take a nap."

Silence reigned for a few moments as Jordan's mind raced. "Paige?"

"Yeah?"

"Why are we going to Boston for college?"

Paige lifted her head and adjusted her sunglasses. "Because we've always said we were going to, I guess."

"Why can't we go to school here? We love California. Our families are right here. Now you've got that adorable little sister. How can you possibly leave her behind?"

"The Brat?"

Jordan gave an exaggerated sideways look at her friend. "Yeah, The Brat. You know, that little girl you worship so much you even used to change her diapers? The one that you buy stuffed tigers for. The one that makes you take her to Baskin-Robbins for ice cream every Saturday after soccer games."

Paige grinned at her friend, then leaned her head back against the seat again. "Oh, that one. Yeah, I would like to stay a bit closer to her--I waited long enough to have a sister. I guess I shouldn't abandon her. At least, not quite yet. Maybe in a few years. Like, when she's getting close to becoming a teenager. I hear they can be quite impossible, you know."

Jordan smiled in satisfaction. "Yeah, I think I've heard that somewhere." She pulled into the parking lot near lifeguard station number twenty-three, the pre-selected site for their Senior Class Beach Trip. "Ready? I see Jonathan over there."

"Yeah, right next to Bitsy Johnson. Don't you ever give up?"

"FYI, they broke up last weekend."

"Ah, so that's why you don't want to go away to college. The muddy waters are beginning to clear."

Jordan threw a beach ball at her friend. "As if! You know Jonathan and I are just friends."

"As if!" Paige repeated and dodged the towel that suddenly flew toward her head.

*

"Ah, our beautiful California girls. Pity the poor surfing dudes who get scoped by our babes." Emerson grinned at the thought.

"You've been spending too much time with the girls, lately, dear. You're starting to sound like them."

"Cool."

"No, that one's from our generation. They've just borrowed it."

"Gnarly?"

"I think that was a few years ago."

6

"Why don't we go spend some quality time together? You know, since we have the house to ourselves. Then you can find better things to do with that smart mouth of yours than criticize my English." Emerson draped his arm around his wife's shoulders and steered her toward the stairs.

As they ascended, Emerson's curiosity took control. "I thought the girls were grounded. How did that wild child of ours wriggle out of it this time?"

Celeste paused on the steps. "She hugged me," she said matter-of-factly.

"She hugged you?" Emerson raised his eyebrows. "That's it? She hugged you? She was an hour and a half late getting home last Friday night, and all she has to do to be paroled is to hug you?"

Celeste smiled up at her husband. "Yeah, that pretty much took care of it. That, and the groveling and the bathroom cleaning."

"She cleaned her own bathroom? She really wanted freedom."

"No, dear, she cleaned yours."

"Ooh," he shuddered. "She was really desperate. Still," he said contemplatively, "I'm amazed at your lack of resolve. You're much too soft on that girl. You give in at the drop of a hat. I, on the other hand, would have been much tougher on her. I would have made her clean all of the bathrooms and help Milly scrub the kitchen."

He continued up the stairs, resolve built into every step. Holding his hand out behind him, he felt satisfaction as Celeste slipped her hand into his.

"Of course, Mr. Defense Attorney. You're just so tough. And *how* many hardened criminals did you represent last year?"

"Hey, everyone deserves a fair trial. And quit changing the subject."

"Which subject were we focusing on? The girls and their commuted sentence, or your plans for this morning?"

Emerson stopped on the top step and swept Celeste into his arms. Nuzzling her neck, he mumbled, "Point taken."

He moved to her earlobe. "But I still say you're too soft on that girl."

Back to her neck. "I wish I'd had you for a mom when I was a kid."

Celeste slid her hand down her husband's back. "No, you don't."

"And why is that?"

"Because you like having me for a wife."

*

Over the years, Liza Kendell and Celeste Blake had teased their daughters about wearing out the blacktop between their two homes. When they weren't traipsing back and forth from one home to the other, they had their ears glued to the telephone.

Earlier that morning, Celeste had found Jordan sitting on the front porch, her ear pressed to the telephone receiver. Across the street, seated on the porch swing at the Kendell home, was Paige, telephone in hand.

"Who are you talking to, honey?" Celeste asked in growing disbelief.

The look she received from her daughter told her that she was being mistaken for an imbecile. She wasn't offended. She knew from experience that any teenage angst and rebellion coming from Jordan would be mild. So, she reverted to the age-old response of children...she stuck her tongue out at her daughter.

"Mom! Who do you think? I'm talking to Paige," came the impatient answer.

Celeste looked once again at the now-waving teenager across the street and waved back.

"Paige says to tell you, 'Hi'."

Celeste didn't know whether to return the greeting via her daughter and the telephone, yell it across the street, or wave again. She settled for a wave and a question.

"Why don't you just go over and talk to her?"

Jordan's you-couldn't-possibly-understand look was firmly etched onto her face. "Because she's on the phone. Besides, you and Mrs. Kendell grounded us, remember?"

"Thanks for the reminder. But I seem to recall that means no telephone, as well."

"This is important, Mom. We're talking about how to get ungrounded."

"Well, finish your conversation quickly, honey. I'll be interested to see how your plan progresses." With a grin and a final wave to the girl across the street, Celeste returned to the house.

The groveling commenced fifteen minutes later. As did the cleaning. Mr. Blake now had a spotless bathroom. Dr. Kendell's home office was freshly vacuumed and dusted.

*

Jordan Blake and Paige Kendell had known each other all of their lives. Literally. They were born on the same day, in the same town, in the same hospital. Placed next to each other in the maternity ward nursery, they were destined to become the best of friends.

The Kendells moved into the house across the street from the Blakes two months prior to Jordan's and Paige's arrival date. Franklin and Liza Kendell seemed, to outsiders, to have a perfect life. She a pediatrician, he a judge, their lives were happy and fulfilling. And yet, the two longed for a child. After thirteen years of marriage and numerous, heart-wrenching disappointments, they nearly gave up hope. Paige was not only a welcome surprise, she was their little miracle.

For Emerson and Celeste Blake, Jordan's arrival was the result of a perfect calculation. Emerson's law practice soared in its success. The investments he made with his inheritance from his parents' estate were all secure and earning him daily kudos and wealth. Celeste had just signed the papers for the opening of her fifteenth floral shop. Life was perfect, and Jordan was the icing on the cake.

When the two women went into labor and arrived at the hospital only minutes apart, the Judge declared that the families were meant to be united. When Paige arrived at one-fifteen a.m. and Jordan made her first appearance a little after five, the Judge stated that the miracle was complete, and that the two little angels and their parents would always be family.

Petite, with blonde hair and clear blue eyes, Paige was generally chosen to be the angel of the annual Christmas pageant at church.

Jordan, slightly taller, with shining brown eyes and soft, dark brown hair, made her first Christmas program appearance as the Baby Jesus. After that, she was a donkey, a sheep, and in later years, Mary. Her Sunday School teachers despaired when she tried repeatedly to convince them to let her be a wise man. On her thirteenth appearance in the play, the teachers having given in to her demands, Jordan proudly carried her precious package of myrrh to the newest baby in the manger.

But on this day, at this moment, Emerson Blake was not remembering how beautiful she was as Baby Jesus. He wasn't thinking about how cute she'd been as a wise man. He was thinking that the donkey was the most appropriate role she'd ever had. Stubborn. That was it, he thought to himself, even as Celeste ran her fingers over his chest. That girl is just plain stubborn.

Celeste fluffed the pillows, snuggled up against her husband and waited, amused by his preoccupation. She knew that their lovemaking was already forgotten and his thoughts were back on their daughter.

"I guess it's a good thing," he finally spoke.

Celeste pushed Emerson's hair from his brow. "What is, dear?"

"Her stubbornness. After all, architecture is still pretty much a man's world. If she's going to make it, she's going to have to be stubborn and fight for what she wants."

"Yes, she will. And she's already off to a good start with that."

9

"Yes, she is."

"I guess it's a good thing that she negotiates things with us. It teaches her how to make her way in life."

"Yes."

"So, I guess it's okay that you ungrounded her."

Celeste raised up on her elbow and teased the hair on his chest with her free hand. "And?"

"Well, I just want to make sure that we're good parents and we're doing everything we can to bring her up right."

"You know what they say, Emerson. The best gift parents can give their children is to love each other." The end of her sentence was muffled as she lowered her lips to his.

Emerson smiled. "Yes, dear."

Four years later...

"Men!" Jordan burst out in disgust and anger as she slammed the telephone down. "I've wasted three and a half years of my life on that jerk."

Paige rubbed her eyes with her fingertips and slammed her book shut. "I assume we're talking about Jonathan."

Jordan threw herself onto the couch, pulling a pillow over her face. Her voice was muffled as she answered. "But of course. You're never going to believe this."

She peeked out from under the fringe of the pillow. "He just called me to tell me that he and Bitsy are getting married."

"Bitsy? Johnson?" Paige nearly shrieked the words. "But we haven't heard anything from her since graduation."

"Well, apparently Jon has heard a great deal from her. They've been corresponding for the past year." She threw the pillow across the room and sat up. "I don't know whether to laugh or cry. I'm not sure I even believe this. How could I have been so completely unaware?"

Paige stood up and walked over to the couch. She sat down next to Jordan and put her arm around her shoulder. "I'm sorry, Jory. I really thought he was going to be the one. You two have grown so close."

"Well, I guess I have two choices. I can sit around feeling sorry for myself, get rip-roaring drunk, and get someone to prescribe tranquilizers for me, or I can go eat a double scoop of Baskin-Robbins' Chocolate Fudge ice cream and then get on with my life. Which do you think I should choose?"

"Can I have Pralines and Cream?"

"Without a doubt."

"Okay, I pick the second option. I'm buying."

"No more men. They take up too much time and

energy, anyway."

Paige wasn't quite ready to completely write off the male of the species. "Come on, Jordan, we just haven't met the right ones yet."

"Do you know how many aging women there are out there who are saying the same thing? Maybe there aren't any right ones left. I've always heard that the best ones are either married or gay. That's it! I'm getting rid of you and getting a gay best friend. That way I'll have the best of both worlds."

Paige dipped into Jordan's bowl and stole a bite of chocolate ice cream. "Mmmm! Good. You can't get rid of me. You can have the gay friend, but you have to keep me, too, 'cause I understand you."

Jordan took another bite. "Yeah, and if I'm too busy to spend time with you, your heart doesn't break. Wow, Paige, I just realized something. You're even better than having a dog."

"Gee, thanks," Paige groaned. "I'm sure that's my finest compliment. For you're information, I'm still not giving up on men. I think there's still a good one out there somewhere."

"Fine. You go find him. Meanwhile, I'm going to be too busy. We've got finals coming up. I need to focus all of my time and energy on those. Then, once I start graduate school, I know I won't have any extra time on my hands. So, that settles it. By the way, how, exactly, are you going to find time for a man once you start medical school in the fall?"

"When the right one comes along, I'll make the time. I have it all planned out. He'll be worth the effort."

"Should I start shopping for my bridesmaid's dress?"

Paige wrinkled her nose at Jordan. "You're really pushing it, you know. Just because I'm still willing to be romantic doesn't mean I'm not realistic. I know he's not going to just come walking through that door and sweep me off my feet. But, I really believe I'll find him eventually. And when I do, do you want his brother?"

"Only if he has absolutely nothing in common with Jonathan." Jordan finished the last of her ice cream. "Maybe I'll try the Banks children's method."

"The Banks children?"

"You know, from Mary Poppins. I'll make up a list of requirements, then you can rip it up, throw it in the fireplace, and the perfect person will show up."

"Perfect?"

"Well, not exactly. I just want someone with a good sense of humor, someone who knows how to relax and have fun and can sit on the beach and not worry about the sand in his shoes. Someone who has a normal, healthy amount of self-esteem and a generous amount of intelligence. Preferably someone who is fairly nice to look at, not pretty, mind you, but attractive. With a nice, strong, but cuddly shape..." Jordan stopped, mid-explanation, chuckling. "Okay, I want Mr. Perfect. And until I find him, my classes are my life."

"Works for me. Speaking of work," Paige looked at her watch, "shouldn't we get back and hit the books?"

"That would be the responsible thing to do."

They were climbing into Paige's car when Jordan paused. She leaned her arms on the roof and rested her chin on her wrists. "You know, this really does hurt. I'm trying not to feel it, but it hurts. It feels like something inside of me just broke."

"I know. I wish I could fix it for you."

Jordan looked at her gratefully. "I know. Thanks."

"Why don't we leave our books for a few days and head home?"

"Home home? As in, where our parents live?"

"Yep. Home, where you can sit by the pool and have Hendricks and Milly pamper you endlessly. Home, where your mother will help you to feel better and your father will treat you like you're the most precious little girl on the face of the planet."

"Oh, that home." Jordan smiled wistfully. "Yeah, I'd like that. But only for a couple of days, okay? Then we've got to study."

"Deal."

But what they found when they returned home changed their plans. They had only begun to experience heartbreak. The two days stretched into two weeks. Studying would have to wait.

CHAPTER TWO

As wicked dew as e'er my mother brush'd
With raven's feather from unwholesome fen,
drop on you both.
- The Tempest

Jordan and Paige drove home on Friday morning, ready to relax by the pool, possibly rousing themselves to raid kitchens, but definitely planning to "psyche themselves up" for their last weeks of classes. They laughed as they drove up the street lined majestically with palm trees. Liza's beloved rose bushes greeted them with newborn fragrance as they went up the drive of the Kendell home.

Jordan looked up at the house, admiring the Spanish ingenuity in building. She turned and looked through the palms across the street to see the Blake home, designed to model her parents' favorite Swiss chalet. "I guess it was looking at these two wonderful houses all my life that made me want to be an architect."

"I always thought it was the building block set your folks bought for you when you were eighteen months old. That set must have been more elaborate than the one Frank Lloyd Wright's mother bought for him."

Jordan laughed at the memory of the blocks. They came in assorted shapes and sizes, some painted to resemble bricks, others to look like the walls of a log cabin. The set included directions for building various types of buildings, houses, churches, schools, gymnasiums. When Jordan was two years old, she ate page one of the instructions. When she was three, she made page two into a paper airplane. When she was four, page three became more intriguing, and she built a house like the one in the picture. But, she explained to her mother, this room is too little, so I changed it.

"I don't know about the influence the blocks had on me, but I do know that I'm going to build the most wonderful houses in the world, like Mr. Wright's Fallingwater House. And they won't just be houses, they'll be homes. Like ours."

Paige put her arm around her friend's waist and gave her a loving squeeze. "You'll do it, too. And my home will be the first one."

Jordan winked at her. "Oh yeah, little Doc. Just when do you think you'll be able to afford one of my creations?"

In her best effort to mimic W.C. Fields, Paige responded, "Not to worry, my dear. It'll be sooner than you think." Then, in a more natural voice, "Come on, Jory, help me carry my bags in. You have to tell Mom and Pop 'hullo' before you desert me."

13

"How you can call a respected judge 'Pop,' I'll never know," mumbled Jordan as she lifted the largest of the two bags from the back seat. They entered the house, dumping the bags at their feet. "Sure is quiet in here. Where is everyone?"

Paige stepped beneath the archway of the den and glanced around. Seeing no one, she yelled, "Hullo, anybody home?" The house remained quiet. She began to reason aloud. "Today is Suzi's last day of school before her vacation starts, so she won't be home until three. Mom must be catching a baby, but Pop..." Seeing Jordan's grin, she corrected herself, "um...*Father* said he'd be home to give me a proper greeting."

"Maybe he's helping your Mom catch the baby."

"What? No, you dope. In the delivery room. The pediatrician has to be there to take care of the baby as soon as it's born. Maybe Daddy ran to the store. He loves hardware stores, you know. He likes to fancy himself a great fixer-upper. But Hannah, or somebody, should be here."

The girls turned as they heard the front door open behind them. They looked surprised as the Kendell's cook/housekeeper walked in, her eyes red from recent tears.

"Hannah, what's wrong?"

"Oh, Paige, your Mama and Daddy will be so glad you're home."

"Where are they? What's happened?"

"I've just gotten back from Suzi's school. She never showed up for her classes today. Mrs. Dugan, the principal, is quite worried."

"Well, stop worrying. I'll bet she just went shopping. She probably wanted to get me a welcome-home present," Paige tried to reassure the nearly-distraught woman.

But Jordan knew that Paige was concerned as well. Suzanne Kendell was definitely a spoiled brat. She pushed the household rules beyond the limits, keeping her parents and Hannah on their toes. But the child loved school. She often attended class even when she was ill, not wanting to miss out on anything, only to be sent home mid-morning because her teachers knew she'd be better off in bed.

"Where are Judge and Mrs. Kendell?" she asked.

"The Judge went to the shopping mall to look for her. He thought the same way you did, Paige. Mrs. Kendell went to the police department."

"Where can we look?" asked Jordan.

"You'd better run home and let your folks know we made it home. I'll wait here for Mom and Pop and we'll take things from there."

Paige walked out to the car with Jordan. "There's got to be a logical explanation for all of this. I'll call you as soon as I hear anything."

Jordan drove slowly down the drive, across the street, and toward the Blake home. Celeste was in the sitting room at the front of the house, and when she heard the car drive up, she met Jordan at the door.

"Hello, sweetheart. I'm so glad you're home. Did you have a good trip?" she asked as she hugged her daughter.

"Yes, Mom. It was fine." Jordan kissed her mother on the cheek and led her back to the sitting room. Let's sit down, Mom."

Celeste rang for tea. Hendricks, the Blakes' 'do-everything man,' as Jordan always referred to him, welcomed her home. "We always miss you when you're not here. And I suppose I'd better tell Milly to put lots of honey on the tea tray, right?"

"Of course, Henny. Couldn't drink it without the good stuff."

When the butler went to the kitchen to tell his wife to dig out the honey, Jordan asked her mother if anyone had seen Suzi.

"Well, no, dear. She hasn't been over for a couple of days. She came over the other night for some of Milly's gingerbread cookies, but I believe that was the last time she was here. Why?"

"It seems that she's missing."

"That girl! She's always fretting her parents so."

"Mom, she didn't even show up for school today. Has she ever done that before?"

"No, of course not. She skips out on a lot of things, but never school. She probably just had a better offer today, and she'll be home for dinner with some good excuse."

But Suzanne Kendell was not home for dinner. She was not home for clean clothes, money, or meals. For five days, the Kendell and Blake households barely survived the chaos. It seemed to Jordan that her mother spent more time consoling the distraught Liza than the police spent looking for the missing child.

"I'm sorry, Mrs. Kendell," Neil Larson, the police captain told her. "We just don't have any leads."

Jordan was angry at the lack of progress on the case. The two families sat in the Kendell den one evening, listening as Neil explained that they would just have to wait for more clues. Jordan's temper finally got the better of her. "Come on, Neil," she exploded. "A ten-year-old child can't just disappear. Someone must have seen her someplace."

"Please, Jordan," said the Judge wearily. "I'm sure they're doing everything they can to find her. We just have to have faith."

"Yes, I know," she smiled at him. "Faith can move mountains, and so can we. Come on, Neil." Taking the young man's arm, she said, "Let's go find a little girl."

*

Suzi and her friend Debi got off the school bus, full of Friday excitement. Today was special. Not only was their vacation about to start, but Paige was coming home.

As always, the girls sat at the back, their favorite seat being the last bench that spanned the entire width of the bus. They giggled and pretended to knock one another's books out of their hands, and waited for the other students to disembark before they walked down the aisle and down the steps leading to the door.

The bus was running late that morning, and consequently the other children walked quickly towards their classrooms. But Suzi and Debi were dawdlers, despite their parents' endless endeavors to speed them up. As always, they walked slowly up the sidewalk toward the brick building.

As they neared the corner by the flagpole, a man in a brown leather jacket emblazoned with orange and green patches and emblems stepped out in front of them. His hairline was receding, his light brown hair looking darker than its natural color because of the grease. He smiled at them, revealing a crooked, badly-stained front right tooth.

Debi instinctively grabbed Suzi's arm and pulled her more quickly towards the front door of the school. Suzi tried to look away from the man, but something about him seemed familiar. Where had she seen him before?

The man was faster and stronger than the girls. Before they could round the corner, he reached out, grabbing Suzi's right arm.

"Let go of me. I have to go to school."

"Come on, little girl. I jus' wanna talk to you for a minute. Come over here."

Debi pulled on Suzi's left arm. Suzi tugged her right arm, trying to get it out of the man's firm grip. Debi was frightened, and her voice reflected her fear. "We have to go. Our teachers will wonder where we are if we don't go inside."

The man looked around, fear now etching his ragged, pock-marked features. He grabbed Suzi around the shoulders, his arm reaching around her chest, clutching her close to his stomach. His other hand covered her mouth. He glared at Debi. "You go on inside. I don't want nothin' to do with you. And don't tell nobody about me. If you do, I'll hurt her real bad. You jus' pretend like you never seen me."

The man began dragging Suzi around the corner of the school. Debi stood rooted in her tracks. She stared at the man's face, as if willing him to release Suzi. Suzi began to cry, and Debi saw the terror on her face. Her feet loosened from the sidewalk, and she took a step towards her friend.

16

The man saw her move. He pulled Suzi another foot and hissed at Debi, "You stupid, girl? I told you I'd hurt her. Now, get to school. And if anyone asks you, you don' know what happened to your friend. Got it?"

As he pulled Suzi around the corner, Debi hesitated. They'd been taught in school that if a stranger tried to take them or hurt them, they were to scream, "No," and run for help. But this was different. He had Suzi. If she screamed, he would hurt her.

Debi walked slowly towards the school, stopping at the foot of the steps and sitting down. The door opened behind her and Mrs. Dugan, the principal stepped out. "Debi, is something wrong?"

Debi started crying as the shock of the past few minutes' events wore off. Mrs. Dugan came and sat next to her, her arm hugging Debi's shoulder. "Debi?"

"Mrs. Dugan," she said, and thought, he'll hurt her, I can't tell. "I just don't feel too good."

"Do you want to go home, dear?"

"Yes, please, I feel like I'm gonna throw up."

Mrs. Dugan took immediate action. With her arm still around Debi's shoulders, she pulled her to her feet, leading her up the steps. "You come and lie down in the nurse's office. She's not here today, but you can rest for a bit."

She led Debi towards one of the three cots next to the nurse's desk, and put a trash can next to the head of the cot. "Just in case," she smiled at the pale, trembling girl. Must be the flu, she thought, and wished fervently that the school district could afford full-time nurses for each school. "You wait right here, Debi. I'll go call your mother, and I'll let your teacher know that you're ill."

*

The man pulled Suzi down the alley behind the school, to a small white car he'd hidden behind an old, abandoned incinerator. He unlocked the trunk, explaining, "I know this ain't gonna be too comfy, but I can't let anybody see you riding with me. Now, you just climb on in. See, I put pillows in there to make it softer for you. Now stop cryin', 'cause everything's gonna be just fine. You and me are gonna be friends." He reached in, wiped the tears from Suzi's cheek, smiled again, and closed the lid of the trunk.

Suzi didn't know how long he drove. It seemed like forever. The pillows helped, except once, when he stopped suddenly and she rolled forward, hitting her forehead on a metal bar at the front of the trunk. The smell of gasoline was strong, and as Suzi felt around, her hands met the cold sides of a gas can. She pushed at it, panicking when she realized it was full.

17

Dad told me that people should never carry gas like this, she thought. Her fear increased as she imagined the worst...a crash, a fire, and she couldn't get out. She began to scream, her earlier tears giving way to hysteria.

The car stopped again, and the man sounded the horn two quick beeps and a longer one. She heard a sliding sound, like their garage door at home, only louder. The car moved again, stopped, and the engine turned off. Then, nothing.

Suzi beat against the trunk lid with her hands and feet. "Hey, let me out of here! Let me out. Let me out!"

She heard the man's voice nearby. "I found her. Told you I would. She's a pretty little thing. The boss is gonna like her. Now, maybe he'll pay me more like I axed him."

Suzi heard the key turn in the lock and blinked, her eyes adjusting to the light. She swallowed her sobs as she looked at the two men. This new man was in his mid-thirties, his blond hair dirty and uncombed. His thin mustache was light and difficult to see. His teeth were yellow, almost the color of his hair.

They looked in at Suzanne. Her face was red from her screaming, her eyes swollen from her tears. The first man reached for her, wiping the hair out of her face, pulling her up by the shoulders. Then, as the man standing next to him punched him in the arm, she fell backward onto the pillows again.

"You idiot. Don't you know who that is? That's Suzanne Kendell. How the hell could you kidnap her?"

"How's I s'posed to know? I jus' saw her at the mall. She's so pretty, I figgered we could use her. Come on, Derek. OUCH!" This, in response to the man's second punch.

"Shut up, fool. Don't use names. Now, bring her to the coop, and we'll try to figure out this mess."

He turned and walked away, leaving his partner to pull Suzi out of the trunk. He grabbed her around the wrist, "Come on, girl, I'll show you where yer gonna be."

Suzi looked around as the man pulled her through the building. They were in a big warehouse. The lower windows were hidden by stacks of boxes, the higher ones covered with old, yellowed newspapers and masking tape. There were long chains attached to the oversized garage door through which they had come, but the door was now shut tightly, braces locking it from the inside. There was a doorway to the right of the garage door, and from where they were, Suzi could see no locks on it. Maybe they're on the outside, she thought. If I could just get away from him, I could try it.

But his grip was strong, and despite her wiggling and pulling, she could not free herself. He took her to the other end of the warehouse where several closed doors were lined up, about eight feet of wall space between each door. Each door had a number scrawled on it with thick, black marker. They stopped outside of the door with a large number three written on it. He reached for a key ring, like the jailer's key rings she'd seen in old cowboy movies, and fit the key into the lock.

"Josie?" he called. "Gotcha a roommate. Say, what was yer name, girl? Sally, or somethin' like that?"

"Suzanne," she whispered, looking into the darkness of the room beyond the door.

"Well, Suzanne, say howdy to Josie. Josie can give you your job description. An' I'll be back for you later, Suzanne, honey. Have fun, girls." He pushed her into the small, cold room, pulling the door shut behind her. Suzi felt her tears returning as she heard the key turn in the lock.

The room smelled like an outhouse, and Suzi realized why when she saw the pot sitting on the floor at the far end of the room. The room itself was small, with only enough space for two battered and ripped army cots, the pot, and a space for walking in between the cots. Each cot had a stained, torn pillow and an army blanket. The room was dark. A single bulb dangling from uncovered wires hung down from a circle cut in the ceiling. The bulb flickered dimly.

Suzi turned her attention to the girl on the cot on the left. The girl had been sleeping when the door opened and now sat up, reaching for the crying girl only a foot away from her fingertips.

She leaned over, grasped Suzi's fingers, and pulled her down to sit next to her.

"You're new, huh?"

Suzi nodded.

"My name is Josie. Did he call you Suzanne?"

"Yeah, but most people just call me Suzi." Suzi choked on the bile rising in her throat.

"How old are you, Suzi?"

"Ten and a half."

"I'm fifteen, so I guess that means I'm gonna have to take care of you. Would that be okay?"

Suzi nodded at her, brushing away at her tears. Someone to take care of her? "Why are we here?"

Josie blinked back her own tears. How could she tell this child what was going to happen to her? How could she talk about the things that she herself had already had to do?

"They make movies here, Suzi. Really bad movies. Do you know about sex?" Suzi nodded, her eyes widening. "Well, here they make movies about children having sex."

Suzi's tears fell again. She wondered if she would ever run out. "Are we the children?"

Josie reached her arm around Suzanne, softly caressing her hair and forehead. Her free hand pulled the stray strands of her own black hair away from her mouth as she

19

leaned forward over Suzi.

"Yeah, honey, we are." Josie suddenly felt much older than her fifteen years. She was now the experienced one. The one to explain and protect and wipe away tears.

"Did they kidnap you, too?" Suzi asked.

"No, my folks didn't have any money, so they kind of sold me to them. So, nobody's looking for me. I guess I'll be here until they're done with me. How about you?"

"That man took me away from my school. But my friend Debi saw him. She might help me, 'cept," her voice shook, "he told her not to tell, 'cause he'd hurt me."

Josie hugged her closer. "Well, at least your folks are gonna be looking for you. You didn't fight with them or anything, did you?" Suzi shook her head. "Well, good. That means they won't think you ran away or anything. Now, I'm gonna tell you some things just so you're not surprised, okay?"

Josie explained everything as gently as she could to Suzi. She told her about having to let grownups and other kids touch her private parts, and about having to touch theirs. She told her about grown men putting their penises inside of her, wherever they wanted to. She told her about other people, laughing, watching, and telling them how to move and what to do. She told her about how all the kids hated it, how they were really scared, but they had to do it anyway.

Suzi listened. Her tears halted, her terror increased. Would she have to do all of that?

Josie continued, "We're really lucky. Jimmy, in room number five, says that at some of these kinds of places, they cut kids up and kill them while they film it for their movies. But they don't do that here."

It was too much for Suzanne Kendell. She ran for the pot, losing her breakfast in harsh, racking convulsions. Josie knelt behind her, holding her hair out of the way, smoothing the wrinkles on her forehead. When Suzi was finished, Josie pulled a large bowl out from under her cot.

"This is our bathtub." She attempted humor. "Now, give me your face." She wiped Suzi's face gently with a dirty, but cool, soothing washcloth. Then she stood, walked over to t!he door and pulled a cord that hung next to it. Like the light, it came through a tiny hole in the ceiling.

Suzi heard a bell ringing outside the door. "It's just for emergencies. Almost like having our own bell-pull. You know, like on the Addams Family? Only Lurch doesn't come, usually Harry does. He's the one who brought you here."

When Harry answered the door, Josie faced him squarely. "We need a fresh cleaning bowl and washcloth for her, and a glass of water." Harry nodded, closed the door, and locked it once again.

When he returned, he had everything that Josie had ordered. He handed the items to Josie, but looked at Suzanne.

"Don't you worry none, Suzanne. I'm gonna take good care of you." He reached into the back pocket of his baggy jeans, pulling out a can of soda. "This is your welcoming present." With that, he backed out of the room, once again locking it securely behind him.

It was mid-afternoon when the door opened again. A cart was pushed in with two glasses of water and two T.V. dinners on it. The girl who pushed it in whispered, "Hi, Josie. Who's the new kid?"

"This is Suzi. Harry grabbed her this morning. Suzi, this is Melanie."

"So she's the one. I heard Harry and Derek talking while I was heating these up. Derek's really mad that she's here. Says she's some judge's daughter. He knows because he saw her family's picture in the paper last month. He's got the article hanging on the wall in his office. Said the judge sentenced him a few years ago. Gave him a real fair deal. Then Derek laughed. Said the judge had more faith in him that he had in himself."

Josie was impressed. "Wow! You had your picture in the paper? Why?"

Suzanne felt immediately strengthened at the mention of her father. "It was an article about busy parents and quality time with their kids. The reporter said she couldn't find a family with busier parents than mine." Then, her hope rising, she asked, "Since they know I'm his daughter, will they let me go?"

Josie and Melanie looked at each other in the dim light, sorrow masking their faces. Melanie sat down on the cot next to Suzi. "Sorry, kid. Harry says he has a thing for you. Says he saw you in the mall last week and followed you home, trying to figure out the best way to get you here. Derek's afraid that, if they do anything to you, the law will really come after them, but Harry bugged him so much, they decided to just use you a couple of times...since you're already here. Then, maybe if you really cooperate, they might let you go. They do that sometimes, you know. Especially when they're ready to leave town. And, they said the fire's getting too hot around here. Time to move somewhere else."

"What about the rest of you?"

Melanie forced a smile. "I'm a runaway. Derek found me hooking myself, told me I could have three meals a day and a roof over my head if I'd come work for him. It's not a great job, but at least none of these guys have AIDS or any other diseases. The boss insists on it."

"Who's the boss?"

"None of us know. Just some guy who rents this building for us, and covers our butts if the cops get too close. He warns us if anybody's sniffing around, and of course, he gets all the money. Now, you two better eat your dinner.

Besides, I've got two more rooms to deliver to. I'll be back to get your garbage in a while."

When Melanie left the room, Suzi wept again. "Oh, Josie. She said they're going to 'use me' anyway. I always thought that I was the safest kid in town. I didn't think Dad would ever let anything happen to me." She ran into Josie's arms, tucking her head under the older girl's chin. "Josie, I'm so scared."

CHAPTER THREE

O, I have suffer'd
With those that I saw suffer!
-The Tempest

Jordan and Neil sat in his office, reviewing what little evidence they had actually gathered. Several cups of hot coffee and fifteen hours later, Jordan stretched aching neck muscles, rubbed burning eyes, and shook her head.

"It just doesn't make sense. Where could she have gone? She probably didn't have any money with her. She certainly wasn't wearing expensive jewelry. There have been no ransom notes or phone calls. There are no witnesses. Where could Suzi be?"

"I wish I could answer all of your questions, Jordan," Neil sighed. "We're having a hard time with this one. Especially since she's Judge Kendell's daughter. The whole city loves that man."

"Well, maybe someone doesn't. Neil, I'm so sorry that I doubted your efforts and got so frustrated with you."

Neil smiled at her gently. "I've known you since you started kindergarten. You were they cutest little squirt running around on that playground. Always sort of wished you had gone for older men."

"Four years doesn't make you an 'older man," and I'm still sorry I got angry with you and grilled you all night long."

"I've felt your wrath many times, Jordan Blake, but I've never been burned. I'll always cherish our friendship." He reached his hand out to her.

She placed her hand in his. "Me too, Neil." They sat that way comfortably for a few moments, then Jordan stood up and began pacing the floor around his desk. "All right, back to work. We probably have clues staring us right in the face. We just have to find them."

"You should have been a cop. You definitely have the patience and the persistence for it," Neil chuckled.

There was a light tap on the door as it swung open. "All right, you two. Exactly as I suspected. Shut up in here, alone, all night long." Celia Carter's blonde head peeked around the door. She and Neil had been married for six years and she had learned early in their marriage that when he didn't show up in their bed at night, she could generally find him here.

"Okay. I want a good explanation," she growled as she looked from one guilty face to the other. She walked toward the desk, grasped the handle of one coffee cup and then the other, peering at the cold, muddy-looking contents.

"Just as I suspected."

Celia walked back to the door, swung it open and yelled, "Better bring 'em in, Kelly."

Jordan looked a bit confused. Neil just smiled. "I knew I married you for some good reason," he said to his wife. He stood and walked to her side, giving her a big, hungry kiss.

Kelly, one of the department's new rookies, walked in, her grin as big as one of Santa's elves on Christmas Eve. Her blonde hair was cut in a short bob. The stubborn curls threatened the strength of her mousse, and typically pulled free to curl around her face. She carried a large silver tray laden with fruit, cheese, and freshly-baked, extremely gooey cinnamon rolls. Celia stepped out to retrieve a bag which she had left on Kelly's desk. "Okay, Kelly. Let's serve it up." She reached into the bag, bringing out orange juice, milk and a handful of plastic glasses. "Kelly called me last night to tell me that you'd be putting in a long night." Celia's tone was only slightly chastising.

"I'm sorry, honey. I meant to call. We just got busy." Neil looked quite repentant, and his wife laughed. She turned to Jordan and gave her a quick hug. "It's good to see you, Jory. But, for a well-educated person, you don't take any better care of yourself than my fine husband does."

Jordan looked wistfully at the tray on the desk. "We got a little caught up in our efforts, but that would make a wonderful break."

For the next hour, Celia, Jordan and Neil reviewed the small bits of information which they had. One of the last people to see Suzi was the school bus driver. She told Kelly and Neil, when they spoke with her, that Suzi had gotten off the bus. She and her friend, Debi Burke, were walking towards the school building, laughing and chattering as they usually did, when the bus driver closed the door of the bus and drove away. The teacher who had acted as playground monitor that morning told them the same story.

Attempts to talk with Debi revealed nothing. She just cried and insisted that she didn't know anything. She begged Neil to find her friend, and ran from the room sobbing. Debi's parents promised to try to glean more information from her, in the hope that they could help find the missing Suzanne. But so far, they had found no new information.

Jordan suddenly stood, stretched, and faced her two friends. "Thank you, Neil for being so patient with me. And for letting a mere civilian to try to help out. If you'll allow me to, I'd like to go talk to Debi myself."

"What do you think she'll be able to tell you?" asked Celia.

"I don't know, but I used to babysit her. She's always been comfortable around me, and maybe she'll think of something while we're talking." She shrugged her shoulders in response to the doubtful looks she received from Neil and Celia. "Well, at least it's worth a try."

"Have a go at it," Neil said. "You have my blessing." He tried, unsuccessfully, to suppress a yawn, turned to his wife, and draped his arm around her shoulder. "In the meantime, I think I'll take my lovely lady home and have a nice nap."

*

Jordan went directly to the Burke home. It was a small, two-story house. She smiled as she looked up at the freshly-painted pink shutters. The house was white, and had had gray shutters for many years. Yet, when Debi had made her Christmas wish list the previous December, her first request was that the color be changed. Her only three color suggestions were fluorescent orange, bright purple, or soft pink. The Burkes graciously chose the milder color, even letting Debi help with the painting. Jordan looked for signs of drips and the exuberant painting of a ten year old.

She was looking at the pink paint spots, not yet worn from the white porch steps, when Mrs. Burke answered her knock.

"Jordan, it's good to see you. Any news on Suzanne?" The older woman looked hopeful.

"No, Mrs. Burke. I'm really here to speak with Debi. Is she home?"

"Yes. Please, come in. Why don't you wait in the living room while I get her?"

Jordan sat on the pink sofa, also Debi's selection, and glanced about the room. Just the previous fall, Mrs. Burke had redone the room in shades of pale pink and cornflower blue. Jordan was pleased to see the silk flower arrangement she had given them for Christmas sitting on the fireplace mantle. Mrs. Burke had long been a collector of baskets, and Jordan had hoped that she would enjoy the gift, with a special touch of pink and blue flowers arranged carefully inside.

She was brought back to the present when Debi touched her shoulder.

"Hi, Jordan. Mom said you wanted to talk to me."

Jordan smiled reassuringly at the small girl. She was quite fond of the child, and had cared for her since Debi was a toddler. She absentmindedly caressed the girl's honey-colored hair, pulled back into an Alice in Wonderland style with a bright orange ribbon.

"Honey, come sit down with me. I want you to tell me all about what happened with Suzi."

Debi's green eyes filled with tears, and she bit her lower lip. "But I already talked to Captain Larson."

"I know that, Debi. But we're having a hard time

25

finding Suzi. I'm trying to help Captain Larson, and I thought you might be able to tell me about it. Can you tell me what happened?"

"We went to school on the bus, just like we always do."

"And what happened when you got off the bus?"

"I went to my class."

"Where did Suzi go?"

"To her class?" It was more a question than a statement.

Jordan looked at the dark circles under Debi's eyes, the tears that welled up. She wondered how much Debi knew that she hadn't yet told anyone.

"Debi, this is really important. Suzi could be in a lot of trouble. If you know anything about this, you must tell me."

"I can't." The words were whispered, and the tears began to spill.

"Honey, if Suzi needs help, we all have to try to find her. If you know anything at all, she won't be angry with you for telling."

"But he might hurt her."

The words came out so softly that for a moment Jordan wasn't sure that Debi had really spoken. She felt her heart jump into her throat, but knew that she mustn't frighten the child any more.

"Who might hurt her?"

Debi hesitated, her chin quivering. She took a deep breath, and looked up at Jordan. "The man who took her."

Jordan swallowed hard, grabbed Debi's hands and held them firmly. "Debi, it's time for you to tell me everything. What happened when you and Suzanne went to school that day?"

"We got off the bus and started to go to our classes. This man came around the corner by the parking lot. He looked at both of us, but he didn't say anything. He scared us, so we started to walk faster. But he grabbed Suzi..." She stopped, wiping her tears with the back of her hand.

Jordan waited a few second before asking, "Did he say anything?"

"He put his hand over her mouth, and held his other arm around her shoulders. I started to scream, but he looked at me really mean. He grabbed Suzi's throat." Here the girl stopped, choking on her fear. "He told me that if I told anyone that I'd seen him, he'd hurt her really bad."

Jordan sank back onto the couch. "Debi, I'm going to call Captain Larson and ask him to come over."

*

Jordan spoke briefly over the phone with Neil. He

arrived at the Burke house ten minutes later, with a police sketch artist in tow. After an hour of unsuccessful attempts to get a realistic sketch of the man Debi had seen, they stopped in frustration. All that she was able to tell them for certain was that he had shaggy brown hair and whiskers. "Not a real beard, just whiskers. Like Daddy has when he comes home from a fishing trip. And he had blue eyes. No, maybe they were brown. I don't know. Jordan, can't we just stop?"

Exhausted from lack of sleep and feeling that further attempts were futile, the sketch pad was closed. Neil and Jordan felt close to defeat.

"Jordan, why don't you go home and get some rest? I'll do the same. We're no good to anyone like this." He turned to face Mrs. Burke, who had been pacing nervously in front of the fireplace for nearly an hour. "Mrs. Burke, you'll be contacted by the F.B.I. later today. This is now a case of kidnapping, and not a possible runaway situation. So, it's their territory, now. In the meantime, could you take Debi down to the station? Kelly can have her look at some pictures we have on file." Seeing the hope that sprang into Jordan's eyes, he waved his hand slightly. "Don't get excited. To tell you the truth, it's not likely that we'll find out anything more. But, we'll try anything. We've got to find Suzanne Kendell."

*

Jordan woke late that evening, feeling only slightly rested. She had tossed and turned, men with dark whiskers floating through her dreams. She dressed, washed her face, ran a comb through her hair, and went down the stairs towards her father's den.

She found Emerson Blake smoking a pipe, sitting in his favorite leather easy chair, watching the fire. She kissed him lightly on the forehead. "You shouldn't do that, you know. Not good for your health."

Blake laughed. "Who ever got bad health from watching a fire?"

"Oh, Daddy. You know what I mean. You smokers are all alike. Don't you pay any attention to the surgeon general?"

Emerson put his pipe down and smiled at his daughter, "Yes, dear. Oh, Paige called. She'd like you to go over and talk to her. She's home now."

"Okay, but don't think I'm through with you." She blew him a kiss and headed toward the front door. Hendricks met her there, handing her a jacket. "Thanks, Henny. Don't know what I'd do without you to take care of me."

The butler called after her before closing the door. "I don't know either, Jordan. But I'm not going to give you the chance to find out!"

Jordan ran down the driveway towards the Kendell's. Her mind raced. Was Suzi home?

Hannah answered the door, and sent her to the back patio to find Paige.

Her friend looked up as she walked out of the house. "Well, we're making some progress, thanks to you."

"What do you mean? Do you know where Suzi is?"

"Nope. But Debi Burke identified the man who took her."

"Neil said..."

"I know. He was as surprised as you are. He just left here. They've already checked the guy's apartment, and the place where he supposedly works. Nobody's seen him for several days. But Neil's put out an all points bulletin and they're finally feeling hopeful."

"That's wonderful, Paige." Jordan hugged her as Paige suddenly began to cry.

"I'm scared, Jory. She's so little."

"I know. But, they're going to find her. Neil's the best, and he's like a hound dog. He won't give up. Especially since he's on the right scent now."

*

One week later, Neil and John Stafford, the F.B.I. agent who had been assigned to Suzi's case, had joined forces and were still looking for Harry Motske, the man Debi Burke identified. There were no signs of Motske, and no further clues to lead them to Suzanne. She had been missing for two weeks.

Liza Kendell went into the tiny chapel at their church to pray every morning. Franklin Kendell assured his wife and daughter that if they had faith, their girl would be returned to them.

Paige urged Jordan to return to school. "Your final exams will be coming soon, and I know you have zillions of research papers to finish."

"I can't leave you. I'll wait until we find her."

But Paige could be very persuasive when she wanted to be. She assured Jordan that she would phone her as soon as they had any news. She had already made arrangements with her own professors to make up her work during the summer months. She felt that Jordan had done enough for her family, and should get back to her work. "You absolutely must graduate. I'll never speak to you again if you don't," Paige teased her.

Graduation day came and went. The Kendells and the Blakes came to share Jordan's big day with her. They were all delighted with her accomplishments. But their spirits didn't soar too high. Suzanne was still missing.

After long discussions with her parents and with Paige, Jordan decided not to return home. She took a job with a local architect. He was one of the most talented men in the business, and she was delighted to be taken under his wing. He was not overly generous with money, but she believed that good experience outweighed small paychecks.

Needing to find an apartment closer to work, Jordan found a small, one-bedroom place which she and Paige could afford. Several friends helped her move all of their belongings from the house into the apartment. There was still no word about Suzanne.

*

Suzanne Kendell no longer felt like a little girl. She hurt down in the place that had only hurt one other time. She had been riding Jerry Rice's bike when they were five, and she had fallen and hit her private parts on the bar. She hadn't ridden a boy's bike since then.

Her throat hurt where the man called Cliff had pushed inside of her. Her face hurt where Derek had slugged her, because she had gagged and cried.

As she lay in her bed, she cried again. Josie, unable to console her, retreated to her own cot, feeling as if her innards were being torn out by each ravaged sob coming from the little girl only an arm's length away. Neither girl noticed when the overhead light went out, as it did every night at ten o'clock.

They didn't hear the angry voices, coming from the office several yards away, in another part of the warehouse. "The boss" had arrived, coming for his weekly visit. He purchased this business from a loan officer at his bank when he mentioned that he was having some financial problems a few years earlier. He was disgusted by the prospect, but greed and desperation often win out over disgust.

Now, as he faced Harry and Derek, his face was red with anger. "What do you mean, we have a little problem? If it were so little, you wouldn't want to show me one of your despicable movies. No, I refuse. You deal with your problem. I'll pay the bills, you deal with the actors."

"Boss," Derek spoke, "this is something we need your help with. If we didn't, we wouldn't bother you with it, honest."

Both men were afraid to explain how Harry happened to "collect" Suzanne Kendell. They argued repeatedly over which one of them would tell him. They considered not telling him. "Let's just dump her. Dead or else too afraid to say anything. It really doesn't matter," Derek suggested. "Let's just get rid of her."

Harry liked Suzanne. He wanted to be her acting

partner, but Derek said he was too ugly. "Give her to me, Derek. I'll take her away, and then the boss'll never know about any of this."

"No. The cops are dragging the gutters looking for that girl. And pretty soon, they're gonna end up at our front door. We've got to keep 'em happy. We're gonna have to send her back."

Their argument continued for days. Should they keep her alive? Would she bring the police to them? Neither of them had the courage to actually kill anyone. Who could they hire to do it? What if they got caught? Wouldn't the authorities go harder on them if they were tied to her murder? Besides, Harry had really fallen for the girl. He didn't want her hurt. They reached an impasse. They'd have to tell the boss.

But the boss told them to never kidnap children. Sure, other organizations did that. But they could get their actors other ways. There were enough unwanted, unloved, hungry children out there. They would recruit their actors.

The next problem arose. How would they tell him? They knew he'd be furious with them. Finally, after days of endless arguing, they decided to show him.

Now, as he stood red-faced before them, they weren't sure they had made the right decision. Finally, without speaking, Derek pushed the play button on the VCR.

Resigned, realizing that he couldn't stand and argue with the two imbeciles all night, he watched. The color drained from his face. He stood before them, his hands grasping the edges of the desk for support. Finally, he sank into the chair behind him.

"Dear God, Suzanne. She's here. What have you done with her?" His rage returned, now greater than it had been a few moments earlier. "How could you have done this to her? She's an innocent baby!"

"Not any more," Harry grinned, then cringed as the large man swung a fist in his direction.

Missing his target, the man walked to the chair beside the desk, digging his fingernails into the upholstery. It took him several minutes to regain his composure. Then, his voice tense, his words forced between clenched teeth, he asked, "How? How did you get her?"

Harry was too frightened to speak. But Derek was not about to allow any blame to land on his shoulders. He explained.

"You knew who she was. How could you be so stupid? Why didn't you let her go immediately? Why did you make her do this?" He waved dejectedly at the television screen.

This time Harry had an answer. "She's beautiful. She's got an angel's face. Who wouldn't pay to see her?"

The man rose from his chair. "Take me to her."

"You can't let her see you."

"I am perfectly aware of that. Now, take me to her."

They stood outside of the door with the number three on it, listening. Derek unlocked the door, and stuck his head inside. He glanced first at Josie, then at Suzanne. "They're both asleep."

The boss stepped through the doorway. Suzanne was asleep, but she wept, even in her dreams. Or were they nightmares? He leaned over her, caressing her hair, softly patting her shoulder.

"No more tears," he whispered. "It will all be over soon. Now, hush, my little one. You'll be home soon."

Suzanne heard the words as they incorporated into her dreams. Somehow they seemed familiar. She felt reassured. Her tears ceased.

As the men stood outside the door, Derek and Harry received their orders. "Harry, I want every videotape with her on it burned. Do you understand that? Every single copy. I don't even want her picture used. Go. Do it now."

When Harry left for the production room, he turned to Derek. His anger in check, his distress quickly consuming him, he knew he had to take swift action. The need to assure his own safety helped him control his emotions.

"She could bring all this down around our ears. So, before you send her home, and you will send her home, I want you to scare her. Don't hurt her, just make her think you will. I want her too scared to talk about this. I hate having to resort to this, but your stupidity has put us in danger. Next, I want you to close up shop here. I've got another warehouse for us over in Pomona. And when you're done with all that, I want Harry taken care of."

*

Paige telephoned Jordan at two-thirty in the morning, in the middle of June. "They've found Harry Motske. His body was found in an alley by some transients. He had his wallet and his driver's license right on him, and his fingerprints matched the ones the police had on file. But, Jordan, his face was unrecognizable. He was beaten to death."

Two days later, unable to speak, weak from fear and hunger, Suzi came home. Her body and her spirit hurt more than she ever imagined possible. But Derek's threats against her family still rang in her ears, and she refused to tell anyone what happened to her. When questioned, she stared forward, not blinking or moving.

That afternoon, following the previous evening's instructions, Derek sent a message to the Kendell home. It read, "You will suffer even greater tragedies if you pursue this. Keep silent, or lose your little girl forever."

31

The victim would not speak, her parents refused to cooperate with the authorities, there were no witnesses, and no new evidence. Neil Larson wondered if the case would have to be closed.

CHAPTER FOUR

Be collected; No more amazement:
tell your piteous heart
There's no harm done.
-The Tempest

Paige returned to Los Angeles three weeks after Suzi's return. "I don't even know what happened to her, Jordan," Paige cried. "Suzi doesn't want anyone to know, and Pop agrees with her. He tells her just to put it behind her."

"But, Paige, what about Neil and Mr. Stafford? Surely they know what's going on."

"Yes," Paige assured her wearily. "They're still working on the case. They say that the man who kidnapped Suzanne was a child pornographer. Dear God, they can't have done that to Suzanne, can they?"

Despite attempts by both Paige and Jordan, Suzanne refused to talk about her experiences. And the Judge thwarted their every effort to break down her walls of silence.

*

Paige completed all of her undergraduate requirements without too much difficulty. She was a dedicated young woman, and by devoting most of her waking hours to her exams and her still-unfinished lab work, she received her degree in biology and was ready to enter medical school that fall.

Jordan worried constantly about her friend. Paige suffered from nightmares about her sister. She made several unexpected trips home to be with her family, always going by herself, barely warning Jordan that she would be leaving.

Paige and Jordan eventually resigned themselves to the fact that Suzanne would reveal nothing. Deciding that the Kendells were intelligent people and would know what was best for their child, their efforts to uncover the truth diminished, even though their concern did not.

Jordan, always guided by her dreams of achieving the success and the acclaim of the late Frank Lloyd Wright, entered her master's program one week after Paige began her med school classes.

They kept the same small apartment, finding med school and graduate school to be even more expensive than their undergraduate work had been. Paige gradually began to rediscover some of her former zest for living. She made a conscious decision to put her concern for her sister at the back of her mind. She didn't know what happened to Suzanne. She

33

really didn't want to consider the possibilities. She couldn't face them. It was easier to try to forget.

As Jordan and Paige settled into a routine, they soon began to enjoy their new home. The apartment was in poor condition prior to Jordan's moving in. Previously occupied by three college boys who preferred partying to cleaning and studying, they found it in great need of repairs. The landlord agreed to deduct their expenses from their rent, but the extra decorating would have to come out of their own budget.

The holes in the walls and doors were soon repaired. Jordan wondered if some of the damage had been caused by fists and heads unnaturally bouncing there. The walls were filthy and painting was required, so she chose light cheerful colors for the kitchen and bathroom. She completed those rooms by the time Paige returned to L.A. The remaining rooms would be decorated in a joint effort by the two roommates.

The first year of school kept them very busy, leaving them little time for anything other than research projects and earning enough money to pay for it all. The renovation of the apartment was put temporarily on hold. The living room still had dingy walls and black hand prints on the ceiling. When Paige first noticed them, she shook her head, smiled at Jordan, and said, "I won't ask."

The bedroom walls were partially covered with faded, peeling wallpaper. The once-bright green roses could never have been attractive. The metallic, silver background was, as Jordan said, "Enough to make you heal yourself from anything normally confining you to your bedroom." The wallpaper became a symbol of better things to come. When frustrated by school projects or tough days, one or both of them would retreat to that inner sanctuary and, with paring knife in hand, begin pulling green petals off the walls.

Jordan continued working with Grady MacIntyre, the architect who hired her after graduation. She loved the work she did for him. Grady knew talent when he saw it, and he found it in Jordan. She had a natural eye for spatial needs and aesthetics. While her preference was to work on private homes, MacIntyre felt that she needed to stretch herself in other directions. "Specialties are necessary to get by in today's world," he told her. "But any architect worth his salt knows about building offices, schools, hospitals, churches. Whatever comes up."

By the end of her second year working with the MacIntyre & Associates Architectural Firm, Jordan passed the ranks of protégé, and was doing her own work. She completed plans on a hospital for a small town in central California, a mere two months after MacIntyre assigned the task to her.

Taking classes full time meant spending many late nights in her cubicle, which Grady assured her really was an office. But the work paid off. Grady was so impressed with her work that he promised to make her one of the associate members of the firm as soon as she completed her degree program.

Unfortunately, the miserly old gentleman barely raised her salary. He told her that he didn't want to make her too cocky. "You might think you're too important and leave me in the lurch."

Jordan kissed his wrinkled, dark brown cheek. "Don't you worry about that, you old scrooge. You're too important for me to leave you," Jordan assured him. And, in fact, she loved the prospect of continuing her work with his firm.

Grady MacIntyre was in his early seventies. He refused to retire, insisting that he had at least fifty good years of hard work left in him. He had lost his beloved wife, Sarah, two years earlier, and devoted all of his lonely hours to the firm. He and Sarah always wanted children of their own. Their only child, a little girl, died as an infant, leaving them with a great deal of leftover love.

Jordan was an answer to prayer for Grady. She even reminded him of Sarah. Not in physical appearance, but in her laughter and her determination. Grady knew that this young woman had exceptional talent and promise. And, without her knowing it, he was planning to entrust her with everything that he had.

Grady was careful not to spoil Jordan. He wanted her to learn on her own, through her own mistakes and her own triumphs. He never failed to encourage her when she did well. But he always saw to it that she found her errors and could correct them. The two spent many late evenings at her drawing table, reviewing her most recent work. He found that, as the months went by, his suggestions came less often, and her successes brought in many prosperous new clients. The fact never failed to please him.

Jordan completed her master's program in three years. As a graduation gift, Paige got a real wallpaper peeler from the hardware store and then re-papered the bedroom walls. "As the future 'greatest architect in the world,' you won't need to peel green roses anymore. This paper is a new symbol of success and the future homes that you are going to plan for us."

Jordan's parents gave her a new, fire-engine red Jeep Wrangler. Celeste moaned as she handed the keys to her daughter. "We are so proud of you, darling. But I really thought that we could honor the occasion in a more sporty manner. For instance, with a Mercedes or a Jaguar."

"Not on your life," growled her husband, standing behind her. "Jordan is going to be driving to all sorts of remote areas to inspect her buildings. This is the vehicle she'll need. A Mercedes or a Jaguar, my eye. What do you women think grows on those trees in our back yard? Must I remind you that it's fruit, and not money?"

Jordan assured her parents that she loved the Jeep, and that she couldn't have been more pleased. Jeeps were more her style, anyway.

The Kendells gave her a gold necklace with a tiny gold sky-scraper dangling from the chain. "We have great hopes for you, Jordan. May this remind you of all you are capable of doing," Judge Kendell told her when Liza presented her with the gift.

Grady's gift, as he promised, was full associate status with his firm. He joined Jordan, her family and all of the Kendells for a festive celebration following the graduation ceremony. He began his presentation by saying, "I'll bet you think I forgot all about a gift, didn't you? Well, I tried, but couldn't do it."

He handed Jordan a small package. She removed the gift wrap to find a black leather box. She paused, but Grady's excitement was evident, and her mother urged her to open it.

Jordan lifted the lid, and found a small card inside. Lifting the card out, she read the words Grady had had engraved on it:

> "WELCOME, DEAR ASSOCIATE.
> THIS IS ONLY THE BEGINNING.
> LOVE, GRADY"

Jordan jumped up from her chair, ran around the table, and gave the old man a joyous hug. "You really have this much faith in me?"

"More! But, you're going to have to earn the rest of it."

Jordan tried all evening to have a moment alone with Suzanne. Now thirteen years of age, she was turning into a beautiful young woman. But the exuberance of her younger years had disappeared. Since that horrible time, three years earlier, she was withdrawn and solemn.

After several unsuccessful attempts to speak with her alone, Franklin realized what Jordan was trying to do. He took Jordan by the arm and whispered into her ear, "Let it be. She's doing just fine."

"I don't think so, Judge. She seems to be in so much pain."

"She's doing fine," Franklin repeated. "Please, don't cause any problems for her."

"Look at her," Jordan insisted, "Can't you see how much she's changed? She's been unhappy for three years. Whatever is bothering her isn't liable to just disappear with time, or because you insist that she's doing fine."

"Please trust us, Jordan. We're dealing with Suzanne's problems as well as we can. Please, just let this go."

Jordan wanted to press the issue further, but Franklin's imploring look and her father's squeeze on her shoulder quieted her.

"They know what they're doing, Jordan. Don't start trouble where there is none. You're an architect, not a Marriage and Family Counselor."

Jordan was puzzled by her father's attitude. Had he talked to the Judge about it? And, most importantly, had Suzanne ever received counseling? She felt helpless to fight the strong tide of opposition.

Jordan began her first year as a full-time employee of MacIntyre and Associates the next month. She and Paige took a three week vacation immediately after her graduation, with Jordan promising an even better trip when Paige finished med school the following year.

Now they drove along the coastal highway, spending several days enjoying the scenery, and stopping to visit every beautiful beach they could find. When they reached Seattle, they thoroughly enjoyed playing tourist.

Jordan insisted that Paige go with her to the top of the Space Needle, making two sets of knees very quivery. She treated Paige to a luscious dinner in the restaurant at the top. She planned to have lobster, but the young doctor informed her that the poor beasts have highly developed nervous systems and really could feel the pain as they were tossed into the boiling water. They settled for steak, trying to forget the beautiful brown-eyed animal that it must have come from.

Mainly they enjoyed the sights and the freedom they experienced for the first time in years. After spending several days exploring Seattle and the surrounding areas, Jordan had her Jeep shipped back to Los Angeles, and they flew to New York City. They hadn't been there for years, and they hit all of their favorite restaurants and saw as many shows as time would allow.

The three weeks ended too quickly, but they returned home feeling refreshed and ready to return to their obligations. Jordan went back to work with Grady, and Paige began preparations for her final year of medical school.

*

One morning Paige burst into their apartment, knocking Jordan's armload of sketches and final blueprints to the floor.

"Oh, Jory, I'm so sorry."

"That's all right, you clutz. What's up, and why are you performing the human cannonball routine?"

"I've met him."

"Met who?

"Whom," corrected a very excited young woman.

"Okay, okay. Whom? Now, tell me what you're so bubbly about."

"I have just met the most handsome, wonderful man in the world."

"Let's see, I believe I've heard this speech before. Let me make it for you this time." Jordan assumed a moon-struck expression and continued, "He's tall, dark and handsome. Has sparkling eyes and a terrific sense of humor. He's kind and generous, and I'm going to marry him." She stopped torturing her friend and smiled, "Well, how did I do?"

"Oh, Jordan, really. Have I been that bad?"

"Ever since we were five years old and you fell in love with Johnny Main when he chased you across the monkey bars on the playground. At least every few months I am treated to your now-famous speech."

"But this time..."

"...it's different. I know. So, who is this paragon of perfection?"

"That's redundant, and stop teasing me. We're meeting him at six o'clock for pizza," Paige laughed as she piled several papers on top of the stack which Jordan already picked up from the floor. "And he just may be perfect," she said to the retreating figure.

Jordan made a face and headed for her office.

*

Jordan and Paige arrived at the pizza parlor twenty-five minutes early. They waited, Jordan calm and laughing at her friend's nervousness.

"You're going to love him, Jory. Really."

When the young man arrived, Paige knocked her glass of water onto Jordan's lap, jumped to her feet, and knocked her chair over backward.

"Good grief, relax," Jordan hissed, wiping her soaked jeans frantically with a stack of napkins. "If he's as wonderful as you seem to think, the night will go without a hitch."

Paige took a slow, deep breath as her long-awaited guest approached the table. "Alex, I'm so glad you could make it. I'd like you to meet my roommate, Jordan Blake. Jory, this is Alex Wynne."

Jordan held out her hand and looked up into the deepest blue eyes she had ever seen. Seeing the beaming face with huge dimples and the smile lines that could only be etched by a good sense of humor, she immediately forgot her self-made promise to treat the young man with distance and

38

doubt.

The evening was a success. The three talked for hours, finally moving their small party to a twenty-four hour pancake house. Jordan started the evening with a bit of apprehension, which she was afraid to admit, even to herself. She had seen Paige "in love" before, and she thought this might be just another crush. Always protective of her friend, she doubted that Alex could feel as strongly as Paige did.

"Good grief." Jordan suddenly jerked to reality. "I've got a meeting with a contractor in two and a half hours." She left Paige and Alex at the restaurant as they ordered breakfast, and raced to the apartment for an hour of sleep and a shower.

After her meeting, Jordan went back home to catch a few more hours of sleep before she had to inspect a building site. She entered the bedroom quietly, expecting to find Paige napping. But the room was empty.

When she got off work that evening, she hoped to catch her roommate for a chat, but Paige was nowhere to be seen. For several weeks they barely saw each other. Jordan became concerned about the relationship which seemed to be progressing quickly.

One evening she found Paige studying for exams, and she knew she had a captive audience.

"Look, Paige, we need to talk. I'm worried about you."

"What on earth are you worried about? I'm happier than I've ever been. Alex is so wonderful. I love my classes. I have fun at work. What else could a girl want?"

"Maybe a little bit of 'feet firmly planted on the ground' type of logic. I'm afraid you're getting too serious. You and Alex have only known each other for a few weeks."

"Twelve weeks and two days, to be exact."

"All right, twelve weeks and two days. That's not exactly a lifetime, you know. What if he doesn't feel the same way about you? I don't want you to get hurt."

"You mean like in seventh grade when Johnny Main took Marilee Conway to the Christmas dance? Stop worrying so much. This is different. I love Alex and he loves me. I did grow up, you know. Jordan, I'm twenty-four years old. Things have changed."

"Not your vulnerability. You're still too sweet and innocent. What if he's just using you?"

Paige looked directly at Jordan and said quietly, "We are in love, Jory. I know it's hard for you to believe, since you've seen me through so many crushes and broken relationships, but this time it's real. You're the best friend I have in the world, and I know you're just trying to protect me, but at some point you'll have to trust my judgment. Please try now."

Jordan was certain that Paige discussed her

feelings of apprehension with Alex. They began to include her in many of their activities. It wasn't long before Jordan was convinced that Paige's heart wouldn't be broken this time.

Jordan relaxed as she discovered an incredible strength in the bond that was building between Alex and Paige. It was rare, she thought, but these two people really were made for one another. They had an open and honest relationship. They rarely disagreed, and when they did, they had such respect for one another that compromise was generally reached easily. They gave to each other the kind of love, support, and encouragement that many people spent their lives looking for, but never found.

Jordan and Paige grew tired of their tiny apartment, and they planned to move to a bigger place as soon as Paige finished school. Prices were incredibly high, and they found that the places they liked were still out of their price range. Even as an associate of the architectural firm, Jordan wasn't earning much. And with Paige's plans to do a full year internship before beginning her pediatric residency, money would still be tight.

Alex came to the rescue. Also preparing for his medical internship, his money wouldn't solve all their problems, but by pooling their resources, they could afford a beautiful, two bedroom condo just a block from the beach in nearby Santa Monica. They felt fortunate to find a home in that community. With the much desired rent-control, vacancies were hard to find. But, to their amazement, Alex pulled some hidden strings and the condo was theirs.

The three of them moved in, one month into Alex and Paige's internships. It felt heavenly to Paige and Jordan, who grew tired of the constant need for repairs at their last apartment. The new condo was small, but many large windows gave them a view that they declared was "worth billions."

The main entrance of the condo was to the east, opening onto a small entryway next to the kitchen. The kitchen, to the right of the entry, was spacious, with large cupboards and counters, inspiring the trio to do what they described as "major" cooking and baking. Just to the west of the kitchen was the living room, complete with French doors opening out onto a deck, where they planned to watch every sunset.

To the right of the living room was the master bedroom, with its own private bath, which Paige and Jordan moved into, reveling in the beautiful wallpaper that awaited them. "No green roses," Paige said reminiscently. "Imagine that." On the other side of the living room was the smaller, second bedroom, where Alex would reside, as well as a second bathroom.

They loved their new home, and decorated it with great enthusiasm. They purchased new furniture, most of it in modern designs of black and white. Jordan would have

40

preferred a few more antiques and lots of oak, but she was so happy with the new place that she happily agreed to her roommates' choices.

Paige and Alex had very similar schedules, but in doing their internships at different hospitals, they rarely saw each other. Jordan thought that she spent more time with each of them than they were able to spend together. When they did manage to be home at the same time, Jordan intentionally found extra work to do at the office, giving them some much-needed time alone together.

Within a few months, Paige asked Jordan if she would mind switching bedrooms with Alex. Paige hesitated before asking Jordan, uncomfortable with the prospect, wondering what her friend's reaction would be. "I really love him, Jordan," she explained. "We are really committed to each other. We may even get married someday."

Jordan laughed at Paige's discomfort. "Silly girl. I'd been wondering what was taking you so long. Of course, I'll be happy to trade rooms. But, I'm warning you, if you don't get married, I'll never forgive either one of you. You are the most perfect couple I have ever seen in my life. And I'm counting on you to live happily ever after."

Paige hugged Jordan quickly. "You are so wonderful. Thank you for understanding. And we'll get to work on that 'happily ever after' real soon. I promise."

On the day when Alex and Jordan officially traded rooms, they passed one another in the living room, arms laden with clothing. "I know," Jordan laughed at him, "you just wanted the bigger bedroom."

Their friendship blossomed in the months since they first met. They became very close, and Jordan was finally able to be completely happy for her childhood friend. That this man loved Paige was evident.

Alex kissed her on the cheek as they passed in the living room the next time through. "Paige is right, you are wonderful. We've just been wishing that you could find someone who would love you as much as I love Paige. He's out there somewhere, Jordan."

Jordan smiled at him gently. "Maybe you're right, Alex, but I think I'll remain skeptical for a while longer. You two know all of the dorks I've dated in the past. Men who only have one thought in mind...the love 'em and leave 'em type. Now, if I could find someone like you, maybe I'd be interested."

"Jordan, you've left broken hearts behind you all over this fair city. You can't fool me. You're just more in love with your work than with any human being," he joked. Then, turning more serious, he added, "We just want you to be happy, Jory. Don't close yourself off from the possibilities of love, just because you haven't met Mr. Perfect yet."

"Yet? Are you sure there's a Mr. Perfect out there?"

"For you? Yeah, he's somewhere. I'd be happy to help you look. I'll pick out a good one."

"No, thanks," she grimaced. "I think I prefer my building plans. At least they don't bore me over dinner, or drag me to various functions that I have no interest in attending, or..."

"Okay, okay. I give up. We'll leave you to your solitude. Just be happy, okay?"

Jordan turned to resume her task of moving and began to sing, "I want a man, just like the man that married dear old Mom."

Alex let her go without speaking further, but a sudden thought occurred to him. "I think I know who Mr. Perfect might be. I wonder...well, maybe...we'll just have to wait and see."

*

Jordan's work with Grady was substantial. He gave her many of his most important projects. She worked mainly on hospitals and private homes, two areas of personal interest for her. Her name was now well known throughout the southwestern states. When the name Jordan Blake was signed to a set of plans, buyers knew they were getting more than their money's worth.

One afternoon, Jordan cornered Grady in his office, hoping to finally get a significant increase in her salary.

"Are you sure you won't put the amount in your portfolio and make yourself available to a more prestigious firm?" Grady asked her.

"You know there's no one I'd rather work with, Grady. But with Paige and Alex barely scraping by, someone in this family needs to be bringing home the bacon. Besides, the only way to impress another firm is with my work, not with the amount of money you're going to pay me."

Grady grew to love this young woman dearly in the years she worked with him, and he knew that she deserved a much larger percentage of the firm's profits.

"All right, dear. How much did you want?"

Jordan named a figure, a bit higher than she really wanted, expecting him to argue. Grady merely gave a large, exaggerated sigh, rolled his eyes back as if he were going to faint, and nodded his head.

"You want it, you got it."

Jordan took Grady, Paige and Alex out for a delicious and extravagant dinner to celebrate. Then, feeling a bit guilty, she pledged an equal amount of money to a Santa Monica church that worked extensively with the homeless people of the area.

The small group enjoyed their evening together,

making plans for their futures. "Next comes building our own house," she told her roommates.

It was at the church in Santa Monica that Jordan first met Rev. Blaine Michaels. Impressed with her forthright manner and friendliness, Jordan quickly introduced her roommates to Blaine and the trio began attending services there on Sunday mornings.

Blaine was a breath of fresh air, as far as Jordan was concerned. With her liberal viewpoints on social responsibilities and Biblical interpretation, Jordan found her to be several steps above the average televangelist seen in the media in recent years. Blaine was often found sharing late-night snacks around their kitchen table, as the foursome discussed various controversial issues. She and Jordan lunched together frequently, sometimes including other members of the church, as they planned more effective ways of serving the homeless people in their community.

With her red hair, light brown eyes, and freckle-tipped nose, Jordan expected Blaine to have a fiery temper, but this was one woman who could always remain calm, compassionate, and true to her religious beliefs. She often shared her personal thoughts with her congregation, always inspiring them to reach beyond themselves, to the needy world around them.

She was a welcome addition to the small group of friends. They valued her friendship greatly, with Paige calling on her occasionally to bring some cheer into the lives of her young patients.

*

The months passed quickly once more, and one beautiful spring evening, nearing the end of Alex and Paige's internships, Jordan found Paige standing on the deck. At first, she thought that Paige was looking at the sunset, but as she walked through the door, she saw her shoulders shaking, and saw a crumpled piece of paper in her hands.

"Paige," she cried, alarm ringing in her voice. "What's wrong?"

"I got it. I got the pediatric residency at the Children's Hospital in Geneva."

"But I thought you applied too late for that."

"Someone decided not to do their residency there, and I got it."

"That's wonderful! It's exactly what you've been dreaming of since you were twelve years old. But I don't think those are tears of happiness."

"It's all just gotten so complicated." Paige paused, trying to formulate her thoughts and her words. "Alex asked me to marry him."

43

"So? He'll be so proud of you. He'll probably drag you to Switzerland."

"It's not just that." Paige's voice trembled now. "I can't leave Suzanne."

"Paige, can't you please tell me what's going on with her? Let me help."

"I wish I could, but I can't even help her. She won't talk to me. She hasn't ever talked to Mom and Pop about it, but she's never really recovered from her ordeal. I know she still has nightmares. The last time I was there for a weekend, I could hear her crying in her sleep. But when I went in her room, she told me not to worry about her, that everything was okay."

"Paige, it's been four years. That's a very long time to keep something swept under a rug. Suzanne must have suffered horribly. Can't you take her to a psychiatrist? Or take her to see Blaine? She can help. She's a very good counselor."

"I can't. Suzi doesn't want to see anyone and Pop tells me not to pressure her. But even if she won't let me help her, I can't just move halfway around the world."

Jordan agonized over her friend's pain and uncertainty. Paige deserved this opportunity. She deserved a lifetime of happiness and success. And yet, she thought, if Suzi were my sister, I guess I couldn't leave her, either.

If Paige was to accept the residency, she would have to respond in three weeks. Jordan urged her to wait. "Something will work out," she assured Paige. But she didn't quite believe her own words.

Two days later, Alex and Paige announced that they would be married on the eighteenth of June. Jordan was dumbfounded.

"What does this mean? What about Switzerland?"

"She's going to accept the offer. She'll be working in the research of children's diseases. This is an incredible opportunity, and I'm not about to let her miss out on it," Alex told her. His pride and enthusiasm were exactly what Jordan expected.

She wondered about Suzanne and her problems, but didn't want to burst any bubbles. This isn't the time for that, she thought. Realism hits all too often. This is a time for celebration.

The next few months were even more chaotic. Paige and Alex worked like maniacs as they came to the end of their residencies. They were exhausted and Jordan often wondered about their abilities to care for their patients. They assured her that they would eat right and sleep whenever possible. "But," Alex told her, "if you want to be a 'real' doctor, you've got to prove that sleepless maniacs can make sound decisions."

44

Jordan worked late into the evening on her regular assignments from Grady. And she worked until early in the morning on a special project for Alex. Together, they were planning a house for Paige. She followed his exact specifications, making her own executive decisions as to how to make some things better. But what puzzled her were Alex's finances.

Perhaps he's just planning to give her the plans as a wedding present, she thought to herself. They certainly couldn't afford to build this with the money they have now. She was thrilled to draw up the plans, despite her questions. Paige's home wouldn't be the first one she created, as they dreamed of when they were younger, but if they followed her plans, it would certainly be the most beautiful.

Jordan finished the plans at the end of May. She presented them to Alex with a gold ribbon tied around them.

"You might as well keep them," he told her. "Because you're going to finish the job for me."

"What on earth are you talking about? Look, Alex, I don't understand..."

"Just stop right there," he interrupted her. "No further questions. Just know that you and I are going to build that house for Paige."

"Someday," Jordan added.

"Yes, someday," he concluded as he walked away from her.

She admired his determination to give Paige such a fabulous gift. He did love her so much. Yet she couldn't help but wonder if he had any idea how much it would cost to build a home like the one he had in his mind, and now on paper. I'll have a realistic talk with him about this. And soon, she resolved.

The next evening Jordan accepted an invitation to dinner with one of the other associates from the firm. With less talent and a bigger ego than many of his colleagues, Quentin H. Galbraith was not one of Jordan's favorite people. But Barbara Langley, a receptionist for MacIntyre and Associates and the only woman in the world that was able to keep him in line and make people think there was hope for him, finally decided that her life had some value and she didn't need to put up with any more garbage from him.

Jordan liked Barbara. She was a quiet, unassuming woman with an inner strength that often went unnoticed. Jordan suspected that she was also the only woman that Quentin respected. Despite his lack of moral principles, he shaped up when Barbara was around.

Now that he was having to do without her, he was indeed in sorry shape. His macho attitude was about to make the other associates at the firm lock him up. Jordan felt sorry for him, so she agreed to the date.

45

She wasn't looking forward to spending the evening with Quentin, but he needed a diversion from his self-pity, and she needed an evening out. She was at home alone, preparing herself physically and mentally for her date, when there was a knock at the door.

Quickly pulling the last curler out of her hair, she raced to the door. She planned to meet Quentin at the restaurant, and was expecting no one. Maybe just someone selling some sort of junk, she thought as she pulled the door open.

The man standing in front of her was obviously impatient, probably angry, and had his fist raised in her face, ready to knock on the door once more. But, she thought, he was very nice to look at. His long, gorgeous eyelashes surrounded deep blue eyes. His shoulders were broad, his hips slim. His tight-fitting jeans accentuated finely shaped legs. His shirt was obviously of fine quality, and she noticed that his sneakers were new and of the latest design. Jordan glanced back to his face, taken aback by the scowl she found there.

He felt a bit surprised as he looked at the beautiful young woman standing before him. Overwhelmed by her long, brown hair which shaped her face with soft curls, and the most beautiful brown eyes and dark, lush lashes he had ever seen, he was momentarily speechless. She certainly wasn't what he expected. She was supposed to have a sharp, cruel beauty. She was supposed to look like the unscrupulous person she was.

"Well," he muttered as he pushed past her into the entry of the apartment, "looks can certainly be deceiving."

"I beg your pardon? Do I know you?"

"I'm looking for my brother, Alexander Wyndham. I believe he lives here."

"I'm sorry, there must be some mistake. An Alex Wynne lives here. I guess it would be easy to confuse the names. Now, if you'll excuse me." Jordan, still holding the door open, motioned for him to exit.

He ignored her movement and stepped further into the living room, looking around. "Modest, but tasteful," he said as he assessed the place.

Jordan was in a hurry, and becoming increasingly agitated. She wasn't quite sure how to get this tall man with the very large shoulders out of her apartment. Nice to look at, but a pain in the neck, she thought.

He turned back to face her, distaste curling his lips. "I suppose you're the little gold-digger, in person. I've warned my brother about people like you. People who marry for cold cash."

"Mr. Wyndham, if that's your name, I don't know what you're talking about. My name is Jordan Blake, and I'm getting ready for a date with a friend with a moderate income. I don't plan to marry anybody."

"Look, I know my brother lives here, so if this is your apartment, you must be the hopeful bride. Well, I'm here to see that your wedding doesn't take place."

"I am not anyone's future bride. And the only people who live here are myself and my two roommates, Paige Kendell and Alex Wynne. They are about to be married, but they couldn't possibly be the couple you're trying to destroy. Alex is poor, and Paige is no gold-digger. Besides, I've known Alex for ages, and he doesn't even have a brother."

The man before her seemed to hear only a portion of what she was saying, as if he were trying to compute an impossible math problem.

"Two roommates?" he finally asked. "You live here, too?"

Deciding that it was hopeless to argue with the man, Jordan shrugged her shoulders and nodded her head. Then, trying to add a little levity to the ridiculous situation, she answered him.

"Yes. That's not so unusual. Three wallets are better than one."

The sarcasm returned to his voice in full force now. "Especially when one of those wallets belongs to Alexander Wyndham."

"I'm really in a hurry, and I'm more than a little tired of this argument. As I already told you, you've made a mistake. Alex is just plain, old Wynne, not Wyndham, and he's poor as a church mouse." Jordan hated the way her voice was rising; but that's what it always did to her when she least wanted it to. This man was infuriating, and she wanted to maintain her composure completely.

It took Mr. Wyndham a few moments to answer her. He looked at her in surprise, wondering why she would be so angry when she was probably in cahoots with the gold-digger.

"I think I finally understand the innocent act. Let me guess. You're single, you're broke, and you've heard of the Wyndham money. I suppose you think you can capture my heart and my bank accounts, just as this Paige Kendell has done with Alexander."

Jordan was furious by this point in the conversation. She barely heard the personal insult, but resembling a mother bear, she went in for the kill.

"Paige Kendell is the most generous, loving person in the world. If she captured anyone's heart, it was the man who was destined to spend the rest of his life with her. Now, since you don't seem to be acquainted with any of the residents of this particular apartment, and since I really must be going..." She had no opportunity to finish her attack, because at that moment Alex's voice spoke from behind her.

47

"You tell him, Jordan. This old brother of mine needs to be put in his place now and then."

Jordan whirled around, looking from one man to the other. Then, resting her gaze on the one she thought she knew, she said, "Brother? I don't understand. You don't have a brother."

"Well, I guess I've been a little deceitful. Alexander Wyndham, at your service, ma'am." He swept an imaginary hat from his head and gave her a deep bow.

Jordan said nothing. She just stared at his smiling face. When his grin widened even further, she spoke. "You don't have any money."

"That's not exactly true. You see, when I first met Paige, she told me about your decision to pay your own way through school. I liked your philosophy, so I adopted it."

"But, your name..."

"I took the name Alex Wynne when I was in pre-med. I didn't want any special favors from professors because of who my parents are. I guess I just wanted to prove myself."

"But..." Jordan began. Then, as her memory kicked into gear, she started to laugh. "You turkey. I've been supporting you. I've been paying your bills and buying your groceries."

Relieved to see that her sense of humor was still working, Alex attempted to explain himself. "I know, and I'm sorry about that. I do have money invested in various places, and tons in savings accounts. I'll pay you back. Every penny, I promise."

"So that's how you planned to build the house. I don't want you to pay me back. I've enjoyed helping two brilliant doctors get started on their careers. Besides, I...oh, I forgot!" Jordan turned to face the bewildered brother standing next to her.

"Mr. Wyndham, I am sorry that I didn't believe you when you said your brother lived here. And now," glancing at her watch, "I really do need to go."

"Where are you off to in such a hurry, and why isn't your date picking you up?" Alex asked her, suddenly looking at the dark green evening dress and the matching shoes and handbag.

They weren't aware of it, but Alex's brother was also studying her more closely. He took in the delicate skin, the faint flush in the cheeks, the slim figure that appeared to be in terrific shape. He wondered if she liked to go jogging on the beach.

Jordan looked at Alex and wrinkled her nose. "Because I'm going out with Quentin and I don't want him to know where I live."

The silent brother chose that moment to speak. "You're dating someone like that? You don't even want him to know where you live? Who is this fellow, anyway?"

"She's a wise woman, Nick. I don't want him to know where she lives either. I don't like the idea of you going anywhere with him, Jordan. What gives?"

"It's a mercy date, of sorts. He's been feeling so sorry for himself since Barbara dumped him. Besides, I deserved a night out."

"You're too nice, Jordan. Don't try too hard to fix his life up. He doesn't deserve it."

"Don't worry. I can take care of myself."

"I know you can. You're a tough little cookie."

"I am NO cookie, Alex," Jordan declared as she kissed him on the cheek.

"You're so wonderful. If I didn't have Paige..." He gave her a playful pat on the rump.

"If you didn't have Paige, you'd be the saddest, most lonely man on earth, and you know it. Now I AM leaving. I was supposed to meet Quentin at eight o'clock. He's going to be consumed with self-pity if I'm much later." She turned to the man that she still hadn't been introduced to. "By the way, if you haven't figured it out, I'm Jordan Blake, a friend of the family."

"I'm sorry, Jordan. I've forgotten all of my manners. May I present my brother, Dr. Nicholas Wyndham, the world's greatest kiddie doctor and my personal mentor."

Jordan reached out a slender hand to shake that of the man still watching her in disbelief. "It's a pleasure, Dr. Wyndham."

"I'm afraid it hasn't been much of a pleasure for you, Ms. Blake. Please forgive me for everything I said to you."

"Yes, of course," she said noncommittally, as she skipped lightly toward the door. "See you later, Alex."

"Be careful, sweetie," Alex called after her. "Tell the moron to keep his pants zipped up or he'll have to deal with me."

CHAPTER FIVE

Then plainly know, my heart's dear love is set
On the fair daughter of rich Capulet:
As mine on hers, so hers is set on mine.
-Romeo and Juliet

The two men stood looking after Jordan as she left. When the door closed behind her, the younger brother turned to face his still-glowering sibling.

"Well, what fine things did you say to the lady that were cause for the not-so-eloquent apology?"

"I'm afraid you wouldn't speak to me again if I told you. You really care about her, don't you?" Nick's surprise was genuine.

"Like I said, she's wonderful. Paige and I love her very much."

"I flew back as soon as Mother phoned with your news. I'm here to talk to you about this Paige Kendell."

"Oh, come on, Nick. I know these warnings by heart. And I will admit that you were right about most of the girls I dated in the past, but this time you're wrong. So very wrong."

"How can you be sure? How long have you known this woman?"

Alex rolled his eyes and grinned at his brother, "Before you say that I should stick with someone I've known forever, like you and Lianna, let me tell you that I've known Paige long enough to know her dreams and goals for life. And long enough to know exactly what kind of person she is. Besides," Alex continued before Nick could interrupt, "I not only didn't tell Jordan about my background, I didn't tell Paige, either. I thought that might make a nice surprising wedding present for her."

"You may not have told them, but you can be sure they knew." Doubt dies hard, and Nicholas Wyndham wasn't a man to be easily swayed. He knew for years that women had one goal in life, and that was to find rich husbands.

"I'm sorry that Lianna hurt you, Nicky. But you've really got to stop being so cynical. Okay, I know you'll need more convincing where Paige is concerned, but there's not much I can say. You'll have to meet her and form your own opinion."

"It would be a waste of time. I've already formed the opinion."

"It'll change. I guarantee it." Alex had no doubt where Paige was concerned. He knew that she could charm his brother in no time.

Jordan's date with Quentin was everything she imagined it would be. She knew exactly why Paige called him a worm, and why Alex insisted that he was pure reptile.

The evening was not a pleasant one. Quentin flirted with every female within earshot. He seemed to think that crude behavior was what was expected of a real man. He made endless passes at Jordan, which she deftly handled. Despite his ridiculous attempts to enchant her, he only repulsed his intended prey. She grew tired of his humorless, raw jokes and wandering hands early in the evening, but wanted to spare his ego from further bruising. She remained calm, rebuffed him gently, and after several exhausting hours, pleaded a migraine and left him.

The fact that Jordan did not suffer from migraines gave her a momentary twinge of guilt. "He may be a snake," she thought, "but I really shouldn't lie to him." She quickly talked herself out of her self-condemnation, deciding that her sanity was at stake, and it was time to retreat to the sanctuary of the beach-side condominium.

As she drove towards home, she hoped that the irritating brother would be gone. Yet, even as she entertained the notion, she felt her heart skip a beat as she remembered his deep, blue eyes and broad shoulders. He shared the beauty of Alex's eyes, and she wondered if he also had Alex's dimples. But then, she told herself, she'd probably never see him smile, so she would never know.

Jordan pushed all such thoughts from her mind, thinking instead of relaxation and rest. She wanted to slip into her soft, white terry robe, sit on the balcony, and sip hot chocolate.

*

Paige beat Jordan home by several hours. She was surprised to find Alex deep in discussion with an unknown man who greatly resembled him. This man was a bit taller, and perhaps two or three years older. His cheekbones were more prominent, his jaw line quite strong, and the quick smile was missing. But the resemblance was there.

The two men stood as she entered the living room. Alex put his arm around her shoulder, kissed her soundly, and asked how her day had been. Nicholas watched with curiosity, marveling at the small, blonde, enchanting creature in his brother's arms. She glanced at him with a gentle smile and inquisitive eyes.

"Alex, you're terrible at introductions. Hello, I'm Paige Kendell," she said to the stranger as she reached to shake his hand.

Nicholas hesitated, then took her small, but seemingly capable hand. He merely said, "Nicholas Wyndham."

"Why don't we all sit down," Alex suggested. "Honey, there are some things we need to talk about."

"Oh, yes, that reminds me. Alex, you need to pay Jordan your share of next month's rent."

"We're not going to have to worry about rent for long. I'm going to build you a mansion."

Paige laughed and said to Nicholas, "Yes, and maybe he'll get me a ski chalet for winter jaunts to the slopes." She wondered why he was scowling at her as she spoke.

Alex's voice was serious as he spoke to her. "If you want one, I'll buy it."

Paige could always tell when he was teasing her, and she was puzzled by this tone. "What's this all about? Did someone die and make you a millionaire?"

"Nobody died. Paige, Nicholas is my brother."

"Alex," her voice scolded, "I had no idea that you had a bro..." Before she could finish her first thought, another burst into her mind. "Wyndham. As in THE Wyndhams, of Wyndham Enterprises, Inc."

The explanations were easier than Alex expected. Paige was amazed. She never suspected. "And I didn't even have to kiss a frog," she murmured as Alexander Wyndham revealed his news to her.

Nicholas watched, first in total disbelief. This girl is good, he thought. But as the hours wore on, her honesty and integrity penetrated his ever-skeptical mind. His mother warned him not to interfere. She promised him that Alex had found a real gem in this girl, that they would probably find her to be sincere and just as sweet as Alex told her Paige was.

Before Jordan returned, Nicholas was beginning to believe that his brother had found the one-in-a-million girl, as their father had before them. He was completely enamored of Paige in a very short time, and even found himself laughing at the playful, happy relationship she shared with Alex.

Sometime after the shock wore off, Paige asked about their missing roommate. After hearing Alex's rendition of the earlier events of the evening, in which he deleted the part about Nicholas' verbal attack on Jordan, Paige grew worried about her friend and her choice of dates.

"I know she likes to think she can take care of herself, but I wish she'd stop putting herself in these situations. She seems to think it's her responsibility to rid the world of despair."

Alex kissed her on the ear and said, "Don't worry. I taught her how to defend herself against any octopus she might end up with. Besides, she'll probably get tired of him and come home early."

Nicholas pondered their words in silence. On a mercy date, huh? He'd been on a few of those himself in his lifetime. She must have some concern for the well-being of others if she'd agree to go out with this Quentin. Nick vowed that he wouldn't fall prey to another woman's conniving plans, but he would like to find out if there were two in a million right here in Alexander's life.

As he contemplated the possibility, Jordan walked through the front door with a big sigh. Her thoughts of hot chocolate on the deck dissolved as she looked at the three faces turned in her direction.

Paige raced towards her, scolding as she walked. "Jordan Marie Blake, how could you? You know Quentin is a slime-ball. Why would you subject yourself to an evening with him?"

Jordan smiled and yawned. "Okay, I promise, this is the LAST mercy date I ever go on."

Alex chuckled, "That's what you said after the last three you went on. Give it up, Jordan. You have the softest heart around these parts. The word is out all over Santa Monica... 'For a soft shoulder and a listening ear, call Ms. Jordan Blake, 1-800...'" He let his voice trail off.

"Oh, Alex, can't you see she's tired? Leave her alone. Now, sweetie, come over here. You must get to know Nicholas." Paige looked at Alex, who winked at her, reading her match-making thoughts immediately.

The next several days passed in a whirlwind of activity. The preparations for the wedding were well underway. Paige demanded to meet Alex's parents, and admonished him with mock-severity for hiding them from her. She was amazed to find that they lived barely twenty minutes from the condo, and that Alex had been visiting them once a week for the past several years, keeping them updated on the progression of his relationship with Paige.

The Wyndhams were delighted with Paige, accepting her into their family without hesitation. Marguerite Wyndham was in her mid-fifties, dark hair speckled by only a hint of grey. A small woman whose strength and composure made one forget her diminutive stature, she charmed people with her warmth and the sparkle in her deep blue eyes.

She scolded her son for not bringing Paige home sooner. Samuel Wyndham, tall, silver-haired and debonair, assured his wife that they had plenty of time to get to know Paige, and maybe their son wanted to do the wooing on his own, without his mother's assistance.

Jordan accompanied them on this significant visit, and was welcomed warmly by Alex's parents.

Marguerite put her arms around Paige's and Jordan's waists and said, "I'm so glad you are finally here. We feel as if we know you so well. Alex has shared your life with us all these months. I only wish he would have brought you girls around sooner."

Jordan immediately fell in love with the Wyndhams and their estate. The endless, rolling lawns were well cared for. She thought of her mother as she strolled among the flower gardens. Marguerite was proud of her flowers, and was thrilled to find someone who could identify and appreciate each variety.

The house itself was magnificent. Knowing that Jordan was an architect, Marguerite took her on a room to room excursion. It was an architect's dream, with spacious rooms, each designed and decorated creatively and with tasteful beauty. Marguerite had done several rooms with decor from different time periods and with different cultural influences. Jordan admired the Japanese dolls and the hand-painted room divider in Marguerite's sitting room, as well as the oak armoire and the Irish linen chest in her bedroom.

"I'm sorry, my dear. This must be extremely boring for you. But I do love this house so."

"I can understand why. It's so beautiful. I especially love all the fireplaces. Even living in a warm climate, there is nothing more wonderful than relaxing in front of a fire."

Nicholas spent most of the day watching Jordan. He'd enjoyed the evening at the condo, as he listened to the cheerful banter of the three roommates. Now, as he watched her, he wondered if her skin was as soft as it looked, and he felt the ice around his heart melt a little bit every time she smiled. He only wished she would smile at him. But, he reminded himself, I've never really given her any reason to smile at me. Whereupon he vowed to be a bit more charming.

Jordan caught him looking at her several times during the day, and she wondered what horrible thoughts he could possibly be thinking about her now. On one occasion, he gave her a slow, heart-stopping smile, and she realized that his dimples, while not as pronounced as his brother's, were indeed there.

Marguerite watched her older son and smiled secretly to herself. At one point she caught her husband watching Nicholas as well. He smiled, shaking his finger in her direction. She knew that was his way of telling her not to interfere and to let nature take its course.

*

The day of the wedding was warm and still. Alex and Paige were to be married in the small church near the condo, with Blaine presiding over the ceremony. They'd worked with her over the past several weeks to write a very personal, lovely wedding ceremony, which Jordan knew would make her eyes fill with tears. She was thankful for her thick, dark lashes, which eliminated the need to wear mascara. This occasion would not warrant smeared make-up.

Jordan expected the typical wedding day jitters for her friends, but Paige was not the same woman who dragged her to the pizza parlor to meet the man of her dreams so many months ago. This Paige was calm and prepared, completely sure that this was right.

She was, Jordan thought, the most beautiful bride she had ever seen. She wore her mother's Victorian lace wedding gown. It was the traditional white, high collar gown, with pearl buttons at the back. The bodice had to be taken in to fit her slim figure, and it now fit perfectly. Liza pulled Paige's hair up, allowing just a few tiny curls to escape. Deciding against a veil, Paige wore flowers in her hair, insisting that while she loved tradition, she preferred to see her groom clearly.

A few rooms down the hall, Nicholas, too, was amazed. Alex had only a momentary flash of cold feet, as he wondered if he could possibly be good enough for the woman he was about to marry.

Jordan made a last-minute check, and finding everything ready, gave Nicholas the signal that all was well. The groom and his brother filed down the stairs. They found their parents waiting there, then after nodding to Blaine, Nicholas sent the flower girl and the ring bearer, young cousins of Paige, on their way down the aisle. He followed after them as Blaine walked in from the side door, meeting him as he walked past the chancel. Next came Alex, escorted by his parents.

The wedding march began, and Jordan entered the room. All eyes were on her, noticing the quick smile that was brought by Blaine winking at her.

She really is lovely, thought Marguerite as she watched Jordan come down the aisle. The peach-colored gown was perfect for her dark hair and lightly tanned complexion. She, too, wore flowers in her hair, which was pulled back into a loosely-knotted French braid.

As Paige and her parents entered the chapel, everyone turned to smile upon the bride. Nicholas' eyes remained on the maid-of-honor.

The ceremony was beautiful. Alex and Paige smiled through their tears as they said their vows, words they had written to each other. Words about their hopes and dreams and promises for the future they would share.

The best man found himself paying more attention to the woman standing beside the bride than to the service. He had no more doubts about Paige. A few days in her company was enough to make him believe that all Alex said about her was true. Nicholas was captivated by his new sister's sincerity and sensitivity. He was inspired by the profound love shared by the young couple, and felt honored to be able to share in their joy.

As the bride and groom lit the Unity candle, Nicholas again turned his attention to Jordan. He surprised himself as he wondered what it would be like to hold her in his arms. He watched her working out all of the details of the wedding. He saw the plans she drew up for Alex and Paige's house. He saw her as capable and creative, and he saw her with laughter lighting her face. As he watched her now, he saw the tears shining in her eyes.

Jordan knew that he watched her. She wondered if he was still angry with her over their first encounter. When she returned to the condo that night, he laughed with Paige and Alex, but had said little to her. And, she now admitted to herself, she hadn't really wanted to say too much to him.

She spent the past several days working like mad to get this wedding planned, and had little time to speak with him. He was always polite, but she suspected that he didn't particularly care for her. At least he warmed up to Paige. That's all that matters, she assured herself, as Paige and Alex exchanged their rings.

Nicholas was abruptly brought back to the present as Blaine said, "It is my privilege to present to you Alexander Wyndham and Paige Kendell, as husband and wife." The newlyweds ran happily down the aisle. Nicholas walked towards Jordan and held his arm out to her. He noticed her hesitation before she took it and wished he hadn't been so rude to her when they first met.

The guests left the church to make the twenty minute drive to the country club, where the reception was to be held. The wedding party stood at the door, greeting everyone as they exited, assuring them that they would join them there. When the guests had gone, the photographer wisked the wedding party and family away from the door for the inevitable picture-taking. Paige insisted on a picture of the maid-of-honor and the best man standing together.

As the picture was taken, Alex whispered in Paige's ear, "Always the little romantic, aren't you?"

"They look wonderful together. I think we should work on this."

Marguerite heard her new daughter's remark and said quietly, "I agree. Now..."

"Now, you beautiful ladies will keep your noses out of this." Samuel interrupted his wife. "Outside forces do budding romances absolutely no good."

"Yeah, but Father," Alex whispered, "this was all part of my plan. I decided ages ago that they'd be a good match. We just had to wait for the right moment to get them together." Then, "Oh, no," as a tall, slender blonde woman walked towards the wedding party.

The words "gorgeous" and "striking" flitted through Jordan's mind as she watched the graceful creature coming toward them.

"My goodness. Aren't you finished with all of this yet?" the creature asked in a silky voice.

"Hello, Lianna, dear," Marguerite said as she put her arm around the young blonde's waist. "How kind of you to come."

"You know I wouldn't miss Alex's special day. Besides, with only one Wyndham man left, I couldn't pass up the opportunity to spend time with the family." She gave a soft laugh and walked towards Nicholas. "Now, darling, if you're all finished..."

She lowered her voice, and Jordan couldn't hear the rest of her sentence as they walked away. She saw Nicholas put his arm around the woman, saw him lower his head closer to hers, and heard the soft laugh responding to whatever he said. Jordan didn't quite understand the small stabbing sensation in her chest as they left the chapel.

Marguerite walked towards her. "I'm sorry I didn't have a chance to introduce you to Lianna. She never seems to stay in one place very long. But, I'm sure you'll be able to meet her later. Her mother and I were very dear friends. There was a time that we thought Lianna and Nicholas would join our families together, but now they're just good friends."

That didn't look much like "just friends," Jordan thought to herself. She quickly changed the subject, pointing out how happy Alex and Paige looked. The mother of the groom was very proud and easily turned her attention to the new topic of discussion.

Liza joined them as they stood in the center aisle of the sanctuary. "Jordan, your mother said to tell you that she and your dad would see you at the reception." She turned to Marguerite. "It was a beautiful wedding, wasn't it?"

Marguerite put her arm around Liza's waist. "It was made even more so because of their incredible love for one another. We're very happy to welcome Paige into our family. She is such a lovely girl. Samuel and I think that she's perfect for our boy. We're looking forward to many grandchildren, too."

Jordan smiled at Marguerite and Liza. "You may have a long wait. I know that they want children, but it may be several years before they decide they're ready. They will make wonderful parents, though. And any child would be lucky to have you for grandparents."

When the photographer finished with Paige and Alex, they were able to leave the church to join their guests at the club. They greeted their families and friends, and Alex led Paige to the dance floor. He relinquished her only once, so that she could dance with Franklin. Meanwhile, he spun his glowing mother around the room, dumping her in his father's arms as soon as the dance ended so he could return to his new wife.

Jordan danced several dances with Grady, complimenting him on his fancy steps. Emerson cut in once, apologizing to Grady for taking away his lovely partner.

"This little girl owes her father a dance," he explained to Grady.

As he swept her around the room, Emerson hugged his daughter tightly to him. "I don't believe we've done this since you were a little girl, and you put your feet on top of mine and we danced together."

Jordan giggled. "I don't guarantee that I won't still end up on top of your toes, but I hope I've learned a few new steps since then."

Emerson kissed her swiftly on the cheek. "Darling, it wouldn't matter if you still had to stand on top of my shoes, I'd always love dancing with you. So," he paused, smiling down at Jordan. "When will we be dancing at your wedding? There are plenty of attractive young men around here. What about that brother of Alex's?"

Jordan's blush was no surprise to her father. "Dad, I just met him, and he doesn't think too highly of me. I think I'd better stick with you."

"How about sticking with me for a dance," Samuel Wyndham's voice spoke into her ear. "Do you mind if I steal your beautiful daughter?"

Emerson stopped dancing abruptly, reluctantly releasing Jordan. "If you must," he said gruffly, and without further acknowledgment of the exchange, he walked off the dance floor.

As Jordan and Samuel began to dance, he looked woeful. "I hope I didn't interrupt something important. And I'm sorry if I offended your father."

Jordan looked at her father, who now stood next to the patio door, watching her with a frown on his face. As Jordan watched him, she saw her mother join him. They spoke for a few moments, then Emerson took her arm as she led him to the dance floor.

Jordan smiled at her parents as they moved gracefully through the growing crowd. Emerson and Celeste moved as one, their love for one another evidenced by their embrace.

Jordan looked up at Samuel. "I think Dad was caught up in his reminiscing. I suppose that sometimes it's hard for parents to realize their children are all grown up."

"Just you wait, my dear. Someday you'll find out just how hard it is." Samuel smiled slightly at his son and new daughter-in-law as they passed them on the dance floor. "And yet, when they are happy, you don't mind the changes quite as much. I believe my boy is extremely happy. Just look at them."

Alex and Paige cut the cake quickly in between dances, and Jordan and Suzanne worked together to cut the rest for the guests. They developed a pattern of discussing non-threatening, sometimes trivial subjects in the years following Suzi's disappearance. Jordan gleaned little information from her friends over the years. Her curiosity had been replaced by concern. As far as she knew, Suzanne never underwent any counseling, to help her deal with whatever had happened to her. The entire Kendell family acted as if there had never been a problem. Yet, Suzanne, now sixteen years of age, remained reclusive and quiet.

Jordan danced several dances with friends from school and work. She was thanking her childhood friend, Johnny Main, for their dance, laughing at his recollections of their early years. Glancing mournfully at Paige, he teased, "Boy, I never should have jilted her in the seventh grade. Now, look what she's gone and done. My heart's completely broken."

Jordan linked her arm through his and giggled. "Gee, Johnny, I guess you'll have to settle for me."

Before he could take her up on her offer, he looked inquisitively at the tall man approaching them. Turning to see what Johnny was looking at, Jordan felt a hand on her shoulder.

"I believe that it is expected for us to share a dance." Nicholas Wyndham spoke from behind her.

Jordan looked apologetically at Johnny, who waved her away. "Of course," she replied as Nicholas led her to the dance floor.

They danced well together, although she wondered why he held her so close. They didn't talk, and as she relaxed in his arms, she felt as if this were where she belonged.

When the dance ended, Nicholas seemed reluctant to leave her side. He wasn't ready to relinquish her yet, liking the way she felt in his arms. Without asking, he swept her back to the dance floor, hoping the music would never end.

Almost before she could stop herself, Jordan blurted, "We really got off to a bad start. If you've no plans for this evening, perhaps I could make it up to you."

Lianna had been out of sight for some time. No doubt looking for a richer man, Nicholas thought earlier. Now, his thoughts were for Jordan. He smiled unexpectedly, wondering what she had in mind. Unfortunately, Lianna chose this moment to return. Before Nicholas was able to answer Jordan, Lianna cut in and Jordan retreated.

Nicholas had cared deeply for Lianna once. Now he was merely annoyed. Her true colors appeared shortly before their own wedding date, several years ago. He had given her a beautiful engagement ring, with what he considered to be a large diamond. Lianna pouted for several days, and then returned it to the jeweler, demanding a more expensive replacement. She then hired a private investigator to look into Nicholas' financial affairs. When he discovered what she was doing, she defended herself with a hurt look and tears. Nick almost felt that he was wrong to be angry. Lianna explained that she had to make sure he could support her in the manner to which she was accustomed. And she didn't believe that a mere doctor would be able to do that. When her investigator discovered that Nicholas had substantial holdings in Wyndham Enterprises, her curiosity was ended. He was indeed worthy of marrying her.

Even now, Nicholas still cared about her. They grew up together, spending endless family holidays in each other's company. Their mothers tried as often as possible to pair them off at dinner parties and on weekend family outings. But Nick was disillusioned and hurt, and ended their engagement.

His parents had such a marvelous marriage. He knew that they would always respect their vows, whether rich or poor. Perhaps his mother was the last woman alive who didn't care about all the wealth. And Paige, Nicholas now made the mental adjustment. But Lianna was just a friend. A friend whom he suspected of trying to get her claws into him again.

As they danced, he tried to find Jordan. He thought he saw her chatting with a handsome, athletic blond man near the buffet table. Nicholas realized it was the same man she'd been dancing and laughing with before he'd asked her to dance. As he watched them now, he noticed that they seemed to be very comfortable with one another. They seemed to touch each other a lot. First, Jordan's hand on the man's arm. Then, the man kissed his own finger and pressed it to Jordan's lips. Nick couldn't see how she reacted to that, because at that moment Lianna tugged him around, grumbling, "Nick, we can't just dance in one place."

Nick lost sight of the couple he'd been watching, and when he saw them again, the man had his arm draped over Jordan's shoulder and she was standing on tiptoe to kiss him on the cheek.

"Ow, Nicholas Wyndham, how many times are you going to step on my toes?"

Still, his eyes were glued on Jordan. He felt disappointment creep up. Had she intended to extend some sort of invitation to him? Was she really ready to forgive him? He mentally kicked himself, thinking that he had to stop trying to right all wrongs before he had gathered all the facts. He had been rude and stupid. If she will give me another chance, perhaps I can show her the other side of me, he thought. He felt a small pang of jealousy as he saw Jordan, still laughing with the blond. "Probably a surfer," he muttered to himself.

"What on earth are you mumbling about? Pay some attention to me for a change," Lianna pouted. They danced one more dance, Lianna's arms locked so tightly around him that he wasn't sure how to extricate himself. Eventually, she asked him to take her to the airport. She was off to the Mediterranean for a holiday, she told him. She begged him to come with her, assuring him that even mere doctors deserved vacations now and then. He secretly would have loved to go, but Lianna was not the woman he would like to spend his time with.

Unable to find Jordan, he quickly told Alex to tell her that he would call her as soon as possible. He kissed both his brother and his sister-in-law, secured their forgiveness for having to leave so early, and led Lianna to the waiting car.

Jordan thanked Alex when he gave her the message. He puzzled over the disappointed look in her eyes.

Well, Jordan thought, I guess I won't see or hear from him again. She followed Paige to a small room that was reserved for the wedding party, and helped her change into her traveling clothes.

Paige was exhausted, but exhilarated. "I can't believe I'm really married."

"I am so happy for you and Alex. If ever two people deserved to live happily ever after..."

"...it's us. I know. I think so, too. I do love him so much. But, Jordan, I want you to be just as excited and contented as I am right now. I want to stand up with you at your wedding."

Jordan almost wanted that, too. "Yeah, well when you find another Alex, be sure to send him my way," she joked with her friend. "Come on, hurry up. Your groom is probably wearing holes in the carpet by now. And the guests are waiting impatiently with their handfuls of birdseed."

"Whatever happened to good old rice?"

"It's not good for the birds. For a doctor, you don't know much, do you?"

"Leave it to you to know about animal safety. All right, lead on. I'm ready," Paige said breathlessly as she straightened her jacket and slipped into her shoes.

The bride raced into her new husband's waiting arms. The guests clapped and cheered as they kissed. Alex stuffed Paige's garter in his pocket. He lowered his voice so that only she could hear him. "I have someone specific in mind for this."

Suzi and her friend, Debi, pushed their way to the front, "Paige, throw your bouquet to me. Throw it to me," Debi squealed. Several other excited young girls pushed forward. "Over here, Paige." "Here, toss it over here." But, Paige also had someone specific in mind. As Jordan giggled at the arms reaching out towards Paige, the bouquet flew directly towards her. An old softball veteran, she instinctively caught it, gave her friend a wrinkled nose, tongue-sticking-out look, and then returned the wink Alex gave her.

The Kendell-Wyndhams took their leave, birdseed and best wishes flying towards them. Their mothers stood crying, their fathers beamed, Suzi and Debi frowned at Jordan, and Jordan kissed her own mother and father and excused herself to return to the condo.

The quiet apartment was at first welcoming. Jordan thought about the privacy and freedom she would now have, the work she'd be able to get finished. Then, as she walked around, memories filling her thoughts, she decided that it might take some time to adjust to living alone.

She thought of Paige baking her favorite chocolate cake, the recipe secretly retrieved from Milly in time for their last birthday. She thought of Alex making her laugh whenever she was tired or upset about something. She walked into Alex and Paige's bedroom. The bed had been stripped of everything except the bedspread and pillows. The corners were stacked high with packed boxes, suitcases and trunks. They would be back after their honeymoon, to collect some of their necessary belongings before they flew to Geneva.

Jordan glanced around the room, taking Paige's long-loved teddy bear into her arms. She knew that it would make the move with them. Paige cherished her bear with the tear in the shoulder and one missing eye. She promised to perform surgery on the poor, wounded bear years before, but never found the time. Jordan vowed to make the needed repairs to surprise her friend when they returned. She enjoyed one last bear hug and placed him carefully on the pillows.

After showering and putting on an oversized t-shirt and a pair of holey-kneed jeans, Jordan found an old movie on television. She stood in the kitchen, beating eggs in preparation for an omelette, with eyes glued to the movie. She poured the eggs into the pan, wishing that Tyrone Power would just kiss his lady, but knowing that the butler would surely tell her dreadful husband. She watched as the beautiful woman posed for her portrait, and as she and the handsome Mr. Power rose to embrace one another.

Knowing that her omelette was done, Jordan grabbed the handle of the skillet to remove it from the hot burner. She was so engrossed in the movie that she failed to use a pot-holder.

"Ow!" she yelled as she released her grip on the scorching hot handle. "Owww!" she yelled even louder, as the pan landed on her right foot, sending hot egg and melted cheese flying all over the kitchen and her bare feet. She was hopping on her left foot, trying to avoid the egg, the movie temporarily forgotten, when the door burst open and suddenly Nick was putting cold water on the dishcloth.

"Stop hopping and let me take care of your foot. Where are you burned?" he asked as he placed his hands around her waist and lifted her to the counter, looking her over from head to toe, seeking signs of any possible damage.

"I don't know. Oh, I don't think anywhere. Just surprised, and my toes hurt."

"Let me see your hand." Then, as he held her hand gently in his own, examining it more closely, "Where's your first aid kit?"

"Don't need it. There's an aloe vera plant in the windowsill."

"Good girl." He turned, broke off a piece of the plant, and carefully eased the fluid onto her pink palm and fingers. He suddenly wished that he could hold this hand much longer. Reluctant to relinquish it, his fingers closed around her wrist, her hand resting on his. He looked up to find her eyes on him. He looked concerned as he spoke, "How's that?"

"Much better. Thanks. You're a good doctor."

Nick smiled at her, making her heart beat a little faster. "You probably could have done all that for yourself. But I'm happy to help. Now, stay put and I'll clean up your mess."

"Heavens, no," Jordan said as she jumped lightly from the counter. "I dumped it, I'll clean it up."

Nick bent over to pick up the pan. "Didn't anyone ever tell you that cast iron skillets are to be used on an intruder's head and not on the cook's foot?"

Jordan's sense of humor was returning. "So, intruder, when would you like me to clobber you?"

As they cleaned up the eggs and cheese, Nick explained his early exit from the wedding reception. "I had to leave early, and we didn't get a chance to finish our conversation. I was hoping that you were going to invite me to dinner, but seeing how you cook, I think I'm no longer interested."

"I don't always throw my dinner on the floor. I just got interested in something and forgot what I was doing."

Nick glanced at the television, smiled and nodded his head knowingly. "Yes, I imagine that Tyrone Power has made many women drop their omelettes."

Jordan liked his smile immensely. Lips made just for kissin', she thought briefly. Then she shook her head and asked, "What happened to your date?"

Nick was eyeing her thoughtfully, wishing that he could find some reason to draw her into his arms again. He'd been extremely agitated when Lianna interrupted their dance.

"Date? You mean Lianna? I dropped her off rather unceremoniously with a skycap at the airport and went back to the country club. But you were gone by the time I got back."

"Yes, I was a bit tired, and home sounded like a nice place to be." Jordan wondered why she wanted to explain her departure to him.

"It is a nice place. And since you ruined your dinner, perhaps you would like to share mine with me."

Jordan hadn't seen the box he tossed on the counter when he entered the apartment. She walked to the other side of the kitchen, to retrieve plates and silverware.

"We probably won't need all that," Nick said as he picked up the pizza box. When he threw it at the counter it landed upside-down, and now most of the cheese was stuck to the lid. "Okay, so I'm not so great with food, either, but at least this is clean."

They sat down to watch the rest of the movie, scraping a bit of cheese off the lid to place on each piece of pizza. Nick told her that they never had much pizza when he and Alex were children, and now he got sudden cravings for it. He apologized for the simple fare, but she reassured him that she was quite used to it, having shared a home with his brother for over a year.

"A whole year. I should have hunted him down long ago. I would have enjoyed checking out your cooking skills." Then, more seriously, as he gazed into her brown eyes, "At least, I would have enjoyed getting to know you in a more natural way, rather than barging into your place like I did on the first night we met. If I haven't apologized, I really am sorry. My mother always says that I charge in like a mad bull, without finding out all the facts. I guess I just did it again."

Jordan placed her hand on his shoulder. "Nick, I'm sure you were just being an overprotective big brother. My greatest concern was about how you would treat Paige."

"Well, I admit I was extremely suspicious of her, but she won me over quickly."

"She does have that effect on people. She doesn't have an evil bone in her body, and most people realize it as soon as they meet her."

They settled down to watch the movie, sitting on the floor in front of the couch, the pizza on the coffee table in front of them. As the credits rolled, Jordan sighed. "I just love these old movies. I can't think of a better way to spend an evening."

And I can't think of a better way to spend an evening than to be with you, Nick thought. Then, "Oh, I almost forgot. Alex wanted me to give you something." He stood up and picked up the jacket that he had thrown across the back of the couch. He reached into the pocket and pulled out a long, slender box with a red ribbon around it. "I was supposed to tell you that this is your thank you present, and that if it hadn't been for you, this wedding might never have taken place. He also mentioned that you've done everything in your power over the past year to take good care of him and Paige, and to give them every opportunity to be alone together. So, here 'tis."

Jordan curiously took the box from Nick's hand and cradled it in her own. Nick, knowing the contents, wondered what her reaction would be when she saw exactly what Alex had done for her.

"Well, I love Alex and Paige and I would do anything for them, but I certainly never expected anything in return. Still," she hesitated, "this is intriguing. Wrong shape for a video tape or a compact disc, too light for diamonds and other precious gems."

"Why don't you just open the box and see for yourself."

Jordan carefully removed the ribbon and the top of the box. There was a piece of paper rolled up inside, with another ribbon tied around it. She slipped the ribbon off, and unrolled the paper. She stared at it, her hands suddenly trembling.

"Oh, no! This is crazy. How could he think I would accept something like this?" Jordan rolled up the paper and started to return it to the box.

Nick watched her, first in amazement, then with a swelling heart. He stopped her shaking hands and held them gently in his own. He spoke quietly, looking directly into her tear-filled eyes. "Jordan, he really wants you to have this. He loves you very much."

"And I love him. But this is ridiculous. He can't just buy me this condo."

"Why? He's building a mansion for Paige."

"Good heavens. She's his wife. The love of his life. I'm just..."

"His best friend. Come on. Just accept it and let him be happy."

"I make a very good living. I probably could have bought it for myself, if I had known it was for sale."

Nick watched her, marveling at her incredible goodness. It's just possible, he thought, that Alex did find two in a million. He knew that the condo hadn't been for sale, but that Alex made the owner an offer she couldn't refuse. "Jordan loves that place," he'd explained to Nick. "After all she's done to support me, it's the least I can do for her."

Nick tried to explain some of this to Jordan, puzzled when she just shook her head. "All I ever did was buy him a few groceries and pay his part of the rent on occasion." She started to laugh, as she thought about how ridiculous this whole situation was. "There I was, supporting someone who turns out to be a multi-millionaire and now he tries to buy me a condominium. This is all too ludicrous."

Nick firmly placed the box in Jordan's hands. "Yes, but it's typical of Alex. Let him do this for you, Jordan. It really will make him very happy."

Jordan took a deep breath, "Well, it makes me very happy, too. I just can't quite believe he did this."

They spent the rest of the evening watching old

movies and talking about their childhoods. Jordan asked about the names of Nicholas and Alexander, wondering if it was just a coincidence that the former Czar and Czarina of Russia had similar names.

"My mother is a lover of Russian history. She planned to have one son and one daughter, but things didn't work out that way, so she settled for an Alexander instead of an Alexandra. I'm just thankful that she didn't name one of us Rasputan, or something like that. She saved that name for the dog. And yes, he is a Russian Wolfhound."

Quite late in the evening, Nick rose to leave. He'd seen Jordan stifle several yawns, yet was reluctant to say good bye to her. The evening had been more than enjoyable. This fits, I feel right here with her, he thought. But he knew that the chaos and the activities of the previous days had exhausted her, and that she probably needed at least one good night's sleep.

Jordan walked with him to the door, not seeing the carefully hidden smile on his face as he pretended not to see her latest, fullest yawn. He turned around to face her and took her hands in his. He realized he'd been holding those hands as much as possible that evening, and that the softness of them made him yearn to hold on to her for much longer.

"Jordan, thank you for this evening. I haven't had such a wonderful time in ages. Would it be possible for us to do it again? I'll still be in town for a couple of weeks. I'm not expected back in Boston until then."

Jordan was surprised. "I'd like that very much," she yawned at him.

Nick laughed, squeezed her hands and bent over to kiss her on the cheek. "You're like a zombie. Go get some sleep. But," his voice was hopeful, "do you think you'd be able to spend tomorrow afternoon with me?"

Jordan nodded. "I'd like that very much," she repeated.

"Good! I'll pick you up around one o'clock. Dress casual."

"Is there any other way to dress in a California beach community?"

"Oh, I've seen you pretty fancy. And I like it a great deal. But tomorrow's just for fun, okay?" He gave her hands a final squeeze and walked into the cool evening air.

*

Jordan was up bright and early the next morning. Feeling surprisingly well-rested after her short night, she dressed in a comfortable summer dress and went to the early service at church. She waved at Blaine, not stopping to talk, wanting to get home to get ready for her date.

Date, she thought. Who on earth would ever have predicted that I'd be going on a date with Alex's brother? Little did she know that several people were praying for just that.

That afternoon, they went to the Los Angeles Zoo. They felt sorry for the animals that seemed so bored in their cages, but were happy that no hunters would ever get at them, and that they couldn't become dinner for any larger animals they might have encountered in their wilderness homes. They walked slowly, hand in hand, for most of the day. They felt as if they'd known one another for months, instead of just days.

They weren't able to get together again for several days. Jordan explained that she'd neglected Grady and her work for too long while preparing for the wedding, and she had a great deal to catch up on. Nick felt a spark of jealousy at the mention of Grady's name, but she was quick to assure him that he was more of an honorary grandfather than a possible suitor. He also questioned her about Quentin, and was relieved to hear that the undesirable gentleman was mending his ways and had crawled back to Barbara with repentance in his heart.

Jordan worked hard, long hours over the next several days, but her thoughts often strayed to Nick. Grady caught her staring into space on more than one occasion and smiled. He'd seen her dancing with Nick at the wedding reception, and he'd liked the look of the two young people together. After all, Jordan was a very special lady, and Nick must be a good man, since he was Alex's brother.

Nick spent his days with his parents, enjoying their company, but wishing that he could be with Jordan instead. Several days later, Marguerite noticed her son sitting in the den, reading the same page in his book for several minutes. "Darling, why don't you just call her?"

Nick jumped, startled by his mother's voice as well as her intuitiveness. He set the book down on the table beside him. "Mother, this is going to sound really hokey, but how long did it take you to fall in love with Dad?"

Marguerite tried to hide her smile, but was unsuccessful. "Oh, Nicholas, I knew I loved him after two days. Some people may take longer, but when you can see a person's character clearly, and you know that there is that special bond between you, it doesn't need to take a long time."

"But you were engaged for so long."

"That was a different time, Nicholas. Things were done differently then. And you can take your time, if you need to. But Jordan is a beautiful young woman. Alex has spoken so highly of her. She's been wonderful to him and to Paige. She's a compassionate, loving woman. You couldn't find anyone better than her." Marguerite paused. "Nicky, darling, I know Lianna hurt you. I'm sorry that her mother and I pushed so hard for you to get together. We were blinded by our love for each other, and thought that our children would make a most desirable match. Unfortunately, Lianna was spoiled horribly by her parents and, while she's incredibly lovely, she's also incredibly shallow." She paused briefly before adding, "And confused."

"Mother, I've never heard you say a harsh word about anyone."

"It's true. I should have seen it years ago. I only wish that I could have realized it earlier, and warned you before she hurt you."

"I was young, Mother. And I was incredibly naive. Besides, that was years ago."

"Yes, but in some ways I think your heart was scarred deeply. Perhaps it's time for healing. I'm certain that in her own way, Lianna really does love you. She's just not very good at it. Her parents never had a close, happy marriage. They basically just tolerated each other and spoiled Lianna. They gave her everything they thought she might need...materially, that it. They gave her money and possessions, but they couldn't seem to teach her about the value of human relationships. Nicholas, I know that Lianna would never have hurt you intentionally. She just doesn't know how to love you for yourself."

Nick thought about his mother's words for several moments. "I know you're right, Mother. But I think she just wanted to possess me, like she possesses everything else. You know, make me one more of her acquisitions. That hurt. I wanted to be everything for her."

"Like your father is for me?" Marguerite asked softly. "You'll find that someday, Son. Just remember that Lianna is not the standard for all women. They're not all filled with ulterior motives and greed. Jordan certainly isn't."

"I think you're right. A few weeks ago, I never would have agreed with you. Hell, I even, I mean darn, sorry Mother," he said as he saw her eyes widen. "I even thought Paige was after Alex for his money. And then I thought Jordan might make a play for me because of mine. But, she's so honest and forthright. All she seems to care about is helping the needy, human and animal, and architecture."

They spoke for a few more moments before Nick excused himself to go call Jordan. He finally reached her on her car phone, after her secretary took pity on him and patched him through to her.

"Hello," Jordan breathlessly answered the ringing of the phone in her Jeep.

"Jordan?"

"Yes, Nick, is that you? How on earth did you find me?"

"You have a very compassionate secretary. However, I had to assure her that I was Alex's brother and not some ax murderer."

68

"And just how did you convince her of that?"

"Well," Nick suddenly felt extremely sheepish, "I had to have my mother get on the phone and explain to your very over-protective Miss Wilkes that I really was her other son. Really, Jordan, I know this sounds ridiculous, my having to have my mommy fend for me, but I hope you'll make my humiliation worthwhile."

Jordan was glad that Nick couldn't see her, and she held the receiver slightly away from her mouth so he couldn't hear the quiet laughter that escaped from her lips. "And just why did you go through this torturous experience?"

"I was really hoping that I'd be able to see you tonight. It doesn't have to be a long evening, I know you've been burning the midnight oil. Miss Wilkes already told me about the long hours you've been keeping. But I need to see you."

Jordan liked the emphasis he put on that last sentence. "All right, how about dinner?"

They settled the details. Nick's heart suddenly lightened as he realized that she was looking forward to this as much as he was. He hung up the telephone, smiling at his mother. "All set. She wants to see me, too."

"And I'm praying that she'll want to see a lot more of you in the future, sweetheart."

"MOTHER!" Nick feigned shock. "I'm surprised at you."

"Oh, dear, I certainly didn't mean it like that." Marguerite colored prettily.

"Well, Mother, maybe I'll hope for that, anyway." He kissed her on a cheek that had become even rosier and exited the room, singing softly, "I want a girl, just like the girl..."

*

Jordan and Nick spent a great deal of time together over the following weeks. They practiced their cooking skills, went to plays and concerts, and spent quiet evenings at her condo, watching videos, sitting and talking on her balcony, walking on the beach, and watching the magnificent sunsets produced by the smog.

"At least the smog is good for something," Jordan murmured one evening, as they sat on a blanket on the beach, Nick's arm around her waist, her head resting lightly on his shoulder.

They were nestled in a pile of pillows by the fire one evening, sharing cheese, crackers, and a delicious bottle of vintage, original Coca Cola, when Alex knocked on the front door and walked in.

"Well, whaddayaknow!" he said to the two people sitting together in front of the fireplace. "I guess my darling wife was right."

"Alex," Jordan jumped up, squealing, sounding like an excited teenager. "You're back. Is Paige with you? How was your honeymoon? What did you do on your trip? Never mind, don't answer that. Is Paige here?"

Alex grabbed Jordan, kissed her swiftly and turned to hug his brother, who had followed Jordan to the kitchen when she heard Alex's voice. "No, Paige is on her way to Switzerland. She's going to find an apartment for us while I pick up the necessary items for life abroad. Our trip was fantabulous, and I take it things have been the same here," he finished, looking at his brother questioningly.

Jordan put her arms around him, leading him to his favorite chair. "Yes, your brother and I have been getting to know each other as human beings, and not just as your beloved family and friends."

Nick followed them into the living room. "I have to admit, everything you told me about her was true."

Jordan looked menacingly at Alex. "Just what did you tell him about me?"

"Only the good stuff, dearie, I guarantee it. I didn't tell him anything about what a fussy housekeeper you are, or how you like to sneak into the cookie jar in the middle of the night, or even about how you like to run around in nothing more than a big T-shirt." Here Alex stopped, groaned and grabbed his chest dramatically. "She always thought of me like a brother and didn't care about what the sight of those legs could do to a guy!"

Jordan laughed and hugged him. "Oh, Alex, you're such a tease. With Paige around I could've walked around on wooden stilts and you still wouldn't have noticed my legs."

Now Alex rolled his eyes, shook his head at Nick and mouthed the words, "Don't you believe it."

Jordan sat down on the couch, pulling Nick down next to her, but she turned her attention to Alex. "I've missed you and Paige so much. It's been so quiet here." She paused, unexpected tears filling her eyes. "And, Alex, thank you for giving me the condo. You really shouldn't have, you know."

Alex smiled at her slightly, his own eyes misting. He reached for her hand, and as he held it lightly in his own, he spoke. "I love you Jordan. You know that. I wanted to say thank you for everything you've done for me. You're more than a friend--you're part of the family."

"I feel that way, too, Alex, but giving me a whole condo? Doesn't that seem a little extravagant to you?"

Alex laughed, waving his arms grandiosely in the air. "You think this is extravagant? You need to spend more time at the Wyndhams', my dear. This is merely servants' quarters."

She didn't see the look of jealousy that was evident on Nick's face as they talked, declaring their feelings for one another, but Alex didn't miss it. He decided to give the budding romance a nudge.

Smothering a grin, he yawned and said to Jordan, "I know this castle is all yours now, but would you mind if a poor, weary knight crashed here this evening? If you'd prefer, I could go to my folks'." He paused expectantly, knowing that she would never turn him away.

"Alex, you know you're always welcome here. In fact, your stuff is still right where you left it. However, I'm warning you, once you're gone, everything you leave behind is going to the garage, and I'm taking over the master bedroom."

Alex, with his eyes on his brother's face, lowered his voice seductively. "You know, Paige is awfully far away, and it might get awfully lonely in that big bed all by myself. I don't suppose..."

Now he really had to fight his laughter, because Nicholas Wyndham's face had grown red with anger, and he was positively glaring at his obnoxious little brother.

Jordan, not realizing what was going on between the brothers but used to Alex's teasing, grabbed a pillow from the cushion next to her and hit Alex square on the nose with it. "Go to bed, you pervert."

Resisting the temptation to fling the pillow back, Alex excused himself to get some sleep. Nick and Jordan sat on the couch for some time after he left, rarely speaking, merely content to be together. Long past their normal sleeping hours, Nick got up to leave. They stood at the front door, facing one another, hands clasped.

"Jordan, I hope that you understand how much these past few weeks have meant to me. This is by far the best vacation I have ever had."

"It's been wonderful for me, too, Nick. I love spending time with you. I'll miss you when you leave. But I think your patients must be clamoring for you to get back. You must be a wonderful doctor."

"That's what they tell me. But, since most of them are too little to talk, we'll just have to guess."

"Well," she smiled up at him, "if they're not crying or spitting up on you, you must be doing okay."

"Jordan, I've got to go away for a couple of days. I didn't tell you this before, because I didn't want to scare you off, but I'm moving back to L.A. I'm leaving private practice for awhile to do research. I did my fellowship in pediatric cardiology, and I want to continue my work. I plan to make L.A. my home now. I'd like to find a place close to you, if that doesn't frighten you."

"Why should it? I'd love to have you close by. These weeks we've spent together have been so special." She looked at his deep, blue eyes, ran her finger down the crease on his cheek where she knew a dimple was hidden, and felt herself melting.

Suddenly he put his arm around her waist, drawing her closer to him. Their lips met, tender, yet tentative.

When Nick spoke, his voice was low and questioning. "Jordan, I didn't think I'd be ready for this for a very long time, if ever. I think I'm falling in love with you."

Jordan, still held in his arms, pushed away slightly until she could see his face. "Let's just take this slow and easy. Relationships take time."

"We've been going slow, Jordan," he said softly. "We've established a marvelous friendship. But, I'm not sure I want to go slow anymore. You're filling my life in a way I never expected."

"And you're doing the same for mine. I sit at my desk, trying to work, and I see your face. Someone speaks to me and I hear your voice. It's crazy. I feel like I've known you forever, but we only met a few weeks ago. I know Paige and Alex fell in love instantaneously, and it was perfect. I don't know why I'm being so cautious. I just want to be sure this is right."

But, deep inside, memories of Jonathan bounced around, and she knew why she had to be cautious. Yet even as old painful memories began to surface, she realized that this relationship was different. She had experienced fun, passion and sincerity in past relationships. But Nick roused new feelings in her. He was making her think about commitment, the kind that few people her generation seemed to think about anymore. Except Paige and Alex, she amended. The kind of commitment that her parents and grandparents had with one another.

When Nick looked at her, he saw them in the future. He saw them walking hand-in-hand through the gardens at his parents' estate, with their grandchildren playing out on the lawn. Premature thoughts, he told himself. Mom and Dad knew each other for five years before they married, and Grandpa and Grandma Wyndham grew up together. Better not push Jordan, he now thought sadly, as he reluctantly agreed with her. He wanted their relationship to build to the kind of strength that could weather all of life's storms. He didn't want to hurt her, or add to the divorce statistics he was constantly reading.

Nick kissed Jordan once more before leaving the condo. His arms ached as he walked towards his car. He wanted to hold her for more than just a few moments. He wanted it to last a lifetime.

Jordan leaned against the door as it closed behind him. Several minutes later, Alex found her still standing there when he came out to the kitchen to fix some hot chocolate.

"That's exactly how I looked when I met Paige. Did I detect a small sigh as I walked down the hall?"

"Oh, Alex. Yes, I'll admit you probably did." Jordan

brought herself back to earth quickly. "He really is an incredible man. He's funny and kind and gentle and understanding and..."

"Tall, dark, handsome, like his brother."

"Yes," she laughed at her friend. "All that, too. *And,* I enjoy being with him and I hate it when he's gone. Sounds stupid, doesn't it?"

"I'd say from the way he looks at you that he feels the same way. Just out of curiosity, how much has he told you about Lianna Ashmore?"

"Just that they grew up together, were engaged at one time, but that he found out she just wanted him for his money."

"Jordan, I don't want you to be hurt. But I need to warn you about my brother. He doesn't give his trust easily. He was cut pretty deep by what Lianna did to him, but he still loved her. We were all kids together, and Lianna always had us wrapped around her little finger. I guess Nick and I sort of idolized her. She was always beautiful, from the day she was born. And she learned early in life that she could get whatever she wanted. She bounced back and forth between wanting me and wanting Nick. Believe me, we fought many battles over her.

"I think I woke up to who she really was long before Nick did. Lianna and I had a showdown shortly after high school. I told her that she was too caught up in money and prestige and what people think. She was pretty angry with me for awhile, but she finally admitted that I was right. Unfortunately, she also admitted that she didn't want to change."

"What about Nick? Couldn't he see those things about her, too?" Jordan interrupted.

"To a certain extent, yes. But she covered her greed with charm and flattery. She really fed his ego, making him feel like he could accomplish anything. And he can. I guess we should be grateful to her for making him see that. Yet when she convinced him that he could do anything with his life, he took a turn she didn't expect.

"He'd always wanted to be a doctor. He said that it was because when I was born I was the sweetest little thing and he just wanted to protect me." At this point Alex paused and made a funny face at Jordan. "Imagine me as a sweet little thing!"

"It is pretty hard," she returned with a giggle. "But why should that have upset Lianna?"

"Well, it seems that she, like my father, always assumed that Nick would leave medical school and go to work in one of the family businesses. Something that could assure her of several glamorous homes, lots of play time, and a

73

husband always at her beck and call. Granted, a doctor doesn't do too poorly in the financial end of things, but we do have to work hard. So, when Nick decided to focus his efforts on pediatric cardiology, she decided she'd better find someone who could devote more energy to her."

"He mentioned that he intends to get into research."

"When I was born, I had a heart defect. They weren't sure for a while if I would be around for very long. Hence, his interest. He really is driven. In his practice and research, he has seen a lot of babies suffer, and many of them have died. He wants to stop the suffering and assure those little ones long, healthy lives. His greatest dream is to invent an artificial heart for infants - one that could work efficiently until their chests grow enough to accept a human heart transplant.

"You're really not helping me to not fall in love with him, you know." Jordan grimaced at him.

"I'm trying to make you marry the guy. I'd love to have you become an official member of the family."

"Yeah, well, let's not rush things here. Besides, official or not, we are definitely family." Jordan kissed him, told him goodnight and headed for bed.

She was still puzzled by Lianna. The Ashmore family had a great deal of money on their own. Could anyone be so greedy as to want two fortunes, rather than just one? If she had enough faith in Nick's abilities to convince him that he could do anything, if she cared enough about him to encourage him and give him hope, why wouldn't she care enough to marry him?

*

The next morning Alex gathered up everything that Paige had included on her list of "can't live without" items. He helped Jordan carry the remainder of their belongings to the garage, promising that he'd make his brother put the boxes up in the rafters for her. Then he showered, changed, and waited for Nick to drive him to the airport.

Alex had been invited to do his pediatrics residency in a clinic near Paige's hospital. While he would be working mainly with neo-natal care, Paige would focus her research in the field of childhood diseases. The two couldn't believe their good fortune. They would both be doing what they had dreamed of, and to be in the same city was a miracle.

As Jordan and Alex said their good-byes, she assured him that she would miss him and Paige, and she sent him off with several hugs and kisses with orders to deliver them to his wife.

Nick pulled Jordan into a fierce embrace, promising to call every day and to return in exactly three weeks. He needed to return to Boston to end his practice. He'd explained

to Alex and Jordan that a friend of his would take over his
practice and that many of his patients had already met and
fallen in love with her, so he had no compunctions about
leaving everything in her care. He had also made
arrangements to visit a hospital in Denver when he left Boston.
He wanted to review the progress they had made in their recent
research before returning to L.A. He asked Jordan to be on the
lookout for an apartment near her condo while he was away.
Then he gave her one final kiss, and he and Alex left for the
airport.

*

Jordan immediately began making arrangements to
build Paige and Alex's house. They asked her to start
construction immediately, as they planned to use it for a
vacation home for the next few years, and then would move in
immediately upon their return to the states.

Two weeks after Nick and Alex left, Jordan hired Bill
Mason, a local contractor, to build Alex and Paige's home.
Mason had a reputation of being both reliable and professional,
but extremely temperamental. Jordan had only worked with him
on three other buildings, but she liked his work. She discussed
her choice with Grady, and he agreed that Mason would do the
best job. The sub-contractors in the coastal area liked working
with Mason, and he demanded the best from them.

Jordan met with him, showed him the plans, and
then drove him to the property Alex and Paige had purchased.
The site was in the hills overlooking Los Angeles. The view
was perfect, according to the Kendell-Wyndhams, and they
were emphatic that this was where their little castle would be.

Mason spent much more time surveying the site
than Jordan would have liked. The day was extremely hot and
she wished she were in her air-conditioned office. By the time
she got back to the condo, all she could think of was a cool
shower and less clothing.

Jordan put the teapot on the stove, then went into
the master bedroom, which she had not only claimed, but
redecorated in the two weeks since Alex left. She dropped her
clothes on the new four-poster bed, looking appreciatively at the
new love seat in the corner near the window. It had cream-
colored upholstery, with pastel stripes. At each end were two
pillows, one matching the couch, the other in a delicate flower
print, the colors matching the stripes. Her bedspread matched
the flowered pillows, as did the valance above the window, and
the wallpaper matched the stripes. When she first saw the
fabric and wallpaper samples, she wondered if it would be too
much for one room, but with the beautiful wood of the bed, the
dresser, the night stands, and the trim on the love seat, the
room seemed well balanced. Neither too feminine, nor too

bland. It was a room that she felt comfortable in. She planned to start on the living room as soon as her budget allowed.

Jordan stood in the shower longer than usual, chastising herself for wasting water, but feeling like she deserved a little luxury today. She climbed out, dried off and put on a forest green silk camisole and matching tap pants.

Still not used to the silence of living alone, she stepped out into the living room and turned on the stereo. She then returned to the bedroom, planning to clear off the bed and relax with a book for a couple of hours.

She walked to the bed to pick up the clothes she had tossed there. She didn't hear the front door opening--she wasn't aware that anyone was in the apartment until a voice spoke behind her.

"Your tea is ready."

Jordan whirled around, faster than her mind was able to register who the owner of the voice was. Nick felt as if he'd fallen on the ice, and the wind had been knocked out of him.

"Ooh, boy," he said the words slowly. "You are beautiful." He realized now, as he stared at her, that he had wanted to make love to her since their first meeting. Lianna be damned, he thought as a brief flicker of doubt and insecurity teased at his consciousness. This woman was made just for me.

Still feeling startled, Jordan asked, "What are you doing here? You're not supposed to be back for another week."

"I finished early."

"You nearly scared me to death. How did you get in?"

"Well, I did knock, but with that loud music of yours, you couldn't hear me." Then, in answer to her question, Nick held up a key. Jordan recognized it as belonging to her front door. "Alex gave it to me before he left. He thought I might like to stay here until I can find a place of my own." He walked toward her as he spoke. "That is, if you don't mind," he added.

Jordan held out her arms. Nick's last two steps were sudden, as he reached for her, pulling her face to his, her body firmly against his own.

"I missed you, Jordan." He somehow got the words out as he kissed her tenderly on the mouth.

Jordan's hands were working at the buttons of his shirt and jeans as his lips moved to her throat and then downward.

"I love you, Nick. I don't think I should, but I do."

This time Nick's lips nearly crushed hers. As they kissed, he slid one hand into the back of her camisole, gently caressing the small of her back, his fingers slipping into the waistband of her panties.

Jordan had a fleeting thought of the teapot on the

76

stove, then dismissed it as Nick lowered her to the bed.

CHAPTER SIX

What see'st thou else
In the dark backward and abysm of time?
-The Tempest

Nick decided to wait until he finished gathering his research before apartment-hunting. Jordan invited him to stay with her, almost wishing that he would never finish with the research, that he would always stay with her in the condo.

Their original intention was for Nick to stay in her old bedroom, which she now designated as her guest room. On his first night there, he climbed in between the cold sheets in the double bed, rejoicing that he had so much space, and that he could toss and turn freely. He lasted for an hour. Then he pushed the covers to the side and walked out to the kitchen, ostensibly to get a drink of water. What he really wanted to do was to see if Jordan's bedroom light was still on.

He was disappointed to see darkness coming from the space under her door. He poured himself a glass of water, took a few sips, set it on the counter and walked towards her door. He raised his fist to knock, decided that he shouldn't disturb her, and returned to the kitchen.

This time, he went to the sink, ran his hands under the cold water, and then his dripping palms over his overly-heated face. Should probably just take a cold shower, he thought to himself.

He took another swallow of water, turning to look at her bedroom door, wondering what she was wearing in bed. Wondering if she wanted him as much as he wanted her. He walked back to his room, made it as far as the doorway, then turned and walked quickly across the width of the living room, hitting the back of the couch with his fist as he passed behind it.

He didn't hesitate at her door this time, but strode through as if he were the king and these were his private chambers. She was not asleep, despite the fact that she had willed her lower regions to stop throbbing, and that she had ordered her eyes to stay closed. She heard him in the kitchen, but told herself that it was foolish to go out to him.

As he came through her doorway, she rolled over, facing him, scooted herself backward several inches, and held the covers open for him. His pajama bottoms, which rode loosely on his hips, were removed quickly, as was the t-shirt she wore.

Nick tried two more nights to remain in the guest room. Each night, as he crawled into the bed, it seemed more lonely, the distance between their two bedroom doors

78

stretched. And, each night, he remained alone fewer and fewer minutes.

*

Nick still had extensive research to collect from several pediatric medical centers. He spent most of his time at the Children's Hospitals in Cincinnati and Boston.

Alex was always on his mind. Born with a hole between the two ventricals of his heart, blood leaking between the chambers, the Wyndhams feared they would lose the young infant. He amazed his physicians and his parents as he grew tall, strong, and healthy.

Marguerite was terrified when Alex wanted to play high school football. But, with his constant assurance that, "I really want to play, Mom. It makes me happy," she consented. She was relieved when he graduated, and his college work kept him too busy for his favorite sport.

Alex's family never forgot that he had Ventricular Septal Defect. His parents continued to worry about him. Nick was concerned for his brother, but he had determined years earlier to put his energy into something more productive than worry. His personal commitment was evident to those who worked with him. They could tell by watching him that he was not a man who would be easily discouraged. In each child he faced, he saw Alexander. And in each child he watched die, he thanked God for his brother's strength and good health, becoming more devoted to his work than ever.

Nick made an unexpected trip to Geneva, after being told they had developed an artificial heart for infants that they were beginning experiments with. While he was there, he stayed with Paige and Alex. They were working long and difficult hours, with few moments together to enjoy their marriage. But, they were happy.

They quickly fell in love with Geneva. Paige found an apartment on the Quai du Mont-Blanc, which ran along the shore of Lake Geneva, or Lac Leman, as the French-speaking Genevoises called it. From their balcony, they could look down into the clear blue inviting waters of the lake.

They found Geneva to be an extremely clean, quiet city, still influenced by sixteenth century Calvinism which frowned upon entertainment, banquets, theater and anything not considered a necessity of life. Now, it seemed, the luxurious stores and restaurants were frequented more by foreign visitors than by the natives.

The third largest city in Switzerland, Geneva was host to many international headquarters, including the Red Cross, the Palais de Nations, the European Offices for the United Nations, as well as the United Nation's World Health Organization. Alex looked forward to spending many hours exploring the latter facility.

As Paige and Alex toured the city, met their patients and co-workers, and devoured the culture, they were confused at the many languages they found. While French was the common language of Geneva, they discovered that German, Italian, and Romansh, a derivation of the Latin spoken by ancient Romans, pervaded the city borders as well. Paige was grateful that she had learned French in high school. Alex vowed to learn immediately. While he was learning, he hired a young boy from the apartment across the hall to serve as his translator whenever he went anywhere without Paige.

Young Jean-Claude Dunant was eleven, enthusiastic, and passionate about America. His American-born father had returned to his own parents' homeland, but filled Jean-Claude's head with stories of American life.

Jean-Claude was proud to take Alex under his wing. He felt very sophisticated as he led him around the city, explaining the Swiss ways to Alex, but constantly questioning him about life in California.

Alex often had time off when Paige was busy in her laboratory, and he took advantage of Jean-Claude's free time. With Alex footing the bill, Jean-Claude happily found many places for them to go. He grilled his mother each night and poured over library books and tour books, finding new and different places to take his new friend. But Jean-Claude's favorite place was a chocolate shop on the rue Kleberg, where the chocolatier served tea and mouth-watering handmade sweets.

Paige and Alex were captivated by the uniquely Swiss activities and atmosphere. When Nick arrived, Paige insisted that he stay long enough to absorb the culture with them.

They learned that music was a Swiss passion, and easily found a folk music festival in a nearby park. Most of the people who were scattered around the lawn of the park were dressed in typical American fashion and, if they hadn't been surrounded by the sky-tickling steeples of the ancient cathedrals, Paige would have thought she was still in California. But, as they watched the musicians tune their instruments and the dancers take their places, they were pleased to spot people dressed in more traditional Swiss costume.

The women wore black dresses with tight-fitting bodices and full skirts. They wore black shoes, white stockings, and lace peeked out above the necklines of their dresses. They wore brightly-colored aprons tied about their waists and the wide, square collars were of matching material.

The men were dressed in top hats and matching tuxedos with tails. Their ties were scarves, made to match the women's aprons. Their breeches were cut just below the knee and they, too, wore white stockings. They had large gold buttons on their unbuttoned jackets and gold buckles on their black shoes, and Paige was certain that they were transplanted leprechauns. The musicians were dressed in black pants. They wore white short-sleeved shirts with gold embroidered red vests. One man, who played an oddly-shaped stringed instrument resembling a dulcimer, wore a short white jacket over his vest. On his head was a small, brimless cap, resembling an oversized Jewish yarmulke. His cap and jacket were embroidered painstakingly with red flowers.

The Americans greatly enjoyed the music and the dancing, and were delighted to learn that the Orchestre de la Suisse Romande would be performing the following day. Their spirits soared with the grandeur of the Orchestre and they were reluctant to leave, finally being escorted out by tired ushers.

Outside the Grand Theatre, which had hosted the Orchestre, they found a beautiful park. As they wandered down the tree-lined paths, they found the Monument de la Reformation, a three hundred foot wall featuring the statues of John Calvin, Theodore de Beze, Guillaume Farrel, and John Knox, great leaders of the Reformation.

Paige, a history buff, began to explain the significance these theologians had played in the history of Geneva, but immediately broke off, her laughter filling the evening air. Two young boys had run to stand in front of the monument. Paige assumed they were in awe of the statues placed there respectfully seventy years earlier. But as she watched, she saw them take small rubber balls from their pockets. Before she could guess what they were doing, they began to bounce the balls, using the broad stomachs of the theologians as a backboard for their game.

The three Californians returned to the apartment, still laughing over the bizarre ball game they had just witnessed. As they stood on the balcony, the fohn--the hot, dry breeze that swept out of the mountains--washed across them.

As Paige drank in the hot air, she felt she was being transported to California. "I wish Jordan was here with us. I've never been away from her for so long, and I miss her. Promise that you'll bring her back for a visit, Nick," Paige begged.

Nick looked out at the lake, watching as its famous jet of water rose suddenly into the air, peaking at nearly four hundred feet. He strained his eyes to see the far side of the lake, where he knew the waters were muddy where the Rhone River emptied itself into the lake. He turned to look past the Pont du Mont-Blanc, the bridge that spanned the southwestern part of the lake, as the now-crystal clear waters of the Rhone River continued on their journey.

He looked at the mountains, which could only be described as grandiose. With the majestic Alps to the east, and the weather-beaten, timeworn Jura Mountains to the west,

Nick couldn't imagine a more beautiful place on earth.

He turned his gaze to the skyline of the city, as it wrapped around three sides of Lake Geneva. He thought of the Romanesque/Gothic Cathedrale-St.-Pierre. Originally a Catholic cathedral, it had been stripped by Calvinists when it was transformed to a Protestant church.

On the west side of the cathedral was the Site Archeologique with portions of a fourth century Christian baptistery and fifth century rooms with ornate mosaic floors. And, as Nick thought of the Maison Tavel, the Tavel House, he knew that this would be paradise for Jordan.

The Maison Tavel, the oldest house in Geneva, dating from the fourteenth century, had been carefully restored, with several rooms furnished in period decor. Other rooms held collections of architectural details and mementoes of Geneva's history.

He turned to smile at his sister-in-law. "Yes. Someday, I will bring Jordan to Geneva."

Paige threw herself into his arms, ignoring her husband's exaggerated groan of jealousy. "Thank you, thank you, thank you," she gasped, kissing him on both cheeks. "Just don't let it be too long."

The next day, Nick was relieved when both Paige and Alex had to return to work. He ruefully admitted that he had a hard time remembering why he had come to Geneva when they were dragging him around the city.

Late that evening, Paige returned home to find Alex and Nick relaxing in front of the television. She was incensed by her battles of the day, and bombarded them with her frustrations.

"I can't believe that personal greed and politics are allowed to affect medical research. That new advances in medicine can be kept hidden from the public, because someone's making more money with the old ways."

Alex was used to his wife's rampages. He knew she was right, and he only wished that she didn't have to face difficulties in her research.

"What happened today?"

"Someone stole all of my files. Everything. All my records of the work we've done over the past seven months. Then, they broke into the laboratory and destroyed everything. They even went through my desk drawers and my personal belongings."

"Why would anyone do that?" Nick asked.

"Because everyone wants to be the first to make any important discovery." The bitterness in her voice seemed well-justified. "There's a fortune to be made by the first person to market cures for childhood diseases. People seem to forget that while we're fighting over 'who wins,' children are losing. Children are suffering and dying from AIDS and juvenile

82

diabetes and multiple sclerosis while we break into each other's labs to steal or destroy valuable research."

"It sounds like the old story of Jonas Salk and Albert Sabin," Nick mused. "Sabin developed the first oral polio vaccine in the fifties. Unfortunately, Salk had already developed an injectible version. He blocked Sabin from even testing his vaccine in the states."

"Yeah, we read about that in college. It seems ridiculous that Sabin had to go into communist countries for his testing. Meanwhile, more children died," Paige said. "It's all so unjust. When will people learn what's really important in life?"

"When a very hot place freezes over," Alex told her as he handed her a cup of tea. "Now, tomorrow you can worry about saving the children of the world. Tonight you'd better get some rest and rejuvenate your mind. Besides, you don't really know that that's why somebody destroyed your lab. Maybe it was just vandalism."

"Yeah, maybe."

Paige did try to rest, but her thoughts drifted back to the lab. She couldn't understand how people could be unjust, especially where children were concerned. She wondered how anyone could intentionally hurt a child, mentally or physically. As she lay in bed, trying to sleep, pictures of her sister floated through her dreams.

Nick spent a few more days with the pediatric cardiology researchers in Geneva, then prepared to leave. Paige packed one of her own suitcases full of gifts for Jordan. She included several boxes of chocolates and three of her favorite cheeses. She also packed two bottles of wine, made from the grapes grown around the shores of Lake Geneva.

Finally, the suitcase weighing more than all of the other bags combined, Nick bid his brother and sister-in-law farewell. After a three-day stop in London, he headed for home.

Jordan had been busy over the past several months. In addition to her regular responsibilities with the firm, she was overseeing every step of the construction on Alex and Paige's house. She wanted it to be perfect for her friends when they returned.

On the evening Nick was to arrive, she left the office early, fixed his favorite dinner which, fortunately for her, was the simple fare of fried pork chops, applesauce, mashed potatoes and corn on the cob, and set up the table on the balcony. She carefully placed flowers, candles, and her Wedgewood china on the table.

She bought the china for herself as a reward for a job well done on the Palmer house, a home she completed two years earlier. On the coast north of Malibu, she thought it was close to being her dream home.

Nick was exhausted, but elated when he arrived at

the condo. Jordan met him at the door and was swept into his glorious, muscular embrace. She nearly forgot about supper, as his kisses covered her face, neck, and hands.

"I am so glad you're back. I've missed you."

"I've missed you." More kisses, then, "Oh, Alex and Paige send their love."

"I'm more interested in your love right now, but I've got dinner ready, if you're hungry."

"Absolutely famished. The only time I get good food on an airplane is when I take Father's jet. He insists on having his chef travel with him."

"Tough life, huh?"

"Well, the chef loves it. He stays on the payroll, gets to fly all over the world, and works very short hours. Hmm, maybe I should have gone into cooking instead of doctoring."

Jordan took him by the arm and led him out to the balcony. "Let's just worry about filling your empty belly right now. Then I have a proposition for you."

"Can't I have the proposition first? It sounds more intriguing." Nick immediately forgot his hunger.

"Sorry. My parents' cook told me that the way to a man's heart is through his stomach."

"Your mother didn't tell you that?"

"No, she said it was through letting him think he's boss."

"And I suppose you believed all that. Are you sure the way to my heart couldn't come in more concrete fashion?" He pulled her toward him, loosening the collar of her blouse. "Cold pork chops are just as good, don't you think? I really could use a little exercise before supper. You know, I've been just sitting on that plane for hours."

*

The next morning, Jordan awoke to the soft petals of a rose stroking her cheek. As she opened her eyes, she looked up into Nick's smiling face.

"Good morning, sleepyhead."

"Goo' mor'ing," she yawned at him.

"I certainly enjoyed the results of your proposition last night."

"That wasn't what I was going to propose."

"What could have been better?"

"The location. Nick, what do you like best about this condo?" Seeing the corners of his mouth turn up, she added, "Besides the bedroom, that is."

"I guess being so close to the beach."

"Good. How would you like to spend the next couple of days in a gorgeous home with a private beach with yours truly?"

"What, did you inherit Hawaii while I was away?"

"I have some friends who have invited me to stay at their place in Malibu whenever I like. I think that we could use some time to get away, just the two of us."

"Where would these very generous friends be?"

"They live in Vermont, but they love the west coast, so they built out here a couple of years ago. It's their vacation home, and they're rarely there. Lauren just called me yesterday to make sure I'd be going soon."

Nick, sitting on the bed next to her, said, "It sounds great. I have to head up to Stanford next week. I meant to tell you last night, but you distracted me," he said suggestively. "I've almost finished gathering all of the data I need. I just have to spend a few days up north, then a couple of months in London. I've been invited to teach a course at St. Bartholomew's Hospital. After that, I can settle down here for a while. I'll be able to continue my work at the Medical Research Institute.

"Now, as for this new invitation...I can't imagine anything I would love more. Do you want to leave today?"

"Yes," she said, kissing him quickly and jumping out of bed. "I just have to take care of a couple of things at the office, get some food, and we can leave this afternoon."

Jordan did as promised, packed Nick and their bags into her Jeep, and started on their short journey. On the way there, she explained to him who the Palmers were and how she met them.

Lauren Palmer was an artist, her husband, Grant, a novelist. They traveled a great deal, gathering information and inspiration. They wanted a vacation home in California and chose Malibu as their ideal spot. The property they purchased was a large cove, with rock cliffs at each side, an expansive beach to the west, and behind their new home were several acres of hills and woods, giving shelter and privacy. The cliffs offered great protection from the storms which could come suddenly, and the house was built far up the beach to avoid any waves which might attempt to wash the house, built upon the sand, out to sea.

The Palmers' property was extensive enough to accommodate five or six large homes, but they liked their solitude. They intended to sell half of the property, but until they could find someone they'd enjoy having as neighbors, they would keep it all.

Two and a half years earlier, they had looked for an architect to build their home. In their search, they asked several firms which was the best. Most people claimed that honor for themselves. When asked who was second best, a variety of names were offered, but the names listed most often were Jordan Blake and Grady MacIntyre.

Jordan loved working for the Palmers. They were

enthusiastic. They knew exactly what they wanted, but when practicality demanded otherwise, they were pleasingly flexible. The three of them developed a close friendship, and they invited Jordan to stay in their home whenever she needed a vacation or just a few days of solitude. As it turned out, they rarely got to their beach home, and she stayed there more than she had ever originally intended.

Lauren was thrilled to have Jordan stay there. She said the home was too beautiful to waste, and it belonged, in part, to Jordan anyway. She also worried about burglars, and having a car parked in the drive and the lights on in the house on occasion made her feel better. Jordan never mentioned that burglars could break in between her visits, and lights could be set with timers so that the house would be lit every night. And Lauren never mentioned that she also knew these things, and that she just placed great value on Jordan's friendship, wanting to give her a place of retreat.

As Jordan and Nick entered the private drive to the house, Jordan caught her breath. The view never failed to thrill her. She loved the house and its location. It was her favorite of all the homes she'd designed. Whenever she was in the Palmers' house, she planned how she would do her own differently.

Nick fell in love with the house immediately. "Jordan, this is incredible. I've never seen any of your work, except the little bit that's been done on Paige and Alexander's place."

"I can see that it's been a while since you were up there. I guess we'll have to drive over that way before you leave again. It's almost finished. I've had a double crew working on it for months. It's going to be exactly like Alex pictured it."

"You've put a lot of work into that place, haven't you?"

"I wanted to do my best for them. They're worth it. Now, come on, I want to take you on a tour."

The entryway of the house opened onto a large library and sitting room, several of Grant's books filling the shelves, along with hundreds of classics. To the back of the house, toward the beach, was the kitchen. The Palmers insisted that if they had to work in a kitchen, they wanted to have something nice to look at. So Jordan gave them large windows from which they could watch the waves and the seagulls. The kitchen itself was expansive, with a center island, complete with a second sink for scrubbing vegetables and quick clean-ups. The cupboards were done in natural pine, a favorite of Grant's.

"But if it were mine," Jordan told Nick, "I'd have oak."

With no formal dining room, the dining table was in the breakfast nook near a picture window. To the right of the

86

kitchen and sitting room was the master bedroom and bath, with a door leading out to the beach. To the right of the kitchen was Grant's office and beyond that, the three car garage, which the Palmers had insisted on. "Enough space for one car for Lauren, one for me, and one for you," Grant had explained to Jordan.

The stairway was on the wall next to Grant's office, centered between the kitchen and the library. Leading Nick to the second floor, Jordan showed him the four large guest rooms, each with its own bathroom and sitting room. Across the hall from the guest rooms, one of which Lauren had made into a studio for her work, was the laundry, with a visitors' bathroom situated in the corner, framed by the laundry and the stairway. The entire area above the kitchen and library was a large, open living room. On the far right side of the living room was the bedroom and bath which Lauren insisted were for Jordan. The room had a private balcony, with a stairway leading to the sand below.

Jordan explained to Nick that other guests used it occasionally, but whenever she needed it, it was hers. She told him of the unique friendship which seemed to evolve so naturally and of the long evenings she spent working with them, not only planning the design of the house itself, but the decor as well. She helped them pick out the paneling, wallpaper, carpet, and flooring. She put them in touch with the most reputable firms, made sure that they got the best service and merchandise. Throughout the process, they relied on her advice and her opinions.

Late into the evenings of working on the house, even down to the arrangement of the furniture, the three of them shared their dreams and goals for their lives. They had a great deal in common, and despite Jordan's preferences for different color choices and styles, the mutual respect that they cherished enabled them to work well together.

By the time the house was completed and the Palmers were ready to return to Vermont, they felt as if Jordan was a part of the family. They invited her to come to their new home whenever she liked, urging her to bring friends and family.

"They even threatened to 'match me up' with Lauren's brother," she told Nick.

"And what happened to that grand plan?"

"Who knows? I still haven't met him," she said, her eyes twinkling at him. "You never know. It may happen yet."

Nick wrapped his arms around her, pulling her close. "I wouldn't count on that, sweetheart. Now, come here. I have a surprise for you."

He pulled Jordan down the hallway to his bags, which he had dropped in Jordan's room. Jordan walked to the bed and, perching on the edge, watched as he unzipped the largest bag and began to pull out the contents. He tossed a shirt on the floor next to his knee, and threw two pairs of jeans next to them.

"That's an interesting method you have for unpacking," Jordan said solemnly, her eyes alight with laughter.

Nick frowned at her. "No complaints. I'm looking for your present."

"You already gave me lots of presents."

"Those were from Paige. This one's from me, and it's more important."

Jordan raised an eyebrow. "I suppose that depends on your point of view."

Ignoring her, he continued rummaging, finally tossing the bag to the side, atop the pile of the items which had once been carefully folded inside.

"I know I brought it," he muttered, and reached for the smaller bag on the foot of the bed. He sat on the floor, legs crossed, the bag resting in his lap. Smiling as he lifted a large box from the middle of the bag, he looked up at Jordan. "This is something I picked up for you on my way to the airport in London."

Jordan took the heavy box from him carefully, and began to unwrap the gold paper. Lifting the lid from the box, foam peanuts fell onto her lap and the bed. She slipped her fingers into the white packing pieces, and slowly extracted a miniature Lilliput cottage.

"Oh, Nick, it's beautiful. Thank you."

"There's a message for you on the bottom."

Jordan tipped the building, her eyes filling with tears as she read the engraved plaque which Nick had attached to the base. "Someday," it read, "we'll build our own. I love you, N."

Jordan set the cottage on the bed and slipped to the floor, kneeling in front of Nick. She placed her hands on either side of his face and kissed him, slowly at first, then with growing fervor as he pulled her into his lap.

"I love you, Jordan. And I mean to keep this promise."

The next few days were ideal, the pressures and responsibilities of the real world far away. They slept late in the mornings, and napped following afternoon swims. They spent hours walking on the beach, snuggling in the hammock on the deck outside Jordan's bedroom, and reading Grant's books. They stayed two days longer than they intended, finding it difficult to tear themselves away. Eventually, deciding that they'd better be rational, they packed their belongings back into the Jeep.

Jordan stood next to the loaded vehicle, still not wanting to leave. Nick stood next to her, leaning against the fender, his arms wrapped tightly around her waist.

"I'm sorry to leave--this has been wonderful. Too bad real life can't always be like this. No worries, no violence, no responsibilities, no telephones."

"There is a phone here. I just didn't have the phone company connect it this time."

Nick rested his cheek against her hair. "I'm glad you didn't. Will you bring me back?"

"It's a promise."

*

Two weeks later, Nick left for London. "I wish I didn't have to be away for so long," he told Jordan, "but two months is really a minimal time requirement for me to study everything that they've done. Maybe you could come over for a vacation."

Jordan promised to make the arrangements, kissed him good-bye, and took him to the airport. Later that night, as Jordan sat working in her living room, papers surrounding her, she heard an aggressive knock at the door. Before she could set the papers on her lap to the side, the door knob turned. She was grateful that she had remembered to lock the deadbolt. Then, as she raced towards the door, her lethal cast-iron skillet grasped firmly in hand, the knock sounded again.

"Who is it?"

"Jory, it's me, Alex. Let..." Before he could finish, Jordan flung the door open. Alex grabbed her arms fiercely, looking her over from head to toe, then hugged her in a grizzly-like grip. "Thank God you're all right."

"Of course I'm all right. Alex, what are you doing here? Where's Paige?" she asked excitedly.

Alex looked puzzled for a moment, then pushed past her, looking frantically around the room. "What do you mean? Isn't she here?"

Jordan saw the fear written on his face, and attempted to stifle her panic. "No, why would she be with me?"

Alex sank into the overstuffed chair which had always been his favorite. "She disappeared from the lab yesterday. No calls. No notes. Nothing. She didn't tell her assistant, Brigitte, she was planning to leave the building. She didn't even take her make-up or any clothes. She's just gone. Maybe she found another man."

Jordan was alarmed, but his last suggestion made her giggle. "Alex, don't be ridiculous, she loves you more than anyone else on earth. "Besides," she added mischievously, "if she were running away with someone, she'd definitely take her make-up and clothes. Now, let's just think this through and figure out where she's gone. There has to be a logical

89

explanation for it."

"I hope so. I know she loves me. I guess I would rather think that she's safe with a lover than in danger somewhere. You know, when Nick was staying with us, someone broke into her lab and destroyed it, stealing all of her records. Shortly after that, someone broke into our apartment and trashed the place."

"Do you think it's all connected?"

"I have no idea. The police have no idea. Lord, I wish she'd call."

"She may be calling you right now. Or she may be home waiting for you."

"No, the Geneva police found the taxi driver who took her to the airport. I can't believe she took a taxi. They've got to be the most expensive taxis in the world," he said, shaking his head. "They questioned all the airline employees, and the people at Swissair said she bought a ticket to New York, with a connecting flight to Los Angeles. I called her parents right away, but they haven't talked to her for over a week. And I kept calling you, but your machine was off," he said accusingly. "I thought for sure that you'd had an emergency.

"Anyway, I'm glad you're all right, but now I'm really worried. I've got one of the neighbors answering our phone and keeping an eye out for her. I've got Brigitte staying right there in the lab in case she gets any news. Everyone has promised to call me here if they hear from her."

Jordan sat in silence for a moment, considering the possibilities. Finally, she spoke softly. "Suzanne. You talked to the Kendells, but did you talk to Suzanne?

"I thought of Suzanne first. Brigitte said that Paige got a call from a young woman. Brigitte just assumed it was Suzi. Then she left the office for a little bit, and when she came back, Paige was gone. We thought that maybe Suzi needed her for something. But when the folks said they hadn't heard anything from Paige, and Suzi was at work, I figured it must have been you on the phone. When I couldn't get in touch with you, I thought you might be in the hospital or something. So I came here, expecting to find Paige."

They sat in silence for most of the evening, each lost in his own thoughts. Alex called their apartment and then Brigitte. After he woke her for the third time, she promised firmly that she would let him know if she heard anything from Paige and begged him to let her get some sleep. Alex apologized for waking her and returned the telephone to the desk.

"Alex, you really should try to get some sleep."

"I just can't. I feel there's something I should be doing. What if she's in trouble somewhere?"

Trying desperately to keep the fear out of her voice,

Jordan did her best to reassure him, but he knew that she was as worried as he was.

Alex dozed for a couple of hours in the early morning hours while Jordan paced in the kitchen, clutching her mug of coffee, willing Paige to call. Shortly after seven o'clock, they were startled by the sudden ring of the telephone. Before it could finish the first ring, Alex grabbed the receiver.

"Paige?" he yelled into the phone. His disappointment and frustration were evident as he held it out for Jordan. "It's for you."

Jordan took the business call quickly, reminding the caller that she did keep business hours. As she replaced the receiver on the telephone, she turned to Alex.

"I still maintain that there's a reasonable explanation for this."

The phone rang a second time. Jordan and Alex looked at one another. "Go on, answer it," she urged him. "This time it's her. I'd know her ring anywhere."

Alex hesitated before answering. "Hello?" Then, joy in his voice, he said to Jordan, "It's her. She's all right."

Jordan smiled at him, nodded her head and left the room, giving him a few moments 'alone' with the woman he loved so deeply.

Sometime later, Alex found Jordan in her bedroom, folding laundry. His spirits obviously lifted, the lines around his mouth were gone. He stood in the doorway and called, "Well, my fine wench, it's good to see you doing such a womanly task."

Jordan wadded up a pillowcase and threw it at his head. As he caught it mid-air, she asked, "Well, what's going on?"

"Suzanne did call her yesterday, and asked her to come out to help her with something, so she caught the first plane out. She said she wrote a note to Brigitte, explaining where she was going and ordering her to call me right away. She thought she left the note on Brigitte's desk, but when she put her coat on this morning she found the note in the pocket."

Jordan laughed, "That's our girl. Scatterbrained as ever. How on earth will she ever make it in the world of medicine and research?"

Alex smiled, "Well, for some bizarre reason, she handles her work better than she does her personal life. Anyway, I'm heading up there to see her."

Jordan saw that he still seemed concerned. "Just what is it Suzi needs help with?" Then, after a few moments of thought, "You don't think this has anything to do with her disappearance a few years ago?"

"I'd thought of that. I really don't know. But, I'll wager it does."

Alex folded the pillowcase neatly, and placed it on

the pile on the bed. "Well, sweets, thanks for your hospitality, but I've got to run. Can I take Nick's car? I saw it in your garage. I assume he won't be needing it for a while."

"No, he's not due back from London for a couple of months. I'll get the keys."

As Alex stepped through the front door, he squeezed her hand. "Thanks for the coffee and the goodies. They'll keep me awake as I drive." He tried to hide a yawn. "Good thing it isn't very far, or even all the caffeine couldn't keep these eyes open."

"Give Paige a hug and a kiss for me. If you're still there over the weekend, I'll join you. I need to run up and see my folks anyway. It's been several weeks since I've been there." As an afterthought, as he walked away she called, "And please, tell Paige to be careful."

Alex gave her a thumbs-up, climbed into Nick's car, and drove away.

*

Paige was working diligently on her latest project when Brigitte stuck her head in the door. Paige knew immediately that something important must have come up, or her assistant would not disregard her "Do Not Disturb" instructions.

"Paige, you've got a phone call. It sounds like your sister, and I think she's crying." Brigitte's French accent was still strong, despite the fact that she'd spent thirteen years living in New York.

Paige didn't hesitate. She thanked Brigitte and answered the phone. The girl on the other end of the line was indeed crying. "Paige, I saw him. One of the men who made me do all those awful things."

Brigitte waved at Paige, shutting the inner office door softly behind her. She headed towards the cafe next to the hospital for a well-deserved break. Brigitte loved working with Paige. She had learned so much from her in such a short amount of time. But by mid-afternoon, she was generally exhausted. She would put her tired feet up for a few minutes, then gather up some coffee and gugelhopf, a bun filled with fresh whipped cream, to take back to Paige.

Paige hesitated, the receiver held tightly in her hand, her breath catching in her throat. "What things, Suzanne?"

"Paige, remember when you and Jordan asked me if the people who took me made movies?"

"Yes."

"Paige, I lied to you."

Paige sank into her chair, the room spinning as she gripped the receiver. "You're sure that the man you saw is one of those people?"

"Yes, he even had the same jacket with the worn-out sleeves and the purple and green patches. I know it was him."

"Well, honey, he can't hurt you now."

"No, this time I want to hurt him."

"Suzanne, what are you up to?"

"I just want to pursue this. I'm not a child any more. I'm almost seventeen. But I'm still frightened. Paige, will you please come home and help me? I really need you."

Paige looked around her lab, at all of the work still demanding her attention. "Pleeease," she heard again in her ear.

"All right, I'll be there. But, no more secrets. If you want me to help you, you've got to tell me the truth."

Paige tried to call Alex, found the line busy, and hastily wrote a note for Brigitte, instructing her to call Alex right away. With the note in one hand, she reached for her purse and her coat. The contents of her purse scattered on the floor at her feet. Absently she tucked the note into her pocket and quickly gathered up her swirling items. Thinking only, "I've got to protect Suzi," she raced for the elevator.

Brigitte spent more time in the cafe than she had intended. She found some college friends sitting at a table in the corner. As they discussed their work and exchanged laughs, she almost forgot about the time. Glancing up at the clock on the wall above the cash register, she excused herself, got the coffee and gugelhopf for Paige, and headed for the elevators. She noted that one seemed to be stopped at the second floor, another was going up and was just passing the twelfth, and the third was being loaded by a couple of clumsy janitors with a large supply cart. She decided the stairs were her best bet.

What Brigitte didn't know was that as she climbed the stairs, Paige was standing impatiently in the elevator on the second floor, hoping the maintenance crew would be able to repair the equipment quickly.

Brigitte returned to her office, surprised to find no signs of Paige. Her vials and papers were exactly as Brigitte had seen them when she told Paige of the phone call. Nothing had been put away. The lights were off and the doors closed, but only the outer door was locked. The doors to the supply rooms and Paige's office were unlocked.

Brigitte set to work completing the day's agenda, taking notes carefully, describing each step she took, as Paige always did. She expected Paige to come walking in at any moment, and didn't think much of the footsteps she heard in the hall. It wasn't until Alex called her name that she pulled herself away from her deep concentration.

"Hello, Alex. Where's that ding-a-ling wife of yours? She seems to have just grabbed her coat and purse and skipped out on me."

They waited, hoping that Paige would telephone or return. As the hours wore on and they found no clues, their concern turned into fear. Alex called home and, receiving no answer, he asked the neighbors to check and see if Paige was anywhere nearby. They insisted they hadn't seen her since early that morning. He called the Kendells, but they had no useful information for him. Finally, he called the police.

*

Alex packed a bag of his belongings and some of Paige's personal items, which he assumed she would want, and took a taxi to the airport. His flight was late getting out of the fog covered air-strip, he fumed and paced throughout his two hour layover in New York, and he missed his connecting flight in Dallas. He called Jordan's condo from there. Still no answer.

Waiting for the next flight, he went to the coffee shop at the airport. As a customer bumped into him, knocking both trays to the floor, Alex muttered something about a comedy of errors to the bewildered cashier, and returned to the gate to wait for his plane. By the time he came to the end of the journey, he was convinced that Jordan must have been terribly injured somehow, and that he must hurry to be with her. Paige isn't the only one who cares about you, he fretted silently.

*

Paige walked into the Los Angeles International Airport terminal, and immediately enfolded a tearful young woman into the sanctuary of her arms. They walked to Suzi's car, drove to a quiet beach, and finally talked.

Paige learned that Suzi had actually seen the man a few other times. She had, in fact, been accosted by him as she walked down the street one afternoon, several weeks earlier. She described the scene to her sister, anger and fear mingling in her voice.

"He grabbed my arm and pulled me into an alley. He said, 'Hello, sweet Suzi,' in a sickeningly sweet voice. Paige, I was so terrified that I didn't know what to do. He told me he was making movies again, and he'd love to have me star in a few." Suzanne paused, shuddering as she thought of his offer.

Paige put her arm around her sister. "You're safe now. What else did he say?"

"Not much. I just wanted to get away from him. He said 'The Boss' might not approve, but I had always been his favorite and we could do everything secretly. He offered to be my co-star. Oh, Paige, he's such a disgusting man. I had to get away. I wanted to scare him, so I told him that my sister had hired a private investigator, and they had information on him and he'd better leave me alone or we'd go to the authorities."

"Did he believe you?"

"Not at first. He was sure I was bluffing and I didn't think I could convince him. So, I told him that you had a whole file on him, with pictures and statements from witnesses that had volunteered to testify against him and his boss. When I said that, he looked really scared. He let go of me all of a sudden and said, 'You and your snoopy sister better keep your mouths shut, or we're all done for.' Then he turned and ran out of the alley. I tried to follow him, but he was gone."

"Oh, Suzanne, I'm so glad he didn't hurt you," then, "Oh, my stars, Suzi, this all makes sense. My lab and our apartment were broken into. The intruders went through everything and took most of my files. It must be connected with all of this. They must have been looking for the file you told him I had. But how could they find me? And why would they send someone all the way to Geneva to search through my things? Just how big is their operation?"

Suzanne had no answers for her. She explained that after that first frightening encounter, she had tried to forget about him, but the nightmares of her childhood soon returned in full force.

When she saw Derek the day before, she determined that he must pay for what he had done to her. Following him, she found out where he lived; at least, she assumed he lived in the dumpy little yellow house. She also found out that he had once again set up his movie studio in the same warehouse in which he had held her and several other children hostage. She peeked in through the windows, but her view was blocked by storage shelves filled with boxes.

Suzanne was quite shaken when she climbed back into her car. Old, terrifying memories flooded into her thoughts. But this time, thoughts of justice accompanied them. She had been wrong to allow her parents to silence her so many years before. She knew, she assured her sister, that they really did think they were doing the best thing for her.

"They thought that if I didn't talk about it, if we could put it in the past and get on with our lives, I would forget. But, I'll never forget the things they made us do. And I don't think I'll ever really be able to get on with my life until I know I've done everything possible to stop what they're doing."

"Suzi, are you sure you want to pursue this? These are incredibly evil, sick people. Honey, you could just talk to Neil Larson. Tell him everything you know. Everything that happened to you, and everything you saw yesterday. Then, just let him handle it."

"No. This time I want to get those guys. When they

took me, I was too little to fight back. Now I'm not. But, I'm still frightened. I wanted you to come out here to help me."

"How can I help you?"

"I guess I just need some moral support and an occasional squeeze on the shoulders."

Paige was silent for some time. When she finally spoke, her voice was soft. "Suzanne, I'm so sorry I didn't do more for you when this all happened. I didn't understand Mom and Pop's decision to try to forget about everything. But they asked us to let it go, and I tried to honor their wishes. I guess I was hoping that they were right, that silence would heal. That was just fear and stupidity talking."

It was the younger sister's turn to offer comfort. "I guess I hoped the same thing. But now, it's time for all of us to grow up."

*

The two young women got out of the car, now parked in front of the Van Nuys police station. They paused at the bottom of the steps, shivering in the cool night air, holding hands as they drew courage from one another.

Paige hated to see her sister go such torment. She took a deep breath, drew Suzi up the steps, and smiled at her. "I'm with you all the way, kid."

They found Neil in his office, working late as he did more often than he liked. His hair was starting to gray at the temples, and worry lines were etched a bit more deeply in his forehead than they had been the last time he and Paige had met. But his smile was the same, warm and endearing. His words of delight and welcome for Paige died on his lips as he looked at the two faces before him.

Instinctively he knew that this visit had something do with the case he had worked on so many years earlier.

After several hours of talking, and mainly listening to Suzanne describe the people involved in the organization and their activities, they sat, exhausted in Neil's office. Paige and Suzanne were appalled when Neil told them that he no longer had a case to work on.

"How could you close such an important case?" Suzanne asked him. "Don't you know what they're doing?"

Neil leaned over his desk, arms resting on the stacks of papers he was supposed to have already dealt with. "Suzanne, I know exactly what they're doing. I'd like to go in and take a baseball bat to all of those beasts. But I can't."

"Why not? Why can't you arrest them? Put them away forever?"

"It's not my case any more."

"So, re-open it. I'll help you this time." She felt helpless, but she let determination echo in her voice. Seeing him hesitate, she added, "Please, Neil. There are so many children to be helped."

"Suzi, I didn't give up all those years ago, even when you and your folks refused to help with the investigation. But kidnapping is a federal offense, and once Debi told us that you'd been abducted, the F.B.I. took over the case. You remembered that, didn't you?"

In response to her nod, Neil tore a corner from a piece of paper and wrote a name and number. "This is the man you need to talk to. Tell him everything you've told me. If I can, I'll take you to meet him in the morning. Now, go home, get at least a little bit of sleep, and tomorrow you'll understand the situation a bit more."

The sisters were disappointed, having hoped that more could be accomplished immediately. But by the time they were in the Kendell driveway, they felt better.

"Well, Miss Suzanne. I guess we didn't do too badly for our first day on the trail." Seeing her sister's doubt, she continued, "Come on, honey, Neil was right. We do need some sleep, and maybe this guy, Ed Colson," she held up the piece of paper, "can tell us more. Like why the case was closed, and what we can do about it now."

"I guess so. I think I wanted to go capture Derek tonight, hog-tie him and make him tell us who all of his employees are. Then Dad could send them all to prison and we could get all of those kids out of that awful place."

"First of all, I get the feeling that Neil is more interested in his employers than his employees. Secondly, you couldn't see past the shelves. You don't even know if they're still working with kids. They might be using adults now. Besides, two untrained women who have never handled anything more dangerous than a paring knife wouldn't make a very good rescue team."

"I guess you're right. I just don't like this."

"I don't either, but we'll be better equipped to deal with this after we've had some rest and some nourishment." Then, looking at her watch, "Suzanne Kendell, it's three o'clock in the morning. Mom and Pop must be worried sick about you."

"Look," Suzanne said, indicating the darkened windows of the house. "They'll just think I stayed at Debi's again. They've probably been asleep for hours. Come on, you can sleep in my room. It's closer to the stairs and we won't wake them. Boy, they'll sure be surprised to see you sitting at the breakfast table."

"They don't know I'm here?"

"No, I couldn't tell them about all this, yet."

"What if Alex called? He'll think..."

"...that you've run away with a handsome lover."

"Oh, Suzi, you're ridiculous. He'd never think that."

97

The Kendells were indeed surprised to see their oldest daughter. She was already seated at the breakfast table when they came down from their room.

"Well, darling, what on earth are you doing here?" Liza asked as she wrapped her arms around her daughter's shoulders. "I just told Alex that you weren't here."

"Alex? Did he call?"

"Yes, yesterday. He seemed quite concerned when I told him you weren't here. Darling, have you had a tiff?"

"Oh, Mom, of course not. He probably hadn't gotten the message I left for him. I'll call him this morning and get this all straightened out."

After a very abbreviated explanation for her presence, Paige excused herself from the table. Her mother's voice stopped her in the doorway.

"Paige, what does Suzanne need you for? And to make you fly halfway around the world. She really is a bit selfish at times. I hope she hasn't gotten you in trouble at the hospital."

"No, Mom. Everything will be fine there. I was happy to come."

"That girl's not planning to elope, is she? She's too young. Much, much too young." The Judge looked worried.

"I'll take good care of her, Pop. Don't you trust me?" she answered evasively.

She kissed her parents and raced back up to Suzanne's room. Seeing that her sister was finally asleep after a restless night, she went down to her father's den to use the phone. She thought that she'd better call Neil first, to see if he'd be able to go with them to meet Ed Colson.

"I'll do better than that. Let your sister sleep a while longer, then meet me here at my office. Ed'll be here about eight. He's quite interested in talking to you."

At seven o'clock as Paige slipped into her coat, she found a wrinkled piece of paper in her pocket.

"Oh, no!" she exclaimed, holding the paper out to her mother. "It's the note I left for Brigitte. No wonder Alex sounded worried when he talked to you. I'd better call him right now."

The receptionist in Alex's office skipped her lunch break that day, in the hopes that Paige would call. She was quite relieved to hear that Paige was all right. Unfortunately, she told Paige, Alex had jumped on the first plane headed west, hoping to find her at Jordan's.

With repentance in her heart, she placed her call to Alex. "Oh, darling. I am so sorry I worried you." She explained about the note. When she was assured that he and Jordan weren't angry with her, and that he would join her at her parents' that day, she told him she loved him and hung up the phone.

Suzanne dressed and ate a quick breakfast, and the two set off for Neil's office. The meeting was a very productive one. F.B.I. agent Ed Colson was a tall, impressive-looking man with slightly graying hair. His face was often expressionless, but seemed to convey the message that he had seen most that life had to offer...the good and the bad. He was the sort of man who wouldn't be easily shaken, but whose compassion could be found easily.

Colson was very interested in Suzanne, and all that she had to tell him. He knew most of the details of her case, having been assigned to the case when his predecessor, John Stafford, retired. What he didn't know was that the man she had seen was back in the area.

"This Derek Frank has been serving time," he told them. "He had just been released when you saw him the first time. He must have gotten in touch with his old boss as soon as he was on the street. We didn't even consider that they'd be setting up shop in their old building."

Colson saw the concern on Suzanne's face. He tried to reassure her. "Don't worry. Neil called me last night after he met with you. We went over there, and they haven't started filming anything. They're just getting things together. They didn't even have guards yet. We'll keep a close eye on the place and make sure that this doesn't happen again."

"Tell us more about their operation," Paige said.

"I can't tell you much, obviously, for security reasons," Colson explained. "But I can tell you that we've been working on this for years. Even before Suzanne was kidnapped."

"So, how can they still be making movies?" Suzanne challenged.

"The operation is much bigger than just those people you saw. They're the 'little guys.' Someone is backing the whole thing. Whenever we find out that a new studio has opened, we shut it down. We prosecute and send them to prison, but somehow we can never get to the top of the organization. Someone's heading this all up. As soon as we bust one group up, a new one starts."

"Could these all be independent groups? What makes you think that they're all headed by the same people?" Paige asked.

"Two things. First, their production methods are always the same. Even though they hire different people to manage things, the films take the same path into circulation. Secondly, they use the same logo and production company name. It's almost as if someone's sitting out there somewhere, laughing at us; as if they're daring us to look for them."

"What about all of the people you've arrested?" Suzanne asked. "Haven't they told you anything?"

"Very little. They've either been paid big money to

keep quiet and take the fall for someone, or they're scared of the head of the organization. They're afraid that they'll face the same fate as Harry Motske."

Paige shuddered, remembering the details of Motske's grisly murder. "So, you think that whoever's behind all of this has enough power and money to keep so many people quiet?"

"Fear for one's life can make a person a very loyal employee," Neil answered her. "The interesting thing is that they generally stick to this area. Now they're starting out with Derek and a few of the other oldies."

Colson looked at Suzanne. "With your help, we may be able to get further into this organization than we have been able to do previously."

"No way," Paige interrupted. "You're not going to involve her any more than she already has been."

"No, Paige, I want to do whatever I can to help. I just don't understand how I could really help."

Colson continued, "These people are very tight. So far we've only been able to get one man into their organization. He worked with them for six months before he was able to gain their trust. They started to give him more responsibilities, but never led him to the head man, or woman."

"What happened to him?" Suzanne asked softly.

"We found his body outside of our offices a few weeks later. It was a terrifyingly effective message for our people. We've been overly cautious since then."

"This is great," Paige stormed. "And this is what you want to involve my sister in? Are you stupid?"

Colson was not offended. He had dealt with so much depravity and despair in his career that he was willing to take risks. And those risks often meant upsetting people.

"Ms. Kendell, please understand. I would never put Suzanne in danger. She'd be wired at all times. We wouldn't be more than a few feet away from her. They wouldn't be able to touch her."

"That's probably what you thought about your agent."

Colson was silent for a few moments. "He thought that they were really buying his identity. He got careless. That won't happen again."

"Use me instead," Paige said unexpectedly. "Let me help you. Leave Suzi out of this."

"Ms. Kendell, I admire the protective feelings you have for your sister. It's only natural for you to want to keep her out of harm's way. But the fact is, you're untrained."

Paige's fear turned to anger again. "So's Suzanne. And she's only sixteen."

Colson waved his hand, not in surrender, but in an attempt to calm her. He turned to Suzanne. "As a minor, we'll need your parents' permission. You could be very helpful to us. You've been inside the organization. You may know some of the people. They will remember you--you caused them a lot of trouble. We want you to go to them and convince them that you know more. Tell them that you want money in exchange for silence."

"This is ridiculous," Paige began. "Mom and Pop will never agree to it."

Neil leaned forward, putting his arm around her. "I know you love your sister. But, think about all of the other children who will be affected by these people. How many more victims will they claim before we reach the top?"

Paige pushed her personal feelings aside, seeing the look of determination on Suzanne's face. "Do you really want to do this?"

"I have to, Paige. For my own sake, and for the sake of any other kids they may get hold of. Please try to understand."

"I do, honey. I understand completely. I guess I can't keep you under my wing forever. I'll talk to Mom and Pop for you." She turned to Colson. "How can I help?"

The meeting continued for several hours, concluding with explicit instructions to Paige and Suzanne to be careful. They were not, under any circumstances, to try to do anything alone. Colson and his partner would back them up at all times, and they were to take every precaution not to arouse the suspicions of Derek and his fellow movie makers.

On their return to the Kendell home, Paige found her husband nervously pacing the driveway. She jumped out of the car and ran directly into his arms.

CHAPTER SEVEN

Here stands a lord, and there a lady weeping.
-Pericles

It took a great deal of coercion on Alex's part to get Paige and Suzanne to tell him the entire story. The details of the events of Suzanne's ordeal had not clouded in her memory. They were as vivid as if they'd happened that day. Paige, who had never heard all of the graphic descriptions, sat with Suzi's hand held firmly in her own. The three people gathered in the Kendells' living room were shaken and tearful.

Suzanne hadn't been able to express all of her fears. Years earlier, her father told her to try to forget about her torturous experiences. She hadn't understood his command of silence, but she accepted it. At the age of ten, she believed he was right about everything. Now, as an adult, she resented his demands. She wanted to be free of the nightmares; to be healed of the intense pain that still caused her heart to ache; to be absolved of the guilt, which she didn't deserve; and to see justice prevail, even after years of silence.

Her story began on the day she was kidnapped. She recalled the scene of the abduction, and Paige was reminded of the story Jordan heard from Debi Burke. The terror that Suzi had felt now gripped Paige, as if the kidnapping were her own, and the crime was taking place as her sister spoke.

Suzanne wanted to tell her story, but found the words difficult. "I was so frightened when the man grabbed me. I kept looking at Debi, as if I expected her to save me. I thought that it must be some kind of horrible joke, and that the man would let go of me. But he didn't. He made me hold his hand and walk beside him. He told me to pretend that we were friends, and that he was supposed to take me to the dentist for an appointment. He said that if anyone tried to stop us, I was supposed to tell them that I had forgotten about it, and that my parents had asked him to drive me there.

"I kept hoping someone would see us. I knew if I had to tell the story about the dentist, that they wouldn't believe me. He was dressed in ugly, dirty clothes, and his hair was messed up. But nobody came within view. The bell rang for school to start, so I guess everybody was already inside.

"Anyway, he held onto my hand, really hard. I think he hurt me when he shoved me into his car, but I was so scared, I didn't really think about it. He drove through town and went someplace I'd never been before. He drove up to a warehouse, and honked the horn. Someone on the inside must have been expecting us, because I heard the door open as soon as he hit the horn. He drove inside, and parked back away from the windows on the garage door. Then, he opened the trunk and told me to get out. At first I didn't. I thought that as long as I was in the car, I might be safe. But he started yelling at me. He said that I was going to have to learn to do everything I was told, and if I didn't, they'd hurt my family."

Suzanne paused, looking at Paige. "That's what scared me more than anything else, Paige. When the other guy, Derek, showed up, he was furious. He knew who I was, but he still wouldn't let me go. He argued with Harry--he's the one who took me in the first place.

"Anyway, they scared me, and I decided right then that I'd better listen to them. I got out of the car, and Derek grabbed me and held onto my chin. He looked at my face, like he was trying to find something wrong with it. Then he pushed me away from him, turned me around, and looked me over from head to toe. I found out later he was the director of the movies. It was usually his job to pick the children. I found out that Harry had seen me at the mall with Debi, and decided he wanted me for their movies. I was the only one there who had been kidnapped. Several of the kids were bought and paid for. Sometimes it was their own parents who sold them into the business. Some of them were runaways who were too young to get a job. They came to work for these guys in exchange for room and board.

"Paige, I don't think you need to hear anymore. The things they made us do were pretty awful."

"If we're going to help you, we need to hear it all."

"I've never told anyone about the things I saw or did when I was in there. I didn't think Mom or Pop could handle it. When they told me to try to forget everything, I did what they said. But I always felt if I could tell someone about it, it might help."

As Suzanne spoke, she kept her eyes focused on the fireplace at the other side of the room. She sought out things of comfort. The crystal vase she had given her mother for her fortieth birthday. The porcelain statue of the mother nursing her infant with such beauty and tenderness, which her father had given to her mother for their twenty-fifth anniversary. Things that represented love and safety. Things that kept her consciousness in the present, while her memories took her to the nightmarish past.

Only occasionally did Suzanne look at her sister or at Alex. The love and compassion on their faces made her task more difficult. Paige was pale and the tears ran down her face, untouched. But she and Suzi knew that Alex was right. The time had come for truth. The time had come for healing.

Suzanne paused, breathed deeply, and began again. "I've done research on child pornography in the last few years. I wanted to know if this was a rare occurrence. I prayed that we were the only children subjected to the whims of a group of sick people. What I found out was horrid.

"Child pornography is a worldwide problem. There may be links between child pornography and organized crime. But, most of the time, it's small-time operators, sometimes just making videos in their own homes and garages, with their own kids or neighborhood kids.

"Like the kids at our center, children around the world are involved for different reasons. While I was the only one in our group who had been kidnapped, it's fairly common. Sometimes groups of pornographers sweep into a town and kidnap all the children they think look 'promising.' Once, a gang did that to some children in Holland. They pulled them off the street, drugged them, tortured them, and raped them. They filmed all of it. Then they dumped the kids back in the streets and disappeared.

"I wanted to know why no one was stopping people like the ones who used us. I thought maybe the Supreme Court protected them. One of the men told me that they could do what they wanted. That it was considered free speech. But I found out that no pornography, not even with adults, fits that category. The Supreme Court determined that speech only fits into the realm of intellectual things. You know, like ideas, and searching for truth. Obscenity doesn't have anything to do with that. It's about arousing people sexually. The Supreme Court Justices decided that hard-core and child pornography can't be protected by the Constitution, because they said they're evils that have to be eliminated.

"I also thought maybe law enforcement people were ignoring the producers of child porn. That maybe they had more important things to work on, or things they thought were more important. But I was wrong. They investigate any and all leads. Unfortunately, getting the proof to arrest and convict people is the difficult part. These people have to work underground. It's more secretive than adult porn, because it involves minors. These people can usually close up shop and disappear before the authorities can pin anything on them. I read the statistics for several years, and during one of the years I looked up, there were two hundred and fifty-four different investigations, but there were only twenty-two arrests and seventeen convictions."

Suzanne paused once again, and this time Alex spoke. "I can't believe how much research you've done on this. Wasn't it difficult for you to read about?"

"I guess it was like therapy. I felt I was accomplishing something; that maybe if I learned a lot about it, I might be able to help someone else who had been through it. That's what I want to do now. My first goal is to help Ed Colson, and my second goal is to help other victims of the pornographers."

When Suzanne finished speaking, Paige and Alex

sat quietly for several minutes, Paige locked in her grief, Alex in his anger. He knew the time for secrecy had ended. He was furious with Franklin and Liza for allowing so much time to pass without trying to help the police.

Paige and Suzanne explained earlier about their meeting with Neil Larson and Ed Colson. Alex was concerned that his wife and sister-in-law were getting too deeply enmeshed in the current plan to smoke out the pornographers. He planned to put a stop to their involvement as quickly as possible.

*

Jordan finished her work early on Friday afternoon. She was looking forward to seeing Paige. She stopped by the condo long enough to pack a weekend bag and tried to call Nick. When she got his message machine, she decided to try again later. She hung up without leaving a message, climbed into the Jeep and headed for 'home.'

She was anxious to see her parents. She had exciting news to share with everyone. She thought Nick should be told first, but she wanted to tell him in person and her trip to London wasn't scheduled for three weeks. And, she reasoned, she never had been good at keeping good news to herself. She figured Nick would forgive her. She would tell her parents, and of course Paige and Alex, swearing them to secrecy until she saw Nick. She smiled as she drove, knowing how happy he'd be when she told him.

Feeling a little queasy, she stopped at a convenience store for a soda and some saltines. She nibbled on her drive home, thinking of Nick and wondering where he was at that moment.

Jordan drove to her parents' home, planning to greet them first and then run over to the Kendells' to see Paige and Alex. She would invite them over for dinner--of course, her parents wouldn't mind. She would steer the conversation around to their happy childhoods, and then she would spring the news on them.

Jordan knew that surprise was inevitable. But she felt certain that her parents and her friends would be happy for her. They knew how she and Nick felt about each other.

As for Nick, Jordan was certain that he would be overjoyed. He very much wanted children to cherish and nurture. The fact that this one was coming so soon would only mean a change of plans.

Jordan grabbed her bag out of the front passenger seat and slid out of the Jeep. She glanced at the Kendell's drive and was surprised to see Paige come out the front door of the house. Seeing no signs of life in her own house, she decided she would go over and greet her friend. She wondered

105

if Paige would know, just by looking at her. Silly thought, she laughed. As if the words were written on her forehead.

Paige still hadn't seen her. She was standing next to Nick's car when Suzanne and Alex came out of the front door. She turned to look at them, and then saw Suzanne smiling at Jordan as she walked towards them. Paige said something to Alex, then turned and walked down the driveway toward her approaching friend.

The following events were almost in slow motion, yet they happened too quickly for anyone to stop them. A black station wagon with darkened windows screeched around the corner, racing down the street towards the Kendell and Blake homes. As it passed between the two friends, Paige looked at the partially-open back window. Before she could scream a warning, a weapon emerged from the window and sprayed her body with bullets, its hideous eruption echoing throughout the neighborhood.

Alex threw Suzanne to the ground swiftly and raced towards his wife. He was caught in the shoulder and the thigh by stray bullets and knocked down. His eyes were riveted upon his wife. He screamed her name, becoming more frantic when she didn't answer.

Jordan was already running across the street and up the driveway. She barely noticed the station wagon careening away and disappearing around the next corner. She saw Alex crawling the few feet between him and Paige.

"Paige, Paige," he cried into her hair, his tears falling onto her cheek. He pulled her into his lap, cradling her body in his arms. With one hand he caressed her hair, gently pulling several strands away from her mouth. With his other hand, he grasped at her fingers, crushing them to his lips. He knew he didn't need to check for a pulse. He lifted her head to his and cried into her lifeless face. "Don't go, Paige. I can't make it without you."

Jordan sank to her knees beside him, grasping Paige's hand in hers. "Oh, God. Please don't let this be happening," she prayed. But it was too late. Her beloved friend was gone. She couldn't bring herself to look at Paige's face.

Suzanne stood over them, her body racked by uncontrollable sobs. "I'm sorry, Paige. I'm so sorry."

Liza and Franklin, who had been in the pool, raced down the front steps, water streaming from their hair and their swimsuits. "No," Liza screamed when she saw her daughter lying in Alex's arms. She fell to her knees beside Alex, her husband standing above her, his hand squeezing her shoulder.

Liza automatically checked Paige's wrist and neck for a pulse, refusing to believe what her eyes told her. But when her fingers confirmed her fears, she sank back onto her

106

heels, staring mutely at her daughter.

Only her love for Suzanne roused her. She heard Suzanne's cries, and clutching her husband's hand, led him to Suzanne's side. They stood together, their tears mingling.

Jordan released the still hand and put her arms around Alex. They sat there, weeping together, until the ambulance arrived.

Ed Colson and Neil Larson were at the Kendell home within minutes of the tragedy. They arrived as Alex was loaded into an ambulance, a horrible, vacant stare in his eyes. Suzanne sat on the top step of the porch, her mother beside her, both of them crying, unable to speak or to answer the questions that were asked of them. The Judge stood in the driveway where his daughter's body still lay, covered with a sheet Hannah had brought out. Bloodstains soaked through the sheet, making eerie designs as they mixed with the black and white stripes. Jordan stood at the Judge's side, their arms around one another, each supporting the other.

Hendricks and Milly stood at the foot of the driveway, telling an officer what they had heard. They explained that the Blakes had gone out for the day and wouldn't be back for several hours.

The police arrived in full force, taking pictures, asking questions, measuring distances between the street and Paige's body, gathering bullets from the walls of the house. Neil stared at the grisly, tragic scene before him, wondering how much more this family could take.

The coroner arrived and, upon receiving Neil's approval, gently lifted Paige into the ominous-looking black bag. Jordan watched, her senses deadened by the vision before her and the events of the last hour.

As the coroner zipped the bag, Jordan stepped closer, reaching for her friend. "Paige!" she cried. Neil wrapped his arms around her, supporting her slender body as she trembled uncontrollably. The sheet that had covered Paige lay at her feet. Suddenly the bloodstains began to swirl before her eyes. She lifted her face to look at the man holding her. "Neil, I don't feel well," she said, and everything went black.

Neil lifted Jordan effortlessly and, without asking permission, took her into the front room of the Kendells' home. Hannah led him to the couch, and quickly brought a cool cloth to put on Jordan's forehead. Neil knelt beside the couch, not relinquishing her hand. He lifted her fingers to his lips, kissing them gently. "It's going to be okay, Jory. You just rest now." But Jordan couldn't hear him.

"Hannah, would you please call Celia? She'll want to come be with Jordan now."

Without a word, Hannah went to make the call.

*

107

As the dark station wagon neared the Kendells' home, Derek, riding in the front seat, turned to look at the man behind him. "Are you ready?"

The man, staring intently at the houses they passed, nodded his head.

Derek continued, "We're almost there. Okay, that one, with the convertible Mercedes in the driveway."

The driver saw Paige walk out to the car. "We'll have to come back. There's someone out there."

Derek shook his head fiercely. "No, we can't risk a second trip. What if the kid sees me? Just shoot over her head. Get the house real good. That'll keep 'em quiet. Now," he yelled, "do it now!"

The man in the back, sweat dripping into his eyes, moisture on his palms loosening his hold on the semi-automatic weapon in his hands, thrust the barrel out as the driver opened the back window. With trembling hands, he braced the weapon and squeezed the trigger.

When Derek saw Paige fall, his mouth fell open and his eyes widened into an unbelieving, glassy stare. "Keep going," he hissed at the driver. Then he turned in his seat to look at the man behind him. "You know now that you're dead, don't you? He'll kill you for this."

Tears formed in the young man's eyes. His gaze was still aimed at the window he had just used. "I never wanted to kill nobody."

As Derek watched his tortured face, he knew that this man faced a certain death sentence. "You have two choices, Monty. You can disappear, or you can die."

"Take me to the bus station," was the only reply.

*

Four days had passed since the shooting. Ed Colson and Neil Larson worked together constantly. They weren't convinced that things were as they appeared. The entire incident had been patterned after a typical gang drive-by shooting.

"But," reasoned Neil, "it's the wrong place at the wrong time. We have no major drug-trafficking in this area, and certainly not on that street."

Judge Kendell had sentenced many gang members during his career, but none of them in recent years, and none who seemed interested in revenge on the Judge. Yet, the shooters had paid great attention to details. The style of car used, the tinted windows, the bandanas on the heads of the driver and the shooter, and the out-of-state license plates, which were traced to a stolen car that had been stripped and abandoned a few days before. And yet, Neil and Ed agreed, things just didn't add up.

Alex spent two days in the hospital, being treated for his wounds and shock. On the morning of the second day, flowers were delivered to his room. Jordan was in his room when they arrived. He showed no interest in their arrival and Jordan, trying to reach into his despair, slipped the card out of the envelope. The words left her speechless and frightened.

Alex: Sorry for your tragedy.
You'd best stick with doctoring.
Stay safe...stay silent.

She said nothing to Alex when she looked at the card and he only stared out the window, seeing nothing that took place around him. She kissed him on the cheek. "I'll see you later, Alex. Please eat your dinner, okay?"

Jordan slipped out of the room, the card tucked in her pocket, and went directly to Neil's office.

Neil and Celia were just leaving for dinner, but when they saw Jordan they immediately changed their plans. She showed them the note. Neil took it from her and, saying little, took it to the lab.

"I want an analysis on fingerprints, type of pen and ink used, and I want to know where this card came from."

He called two of his detectives into his office. "Find out where these flowers came from. Who delivered them, who bought them. Do it now."

The detectives and the lab hit dead ends. The flowers were purchased by phone. They were paid for with a credit card, and the number was traced to a woman whose wallet had been stolen in the mall that morning. The card had come directly from the flower shop. The message had been written by the florist himself, and was dictated by the caller. The florist thought it strange, but the caller offered a ten dollar tip to write it as stated. The caller was a man, with an indistinguishable voice. No lisp, medium voice range, no accent.

One thing they did know for sure--this murder had nothing to do with gang rivalries or drug deals gone bad. This was a warning.

CHAPTER EIGHT

O! she tore the letter into a thousand half pence;
railed at herself, that she should be so immodest
to write to one that she knew would flout her.
-Much Ado About Nothing

Marguerite and Samuel Wyndham were at the hospital on the morning that Alex was released. Marguerite spoke quietly to Jordan, just outside the door of his room.

"I've phoned Nick, to tell him about everything that has happened. I've been unable to get hold of him. So, I left a message on his machine telling him that it was urgent that he call home."

Jordan had also attempted to contact Nick two days earlier. She wondered if she should tell Marguerite about the phone conversation she'd had with Lianna.

Remembering the phone call, she decided against it. She said, "I called and left a message for him, too. I'm sure he'll make it home in time for the funeral."

But Jordan wasn't so sure. Lianna answered the telephone on the first ring. Jordan thought at first that she had the wrong number. But, when asked, the woman told her that she had reached Nicholas Wyndham's flat.

"This is Lianna Ashmore. I'm a very dear friend of Nicky's. Can I help you with something?"

"Miss Ashmore, this is Jordan Blake. It's essential that I speak to Nick. I have some bad news."

"Jordan Blake. Jordan Blake." Lianna pretended to consider the name carefully. Then, "Not Alex's little friend Jordan? The quiet, little brown mouse from the reception?"

Jordan had never thought of herself as a mouse before, and doubted that anyone else had, either. But she felt this woman was not one who would appreciate having other attractive females nearby. "Please, Lianna, may I speak to Nick?"

"Heavens, no. He's in the shower right now, and he's so exhausted that I've ordered him directly to bed afterwards. And I have every intention of seeing that he gets there," she added meaningfully.

"Lianna, this is urgent. There's been a...an accident, and I must talk to Nick."

Lianna yawned loudly. "You know, it's very late here in London. Why don't you just give me the message. I'll be sure to give it to Nicky."

Jordan was uneasy about giving Nick the message in this way, but didn't know how else to get the news to him.

"Lianna, there was a shooting at the Kendells' house

and Paige was killed. Alex was wounded. Alex is going to be all right, but the funeral is in two days. It's urgent that you tell Nick so he can be back in time for the funeral. I'm staying at my parents' house right now, so please have him call me as soon as possible."

Lianna had been prepared to yawn loudly as a response to Jordan's message, but Jordan's words shook her to the core.

"Dear God," she gasped, "how could something like that happen?"

"The authorities are still trying to determine that."

Lianna wanted to get this woman off of the phone quickly, before Nick came back. But her concern for Alex delayed her action. "Please give Alex my love and tell him how sorry I am for his loss."

"And you'll tell Nick?"

Now Lianna was frightened. Nick was her security. In her own way, she loved him. True, as her parents' fortune dwindled, his became more enticing. But in the years since their broken engagement, she had missed him. When she saw him at Alex's wedding, she knew she had to have him back.

Lianna had seen Nick's face as he watched Jordan throughout the wedding ceremony. She was unbearably jealous when Nick and Jordan danced together at the reception, and had been relieved when he agreed to give her a ride to the airport.

Since her arrival in London, Lianna felt she was making progress in establishing a stronger relationship with Nick. She sensed he was falling in love with Jordan, but prayed that she wasn't too late. He had loved her once, she told herself, and he could learn to love her again.

If he went back to Los Angeles, he would be going back to Jordan. And Lianna knew she would be forgotten. She would have to keep him here with her.

"Lianna?" Jordan's voice broke the silence that echoed across the telephone wires. "You will tell Nick, won't you?"

"Yes, of course I will," Lianna said, crossing her fingers behind her back as she had done so often as a child. She glanced at the clock on the wall. Nick had gone to the little tea shop around the corner to pick up a package of his favorite tea to give to Jordan. But, Lianna was not about to share that information.

"I'll be sure to tell Nicky. I promise that *we'll* be there for the funeral." Lianna heard Nick's key turning in the lock on the front door. She spoke quietly into the receiver, "Now, I really must go. Nature calls, you know."

Jordan had had to be content with that. Lianna left her feeling unsettled, but Jordan reminded herself that Alex had told her how conniving Lianna could be. She's just trying to make me suspect something that isn't there, she told herself. But why is she in Nick's flat, answering his phone? Jordan was comforted by the thought that Nick would be back in a few days. She wasn't sure that she could face Paige's funeral without him.

But Nick never called. Jordan began to wonder if she should try to call again.

No, she thought, Lianna might be conniving, but she'd surely never keep something like this from him.

*

Three days before Jordan's call, Lianna arrived at Heathrow Airport in London. She had hastily scrawled Nick's phone number on the back of her checkbook when she'd spoken with Marguerite the week before. She was annoyed that Nick had dumped her at the Los Angeles Airport after Alex's wedding, and she fumed at the way he'd watched that maid-of-honor.

"She's not so pretty," Lianna muttered, checking her perfect little nose in the mirror of her compact.

She called Marguerite, presumably as a belated thank-you call for inviting her to the wedding. She asked about Paige and Alex, and swiftly steered the conversation to Nick. "What's he been up to lately?"

She was not happy when Marguerite told her that he'd been spending quite a bit of his time with Jordan Blake. But Lianna was delighted when Marguerite said that Nick was currently in London, and would be there for a month or two, teaching a course at St. Bart's.

"Well, Marguerite, what an incredible coincidence. I'm heading for London in the morning." Lianna was making plans as she spoke. "Just a little holiday, you know. Do you happen to have his telephone number there? I'd love to give him a ring and surprise him."

Marguerite didn't hesitate. She knew that Nick had been hurt by this girl, but thought a quick telephone call would be harmless.

As soon as Lianna picked up her bags at Heathrow, she found a telephone and called Nick's number. He had just arrived, and ran to catch the phone, hoping it was Jordan. He was disappointed when he heard the familiar, pouty voice on the other end of the line.

"Hello, Lianna. What can I do for you?"

"Oh, Nicky. You won't believe the ridiculous predicament I'm in. I've had this little trip scheduled for months, and the hotel has botched up my reservations. Something about some incompetent clerk and his messed-up calendar. Anyway, they won't have my room ready for me for

two more nights. Can you believe this is happening?" She
paused to catch her breath, but not long enough to allow Nick
to respond, not really expecting that he would. "Oh, Nick," she
said, her voice dripping with syrup, "could I please sleep on
your couch for the next two nights? I really wouldn't be any
trouble, I promise. I could have nice, warm suppers ready for
you when you get home at night."

"What are you planning to do, Lianna, hire caterers
every night?" Nick suspected that she'd have difficulty boiling
water. "Why don't you try another hotel? This is London, you
know. There shouldn't be a shortage of rooms."

"Oh, Nick, you know I can't stand going someplace
where I don't know anyone. Besides, your mother called me
the other day, and she told me to be sure to look you up. How
do you think I got your number? Please, Nick, just two nights?"

Lianna was beginning to doubt herself and her
powers of persuasion. They had never failed her with any other
man, but Nick was different.

Nick, from years of family togetherness, had always
felt responsible for this impossible woman. "All right, Lianna,
two nights only." He gave her the address, and hung up before
she could ask him to pick her up at the airport.

*

Nick returned from the tea shop, Jordan's package
tucked safely in his pocket, along with an exquisite emerald
necklace he had seen in the jewelry store window next to the
tea shop. He wondered if he should give it to her for her
birthday, or just because he would be so happy to see her
when he returned to the States.

As Nick unlocked the front door of the flat, he
thought he heard Lianna's voice and as he opened the door, he
heard her place the telephone receiver back in its cradle. "Who
was on the phone, Lianna?"

"Oh, just a wrong number. Seems to be a world-
wide phenomenon. Did you find the tea, Nick?"

Nick held the bag out for her to see, saying nothing
about the necklace in his pocket. That was something for
Jordan's eyes only.

This was Lianna's third night at his place, and he
was beginning to wonder if there had ever been any hotel
reservations. When he'd pressured her about it, she pouted.

"Where will I go if you kick me out? I'm sorry I'm
imposing on you, Nick, but you're such a dear to put me up.
Who else could I turn to? That ridiculous hotel. To
inconvenience me, one of their best customers."

She was concerned that Jordan or the Wyndhams
would phone again, and her fear was substantiated when she
heard Marguerite's voice on the answering machine the next

113

afternoon. Lianna swiftly erased the message. Checking her watch, she calculated that it would now be eight-thirty in the morning in Los Angeles. She called the Wyndhams' estate, asking for Marguerite when the housekeeper answered the telephone.

"Hello."

"Marguerite? This is Lianna. I'm calling for Nick. We are both so upset about what's happened. In fact, he's at the hospital right now, making arrangements to take a few days off. I just wanted to call and give you our flight information. We'll be there tomorrow. Is that soon enough?"

Marguerite was surprised. "Yes, dear, that's fine. But I don't understand. I didn't realize that you were in London with Nick. What happened to your vacation?"

"Nick seemed so lonely here all by himself. I decided to stay and keep him company."

Marguerite's surprise increased. She was certain that her son had a future with Jordan and it seemed unlikely that he would desire Lianna's company. Time enough for questions later, she told herself.

Lianna spoke again, uneasy with Marguerite's silence. "Marguerite, could you please telephone Jordan and tell her? Nick wanted to be sure that she knew when we were landing."

Lianna was still worried. After she concluded her conversation with Marguerite, she felt certain that Marguerite would not be calling again. And she knew that Nick rarely called his parents. But he called Jordan several times a week. How could she keep him from calling her?

Lianna picked up the notepad by the telephone and wrote, "Jordan called, three o'clock. Said hello and not to call her for a few weeks. She's extremely busy at work and wouldn't have time to chat. Also, mentioned that she's been dating some guy at the office named Quentin."

Lianna had met Quentin at Paige and Alex's wedding. The jerk raved about Jordan, telling her how she'd stuck by him when he was having personal problems. How, even though he treated her badly, she still went out with him because she was so compassionate. And, thanks to her, he and his beloved Barbara had gotten back together.

Lianna hadn't even guessed, on the day of the wedding, how important that meeting would be to her. She left the note on the table, so that Nick would find it when he came home that night. As she expected, he was furious. He immediately reached for the telephone, stopping with his hand in mid-air as Lianna touched his arm.

"Nick," her eyes rested in the note in his hand, "are you calling Jordan?"

"Yes, of course. I want to know what this is all about."

114

"Nick, you look so upset. Did she mean something to you?"

"Everything," he said simply.

Lianna's guilt as she saw the hurt and confusion on his face almost made her relent. But then she remembered how he had dropped her off so quickly at the airport in Los Angeles, explaining that he needed to get back to see someone at the wedding reception. No, she resolved, he can't go back yet.

"I'm really sorry, Nick. But she begged me to keep you from calling. She said she had a lot of thinking to do." Seeing the stubborn look on his face, she insisted. "Please, Nicky. Just give her a few days. Then, if this Quentin means nothing to her, she'll be ready to talk to you. Besides, she might even call back when she gets her thoughts sorted out."

Nick wadded up the note, throwing it at the garbage can, not even caring that he missed. As he went into his bedroom, slamming the door behind him, Lianna smiled sadly. She left the note on the floor, knowing that when he noticed it there later, his fury would be renewed.

Late that night, Lianna sent two telegrams, the first to Jordan, the second to the Wyndhams. They were extremely apologetic. Briefly, the messages explained that Lianna was in London, and she was having problems. Nick deeply regretted that he would be unable to return for Paige's funeral, as he didn't feel he could leave Lianna at this time. Nick's name was signed to each telegram.

With the funeral only a few hours away, Marguerite and Samuel were furious. Alex was resigned. Jordan was devastated.

*

Paige's funeral was quiet and solemn. Blaine Michaels, pastor from their church in Santa Monica, officiated. She gave a reassuring message to the congregation, reminding them of the joy Paige had brought to their lives. She challenged them to remember her always with love and affection. And she encouraged them to put the tragedy behind them, reminding them that Paige no longer suffered, but had gone to a place of great happiness.

Jordan made it through the funeral, though it was her mother's arm she held, rather than Nick's. Celia and Neil stood on Jordan's other side, Celia giving her arm an occasional squeeze. But Jordan only felt a void where she knew her heart should be. She watched Alex, and knew that perhaps only he could understand her grief fully.

Alex had eaten little since the shooting. Jordan suspected, from his appearance, that he had been drinking excessively.

115

When the final words were spoken at the graveside, Emerson stood looking at the casket. Jordan saw his tears and went to put her arm around him.

Emerson leaned over, resting his cheek on the top of his daughter's head. "It's all so wrong," he said. "This should never have happened."

Jordan wiped at her own tears. "I know, Dad. But I'm mainly concerned about Alex right now."

"He'll be all right, honey. He's got all of us to strengthen him." He took Jordan's arm and led her back to the car, where Celeste stood with Celia and Neil.

Celia hugged Celeste as she followed her daughter into the car. Impulsively, Jordan reached out and squeezed Celia's hand. "Thank you for staying with us today. This was more difficult than I could have ever imagined. You really helped me to make it through."

Neil leaned in and kissed her on the cheek. "You know we're always here for you, sweetheart. You can call us any time."

Jordan smiled at him weakly. "I know that, Neil. Thank you. I'll be going back to Santa Monica tomorrow. Could I come see you this afternoon?"

Later that day, as Jordan sat in Neil's office, she felt her body could no longer fight off its exhaustion. Pushing her fatigue aside, she faced Neil.

"Did Paige's murder have anything to do with Suzanne's disappearance?"

Neil looked at her warily. He wanted more information. Dissatisfied with the progress being made on Suzanne's case, he wanted answers.

"What do you know?"

"Very little," Jordan answered weakly. "None of the Kendells will talk about it."

"Jordan, I'm going to tell you because you're a friend of Suzi's and because she was ready to help us before Paige was killed. Perhaps you could convince her to help us even after what's happened."

As Neil spoke, he phrased his explanation carefully. He told Jordan about the original case, and how they had been forced to give up because they were unable to locate the pornography ring.

Jordan listened with a constricting heart. "Did Paige know about all of this?"

"Not until she got here the other day. Jordan, this tore her apart. She was ready to pack up Suzanne and take her back with her to Geneva. But Suzi's very persuasive. She needed to face it all this time. She wanted to help us, and Paige agreed.

"But that's as far as we got with them. Paige was killed before we could re-open the investigation, and now Suzi refuses to help. She keeps telling me that this is all her fault. That her sister would be alive if she hadn't gotten her involved in this."

"She must be terrified, Neil."

"Will you try talking to her? Try to get her to help us."

"I'll do what I can."

Jordan sat in the Kendells' front room, watching as Suzanne paced the floor in front of the picture window.

Jordan spoke with conviction as she pleaded with Suzanne. "I know this is awful for you, Suzi. But you may be the only one who can help them find the pornographers again."

"I'm so frightened, Jory. I've lost my sister, and it's my fault. If I'd kept quiet, none of this would've happened."

Jordan was at a loss to comfort her. There was some truth in Suzanne's words. But she couldn't leave it at that.

"Then maybe you owe it to Paige to try to catch her murderers."

Suzanne sat in the chair facing Jordan. She buried her head in her hands, her shoulders shaking with her sobs. Slowly, filling her lungs with deep, strengthening breaths, she lifted her head and wiped away her tears.

"What if it's Mom and Pop next time? Or me? I'm sorry, Jordan. I just can't do it."

*

True to her word, Jordan went home the next morning. Her parents tried to encourage her to stay longer. "You need to be with people who love you, dear," Celeste told her.

"Right now I think I need to be alone. I need to go back to where Paige and Alex and I shared so many wonderful times. And, I need to get back to work." She rubbed her belly. "Got to start making a bright future for this little one."

Jordan had not had to tell her parents that she was pregnant. Her daily bouts of nausea and sudden repulsion to fish odors of all kinds had given her away. The morning after the shooting, Celeste had come into Jordan's bedroom. She watched as Jordan brushed her hair, and took the brush from her daughter's hand, gently brushing her hair as she had when Jordan was a small child.

"When are you due?"

Jordan smiled at her mother. "Is it that obvious?"

"Well, your frequent trips in there do seem suspicious," she said, nodding her head toward the bathroom. "Do you want to talk about it?"

"Not yet, Mom. Just know that I'm very happy, okay?"

Now, as Celeste closed the door of the Jeep after her daughter, she looked concerned. "If you need anything, please come back home, honey."

"Thanks, Mom, but right now I'm going home."

Entering the condo was more difficult than Jordan expected. She could hear Paige's laughter everywhere. She lovingly ran her hands over the grape juice stain that Paige had left on the arm of the couch last summer. She stood on the deck, where Paige had first told her of Alex's proposal, and of the offer to come to Geneva.

So many times they'd laughed together and cried together in their lives. Paige had been her companion, her sister, since they were in their cradles. Paige had encouraged her when she was ready to give up on men, and when she was convinced she would never finish school. Paige had laughed at her when she burned meal after meal while they practiced their cooking skills in their first apartment. Paige had shared in every important moment in her life. And here she was, in an empty apartment, where that glorious laugh would never ring again.

Jordan sank to her knees beside the couch, resting her head on the cushions. She gave way to her grief. There was no longer a void. There was no longer any courage to share with her parents or the Kendells, or even with Alex. There was only grief: a horrible, agonizing pain that would not go away.

*

Over the next two days, Jordan slowly resumed her regular schedule and responsibilities. Grady tried to shield her from excess work, but she seemed to welcome it. He watched her with great concern. He too had noticed her bouts of nausea and the ever-present soda crackers, and he knew that she should be gaining weight right now. But she seemed to grow thinner and more pale each day. On the Friday afternoon after her return to the office, he ordered her home. "You've got to take care of yourself, Jordan. Don't you want to have a healthy child?"

Jordan was angry. "Of course I do. I'm taking all of my vitamins, it's just that I'm not hungry. If I get tired, I'll rest. Grady, I like to work. It helps me to forget."

"Forgetting is one thing you'll never be able to do, Jordan. You've got to face your loss. Face the pain. Feel it. Only then will it begin to diminish. Please, go home. Do it for the child, if not for yourself."

Jordan couldn't argue with him. She spent the weekend pacing the floor in her apartment. She cleaned kitchen counters that were already sparkling, shampooed carpets that had been shampooed only a month before. She

118

was cleaning out the linen closet on Saturday night when the doorbell rang.

Jordan opened the door, and had to catch Alex as he stumbled in. "Hi, Jory." She knew he was drunk.

She quickly brewed some coffee, doubting its effectiveness against the alcohol, but desperate enough to try anything. She made Alex sit on the couch as she poured cup after cup of coffee into him. But all it seemed to do was make him have to use the bathroom.

She decided it would be better to let him sleep it off, and she brought him a pillow and a blanket, leaving him on the couch.

Early the next morning, she awoke to the sounds of the blender and the smell of melted plastic assaulting her nostrils. She quickly grabbed her robe and went out to the kitchen. She was dismayed to find that Alex had dirtied most of the dishes, and stacked them in various places around the kitchen. One Tupperware bowl was melted on the burner of the stove, and standing next to the sink was an empty bottle of what had once been cooking sherry. Alex was drunk again.

Jordan quickly checked to make sure that the burners of the stove were turned off, then picked up the bottle.

"Alex, you drank this?"

She dragged him out of the kitchen into the living room, shoving him into his old chair.

"No more, Alex. Do you hear me? No more. You can stay here as long as you want, but you absolutely may not have one more drink. Is that clear?"

Alex nodded his head miserably, only aware that Jordan was angry with him for something. When he buried his face in his hands and started to weep, Jordan sank down beside him. She put her arms around him. "Oh, Alex, I'm so sorry. We're going to get through this, okay? Maybe we just have to do it together. I've been going crazy here alone, and you're destroying yourself."

Alex's senses were returning. He caressed Jordan's head as it rested on his knee. "It's going to be okay, Jory. Yeah, we'll do it together."

*

Alex spent the next several days wandering aimlessly up and down the beach. When he was in the condo, he either sat in his chair, staring at the fireplace, or he sat on the deck, watching the sky. He and Jordan spoke very little, each of them finding comfort in the presence of the other.

One morning, as Jordan emerged from her bathroom holding a cool washcloth to her face, Alex asked, "How long have you known, Jory?"

Startled, Jordan asked, "What?"

"How long have you known you're pregnant?"

"How did you know?"

"Well, I know I've been pretty wrapped up in myself lately and I haven't paid much attention to you, but I am a doctor. I'm supposed to know these things."

"I've known since a few days before..." She couldn't say it.

"Before Paige was killed?" Jordan nodded. "I thought so. That's the real reason you came to see us at her folks' house isn't it? To tell us?" Again Jordan nodded. "Does Nick know?"

"No, he hasn't called since before she died. I've left several messages on his machine, but he never returns my calls. And I was so hurt that he didn't even come home for the funeral. I know he and Lianna are friends, and that he has to help her with whatever problems she's having, but couldn't he at least call me?"

"I don't know, Jordan. It seems odd. Lianna has never had problems that she couldn't handle by herself. She excels at taking care of herself. She's generally the one who's causing problems for everyone else."

"Well, I guess I'm going to have to give in and call him again. I need to give him my flight information, anyway.

"I'd thought about canceling my trip over there, but I think I should go ahead and go. If I wait to tell him when he gets back here, I think he'll notice my growing belly, and I don't think he'll believe that I swallowed a watermelon seed."

Later that day, Jordan placed a call to Nick. Much to her dismay, Lianna again answered the phone. She was still there? Just what was going on in London, Jordan wondered.

This time Lianna seemed delighted to hear from Jordan. "Jordan, dear, you're the first person from home I've been able to tell...Nicky has asked me to marry him. I do hope you'll be able to come to the wedding. It's going to be a grand and glorious affair. I've never seen Nicky so happy. It's almost as if he's a little boy again, just getting his first pony. Oh, dear," she gave a little giggle, "I guess I just compared myself to a horse."

Jordan hung up the phone. All thoughts of civility were gone. He's going to marry Lianna? Her anger grew, helping her to keep her tears at bay.

Tenderly she rubbed her fingertips over her abdomen. "Looks like it's just you and me, sweetheart," she spoke softly. "I should've learned my lesson with Jonathan, but I thought Nick was different. So, he wants to marry Lianna?" Her tone slipped from gentleness to sarcasm. "Good luck, Nick. That's quite a choice you've made."

Lianna, across the miles, pushed aside her guilt. Telling herself that Nick was a prize worth fighting for, she smiled at herself in the mirror hanging above the telephone.

"Touchdown," she said. "Good play, Lianna my dear."

CHAPTER NINE

Call me but love, and I'll be new baptiz'd.
-Romeo and Juliet

Shortly after Paige's death, Alex transferred to the U.C.L.A. Medical Center to complete his residency there. He worked hard at keeping his thoughts away from his pain, yet his grief over her death slowly twisted into anger and a desire for revenge.

He didn't believe that she had been killed in a random drive-by shooting. He knew there was much more going on. He tried repeatedly to talk to the Kendells, and each time they told him to put the tragedy behind him; to find some happiness and go on with his life.

"Son, nothing that you do, no questions that you ask will ever bring our girl back to us," Franklin told him.

Liza and Suzanne pleaded with him to try to forget about what had happened. When he persisted, they told him about the note Jordan had found in the flowers that had been delivered to his hospital room.

Alex was furious. "Why didn't you tell me about this before? My own life was threatened, and you didn't think it was important enough to tell me?"

Liza tried to comfort him. "Alex, you were so full of despair. We couldn't bring you more trouble. We couldn't worry you even more."

Alex's questions reverberated through his head. Why had Paige been killed? Did it have something to do with Suzanne's abduction and the porn ring? How had the pornographers linked Paige to the F.B.I.'s investigation? Or had they? Was someone else meant to be the target?

He went to see Ed Colson. "I want you to tell me everything about this case. I want to know why my wife was killed. She didn't know anything about the pornographers, except what Suzi told her. She couldn't identify any of them."

Colson wasn't surprised to see Alex. Neil had told him that Suzanne and Paige would haunt him endlessly if he didn't work with them. When Paige was killed, he expected that Alex would take up where she had left off.

Colson explained about his earlier meeting with Paige and Suzanne, and he told Alex what he and Neil suspected about Paige's murder.

"It was a warning to the entire family to stay away from us, to give us no assistance in our investigation. Somehow, without any of us being aware of it, either Suzanne or Paige got too close. They touched a nerve. Someone decided that they had to be stopped."

"Well, they won't stop me. I want to help you now. I want answers to all of questions the Kendells refuse to discuss."

*

When Lianna told Nick that Jordan was seeing Quentin Galbraith, he was stunned. He started to call her several times, but his hurt pride and Lianna always stopped him.

"Give her some time, Nick. You just have to be patient. If your relationship is meant to be, she'll have to decide that for herself," she had told him.

But Nick argued with her logic. "If something went wrong between us, we need to talk about it. I know that whatever it was, we can work it out. We just need to talk."

Lianna was desperate and felt like she was grasping at straws. Finally, she had her answer. She faced him, her voice solemn and soft. "Nick, she asked for some time. If you really care about her, you have to respect her enough to give her what she asks for."

Following that conversation, Nick left the flat and walked down the steps, not even seeing the beautiful brick and weather-boarded exterior of the house as he left. The house had originally been a family home, but when the owner was left alone and nearly penniless she had converted the second floor into rooms for a bed and breakfast, making the entire third floor into a self-contained flat for long-term guests.

Nick did not see his landlady, Mrs. Vickers, as he walked through the gate, nor did he notice as his feet took him automatically on the familiar journey to St. Bartholomew's Hospital. The oldest teaching hospital in London, St. Bartholomew's was affectionately called Bart's by the locals. Nick knew he was privileged to have been invited to teach their students. He smiled faintly as he walked past the stone statue of Henry VIII standing over the gateway.

The gatehouse was something Nick would love to show Jordan. A small, pretty building, it was built by the masons who built St. Paul's Cathedral. But the gatehouse was built without benefit of any architectural drawings, and Nick knew that fact would fascinate Jordan.

Jordan. What had gone wrong? Nick had sensed that everything was going well. Could he have been that wrong about their relationship?

Absently, Nick walked past the hospital, turning to walk back towards Smithfield. As he walked through Smithfield, past the extraordinary glass and iron arcades which lined the north side, Nick's thoughts turned to his sister-in-law. He would love to bring her to this place. With her love of history, she would be captivated by the stories of Smithfield.

Nick would tell her about the Protestants and Catholics who burned each other alive here in the sixteenth century. If Alex and Paige were to visit, Nick would be sure to take her to St. John's Lane, which had once been the headquarters for the Knights of St. John.

But Nick could not think about Paige without his thoughts returning to Jordan. And, as much as he hated the situation, ultimately he knew that he could not argue with Lianna. He loved Jordan. If time was what she needed, so be it. He would give that to her.

He wasn't worried about her feelings for Quentin. From what she had told him about her co-worker, he knew that she could never love a man like that. He remembered how he had needed time to sort his thoughts before he had asked Lianna to marry him. This was a request he could understand and respect. But he was unsure that his patience would last for very long.

When Nick finally agreed with her, Lianna was overcome by her relief. She was shaken by their discussion and grew more terrified daily that he would pack his bags and head back for L.A.

As the days turned into weeks, Nick's patience wore thin. He told himself that if Jordan truly loved him, she would not put this moratorium on their contact with one another.

With each day that passed, Nick's pain slowly twisted into numbing anger. He had thought that their relationship was special; a relationship that could grow into something permanent and strong. Jordan had seemed so different from Lianna, but now he found that the similarities were evident. Both women had used him for their own pleasures. Both had deceived him, made him think that they cared for him. And both of them had hurt him. Only this time, the hurt was greater.

Nick buried himself in his work, spending more time planning his lectures than was really necessary. The two days that Lianna had asked to stay with him stretched into a week. He didn't care if she stayed or went. He didn't enjoy her company, but he was rarely home to experience it. He left his flat each morning before daybreak, and didn't return until he was exhausted and ready for bed. He knew Lianna was unhappy with his inattention, but he reminded her that he had only promised her a place to stay, not a companion for her vacation.

Lianna tried to be very understanding of his moods. She planned to show great love and support for Nick should he ever seem unhappy about the message she'd written "from Jordan." She would make herself available to cheer him up and bring him happiness when he most needed it.

Her main concern now was dealing with the problem of Paige's death. She'd kept him from going home for the funeral. She was thankful that her plans had gone so well, knowing that if he had seen Jordan then, he might not have returned to London. Lianna knew that she needed to keep him here with her for as long as possible.

But he would find out eventually about Paige, and she would prefer to have him find out her way. She decided she'd make a telephone call to Marguerite. She checked the time, and realized that she'd have to wait a few more hours before it was suitable to call California. As each moment passed, Lianna grew more anxious. This plan would work; she had great faith in it.

Some time later, she placed her call. "Marguerite, I've been thinking about Alex. How is he?"

"I'm sorry to say that Alexander isn't doing very well. He's recovering from his wounds, but he started drinking even before the funeral. And it escalated afterward. He stayed here for a while, but now he's gone to stay with Jordan. We're praying that she can bring him out of his despair. She has always been such a good friend to him. Maybe she can reach him when none of the rest of us can."

Lianna quickly calculated this new piece of information. Alex living with Jordan. This could be very helpful, she thought. "I do want to apologize for keeping Nick from the funeral. He was really distraught that he couldn't make it, but he's so wonderful, and he absolutely refused to leave me."

"Is everything all right with you, dear?"

"Oh," Lianna sighed, "I think it will be soon." Her speech was well rehearsed. She explained that she'd been having some personal problems that had just been too overwhelming for her to deal with on her own. She carefully avoided any direct mention of what those problems might be. The lie would last longer if it were less complicated, she thought. "Nick is so kind. He's put his own grief on hold just to help me. You've raised a really wonderful son, Marguerite."

Marguerite, still unhappy with Nick for missing the funeral, wondered what could have kept him with Lianna. But, as Lianna expected, she was much too polite to ask any questions of a personal nature.

"Yes, Lianna. We're proud of both of our sons."

"Well, I hope you understand why Nick couldn't come home. And I hope that you'll forgive him."

Not understanding at all, Marguerite answered, "Yes, of course."

Their conversation was brief after that, staying with safe, trivial topics. Lianna congratulated herself once again for laying useful groundwork.

Late that night, Lianna greeted Nick at the door. She normally went to bed long before he returned, too exhausted to stay up and too self-indulgent to do anything more than take a long soak in the tub and plop herself on the piles of pillows that she'd purchased and piled on top of the bed in Nick's extra bedroom. But this night, she needed to talk to him.

She wore an expression of despair on her face. She'd mustered up a few tears and blown her nose repeatedly to make it appear red from crying. "Nick, oh, I'm so glad you're home. Come in and sit down with me. I'm afraid I have some terrible news."

Nick's first thought was for Jordan. He followed Lianna into the kitchen, where she had two cups sitting out on the table, the coffee brewed and ready to pour.

"What's happened, Lianna? Just tell me what's wrong."

Lianna forced a few more tears and turned to face him, sitting in the chair nearest her. "Please, sit down first."

Nick, worried and anxious, did as she said. "Okay, tell me."

"Nick, it's so horrible, I just don't know how to tell you." Then, seeing his frustration, "I spoke with your mother today. I'm afraid that your brother's wife, Paige, has been killed."

Nick's anguish came swiftly. He stood up, tears filling his eyes, and walked to the window.

"How did it happen?"

"It was one of those drive-by shootings. She and Alex had gone to visit her parents, and she was standing in the driveway when they drove right in front of the house and shot her." She paused, allowing Nick time to digest her news. She actually felt some of his pain as he stood with his back to her, his shoulders sagging. "When is the funeral?"

"Oh, Nicky, I'm so sorry. It was a few days ago."

"They didn't even call me?" Nick's astonishment mingled with his grief.

"Your mother thought it would be too difficult for you to get home for the funeral, and she didn't want you to feel guilty about not being able to come, so she didn't tell you sooner."

"Good Lord. Paige was my sister-in-law. Didn't they know I would've moved mountains to be able to be there?"

Lianna knew she had to tell him about Alex. "Nick, that's not all..."

Nick turned swiftly to face her. "Jordan, was she with her? Was she hurt?"

Lianna didn't allow her annoyance to show. She had to remain compassionate now. "No, Nick, it was Alex. He was shot, too." Seeing the look of urgency on his face, she continued, "He's going to be all right. Physically, that is, but your mother said he's started drinking."

As soon as she told him about Alex's drinking, she regretted it.

"I've got to go home immediately."

Lianna thought quickly. "No, you mustn't, Nick. Your mother said that Alex just wants to be left alone. He's asked that she and your father give him some time to get on with his life."

"Well, he didn't ask me."

"Oh, Nick, I know that you love your brother, and you feel like you need to help him right now, but Marguerite said that he's really suffering right now, and she wanted me to promise that I wouldn't let you go see him quite yet. She's really concerned about him, and she says that if anyone can reach him right now it's Jordan."

"Yes, she may be right. Jordan's been a good friend to Alex. He might listen to her when he wouldn't listen to anyone else."

Lianna decided that it was time to use her information. "Yes, he's living with her now. So, she'll be there to help him whenever he needs her."

"That's probably best. She knows him well, and she'll know how to be a good support for him."

It was not at all the reaction that Lianna had wanted from him. She had to act quickly.

"I suppose. But I doubt that Quentin fellow is going to appreciate having Alex around when he wants to be alone with Jordan." She watched his face darken. The anger was what she'd been working for.

"What are you up to, Lianna? Are you trying to turn me against Jordan?"

Lianna paled, walking quickly to his side. "Oh, Nick. No. It's just been so long since she's called. I don't want you to be hurt."

Nick waved her excuses aside. He couldn't think about any of this right now. He vaguely asked Lianna to excuse him. He told her that he needed some time to come to grips with all that she had told him.

He left the flat, walking quickly to stand in Smithfield. His grief and confusion burned his soul, just as those unfortunate people had burned here so many centuries past. Paige was dead. His brother was being consumed by his grief. And he, Nick, could do nothing to help. Jordan, the woman he loved, was asking for time. As much he hated it, he could only give her what she asked for.

By the time Nick returned to the flat, his decision was made. He would lift his prayers to the heavens each day as he rose and each night before he climbed into his bed. He would pray for strength for Alex, for a phone call from Jordan, for patience for himself, and for Lianna to go home and leave him alone.

Lianna greeted him the next morning as he was leaving to go to the hospital. "Nick, you know that I never intended to impose on you for this long. But I feel that I can't leave you right now. I hope you won't mind, but I've canceled the rest of my plans for this trip, and I've made arrangements to stay here with you. I really want to help you with your grief."

Nick was annoyed. His emotions took control. "Lianna, please, just leave. I appreciate your concern, but I don't need your help."

Lianna looked like a wounded deer. Tears filled her eyes, desperation filled her heart as it pounded painfully in her chest. "Nick, please don't send me away. I can help you. Really, I can."

Nick was resigned. As much as he wanted her to leave, their history kept him from hurting her. Lianna stayed.

*

Jordan had eaten little in the days following her telephone conversation with Lianna. She'd told Alex briefly of the conversation; his anger roused him out of his grief more than anything Jordan had said to him. He knew that Jordan loved Nick. And, he thought he'd read his brother fairly well. He was convinced that they had a future together.

He tried to call Nick a few days after Lianna shared her news with Jordan. "He's just being an idiot. I can't believe that he'd fall for her again. Something's really screwy here."

But before Alex was able to make the call, Jordan showed him the telegram that had arrived earlier that day.

"Dear A and J, Just sharing my joy. I popped the question. L said yes. Be happy for me, N."

"Jordan, Lianna could have sent that. I told you ages ago how scheming she can be. Besides, with telephones and fax machines, nobody sends telegrams anymore. This smells suspiciously of Lianna's handiwork."

"I don't think so. Not this time, Alex. Nick hasn't called me or written to me. The only explanation can be that all of this is true. Maybe his old feelings for her never died. Please, I don't want to think about it anymore. I've made a horrible mistake, and I need to put my life back together. I've got a baby on the way, and I want to bring her into a world of happiness and absolutely no stresses or worries."

Alex's heart broke for his friend. He tried to sit back and allow her to grieve, just as she had allowed him. But the pain she felt over Nick's desertion, the grief she still suffered in her loss of Paige, and the anticipation of her child's birth were weighing heavily on her. Alex knew that she wasn't eating enough. She appeared to be losing weight. His concern for her grew daily. In his mind, he began to formulate a plan. His solution seemed ideal to him. But how could he get Jordan to agree?

*

A week later, Alex was convinced that it was time to put his proposition to Jordan. But he knew he needed to approach her carefully.

"Jordan, let's go out to dinner. You said that I need to join the land of the living. Well, now I'm telling you the same thing."

Much to his surprise and relief, Jordan agreed. They decided to drive to Malibu and eat at Geoffrey's Restaurant, north of Malibu Cove. As they waited for their food, Jordan found Alex watching her.

"Alex, stop worrying about me. You've been watching me like a vulture for a week and a half."

"I don't feel like a vulture. I feel more like a shepherd watching over a very precious flock."

"Gee, Alex, sheep are pretty stupid animals. I'm not sure I should feel too flattered."

"Well, I'd never think of you as stupid. But, you've seemed a bit like a little lost lamb lately."

Jordan looked down at her hands as they played with her napkin. "I know. I guess I've felt a little lost. I used to be able to go to work and all of my problems would evaporate as my work absorbed me. Things are so different now. The problems are bigger."

Alex reached across the table, grasping her hand in his own. "Jordan, I'm always going to be here for you. I want to help you with your problems. I don't want you to have to bury yourself in your work. You should work because you love it, not because it's an escape. I want to help your worries and your hurt go away."

Jordan squeezed his hand. "You're so good to me, and I really do appreciate you. I just need some time to figure everything out."

"I think I can help with that. Jordan, you know that I love you."

Jordan smiled at her friend, once again giving his fingers a quick squeeze. "I know. I love you, too."

"Jordan, I have something to ask you. Before you answer me, I want you to promise to hear me out. Do you promise?"

"Sure, Alex. You seem so serious."

"I am. Jory, I've been doing a lot of thinking. I think that you and I could make a very happy life for this baby. I want us to get married." Jordan gasped, but before she could speak, he continued. "I know. We're just friends. But I would be the best daddy in the world for your baby. I promise. I would be a loving and faithful husband for you. And, Jordan, don't worry about Paige. I have a feeling that this is exactly what she'd want us to do. Come on, Jordan. Tell me yes."

"Oh, Alex, you're so wonderful. But I don't want to

get married just because I've been jilted and I'm going to have a baby. I'm going to be a good mother, and I can raise my baby myself."

"There is no doubt in my mind that you'll be a fabulous mother, and I know that you could raise him yourself. There are millions of single parents in this world who do a really great job with their kids. But, Jordan, I don't know one single parent who won't admit that things would be easier with someone else to share their burdens, to help them with their struggles, and to join them in their fun times.

"I know you love Nick. I know that you might always love him. I'll always love Paige. But maybe it's time for us to put all of our pain behind us, and to build some happiness for ourselves."

"I don't know, Alex. It seems like such a drastic step, just to solve the problems of today."

"Jordan, I'm not suggesting that we jump off a cliff. I'm suggesting that we build a future together."

Alex waited. The waiter came to refill their water glasses and to apologize for the wait on their dinners. Alex thanked him quietly, his eyes still on Jordan.

Finally, to his relief, she smiled at him. "You're right. We could build a wonderful future for this baby, and for ourselves. Heaven knows that people have built happiness on less than we have. We're starting out with a history of friendship and good memories. Yeah, I'll marry you."

Alex jumped out of his chair and ran around the table, pulling Jordan into his arms. He pressed his lips to her hair. "We are going to be happy, Jordan. I just know it." Then, to the smiling patrons at the surrounding tables, he announced, "She said yes."

As the people around them applauded and called out their congratulations, Alex's smile grew broader. He hugged her tightly until she whispered, "Alex, you're squishing the baby."

Alex suddenly sobered, concern on his face. He gently pushed Jordan back into her chair. "Jory, I'm so sorry. I got excited. Is he okay? You know I wouldn't hurt him for anything in the world."

Jordan laughed at his concern, "Alex, I was just teasing you. Of course the baby's okay. But, *she* won't be if you keep calling her a him." Seeing that he was about to argue with her, she said, "Mothers are supposed to always know these things, remember?"

But her words didn't stop him. "It's a boy, Jordan. This time the mother is wrong," he teased.

Jordan laughed with him. "And just what makes you so sure this is a boy?"

Alex said simply, "Wyndhams have boys. For many

generations back, all boys. Just trust me. My new baby is a boy."

*

For the next two days, Alex and Jordan talked about their future. For the first time since Paige's death, they began to find peace of mind and spirit. Their thoughts strayed frequently to Nick, each of them asking questions that could not be answered. But they kept their thoughts to themselves, telling themselves that now was the time for hope.

On the third day following Alex's proposal, Jordan asked him if he'd told his parents of their plans.

"No, not yet. I'm not exactly sure how to tell them. They're going to be pretty surprised."

"I don't think they're going to be pleased, Alex. They loved Paige so much. They're never going to understand why we're doing this. And, Alex, I would prefer it if we didn't tell them about the baby. Is that all right? I mean, I don't want to be dishonest with them, but I'm feeling a little foolish about all of this. You know, getting pregnant by a man who didn't even have honorable intentions toward me and all that. Especially in this day and age, when everyone knows that the safest sex is no sex. Do you mind?"

"Of course I don't. I won't tell them anything that you don't want me to. But don't you think they'll wonder about a baby coming so quickly after the wedding? You're too far along for him to even be considered a honeymoon baby."

"I know. It's just that I'm not ready for people to know yet."

"What about Nick?"

"I know it's wrong for me to keep this from him. I'm sure he'd want to know. I even wrote him a letter, explaining it all to him. I said that I wasn't asking anything from him, that I would take full responsibility for the child. I told him that I just wanted him to know, so he wouldn't find out from someone else, or think that I was trying to maintain some kind of hold over him. You'd be proud of me. I even went so far as to wish him a happy future with Lianna."

Alex didn't look pleased. "Jordan, did you mail that letter?"

"No, it's still here in the desk," she said, reaching for the envelope.

Alex turned to face her as she picked up the letter. He struggled with his thoughts. When he spoke, his voice was low, full of emotion. "Don't mail it, Jordan."

She looked up at him in surprise. "Why not? Why don't you want me to tell Nick?"

"It's not that I don't want him to know. It's Lianna. Jordan, she's not a good woman. She'd be a bad influence,

131

and a horrible stepmother for this baby. She'd use him as a way to get at Nick, but she'd never love him. I know my brother. He'd at least want joint custody. Then Lianna would be around the baby all the time. Please, don't subject our baby to her." He was pleading.

"All right, Alex. I won't send the letter. But what if he figures it out later? What if he asks us?"

"Jordan, quite honestly, I don't think this marriage of theirs will last too long. They may be ancient history by the time he asks. If not, we'll deal with that at the time. Just like we'll deal with my parents and anyone else who asks. Right now, let's just take care of ourselves and this little one."

He rubbed his hand over her belly tenderly. It was the first time he had touched her since their embrace in the restaurant, and it brought tears to Jordan's eyes.

"What's wrong, Jordan? Does it hurt?"

Jordan wiped her tears away slowly with the tips of her fingers. "No, Alex. I think I'm a little hungry for some love and affection. Sometimes I feel a little lonely."

Alex pulled her into his arms, his cheek pressed against the top of her head. "I want to help get rid of that loneliness. I know that it's going to take time for us to get used to this relationship, but we can make it work."

Jordan stood on tiptoe, and kissed his cheek. "I know we can. That's why I agreed to marry you. You and I and this baby," she rubbed her stomach lovingly, "are going to be the happiest family on this earth." Suddenly she jumped, a look of surprise and delight on her face. "Alex, the baby wiggled."

Alex quickly put his hand on her stomach. "Where? I !can't feel anything." Then, with disappointment, "I guess I'll just have to wait until he kicks harder."

Jordan wrinkled her nose at him, "Gee, thanks a lot. Are you wishing me pain and agony?"

Alex's smile was quick, and Jordan saw a flash of the Alex she'd met so long ago in the pizza parlor. An Alex who knew only joy. An Alex full of dreams and hope.

"Sure! Isn't that what motherhood is all about?" He ducked as Jordan pretended to punch him. "Jordan, if this baby is starting to dance around, don't you think it's about time we got married? We don't really want him showing up for the wedding, do we?"

"I hadn't really thought about it, but I guess you're right. We could go talk to Blaine. I'd really like her to marry us. Do you think she'd do a small private ceremony for us?"

Alex called the church, making an appointment to meet with Blaine later that afternoon. He and Jordan ate a quick lunch before she showered and changed into a loose-fitting, comfortable sundress. When Alex saw her, he pulled at the front of the dress.

"Making room?"

132

"No, silly. I shouldn't really need it for awhile?" She said it with a hint of a question in her voice. "I'm only a month and a half along. I can't start to show this quickly, can I?"

"Jordan, everybody's different. You know that. Some women's bodies start to change immediately. Others don't show until the last couple of months." He laughed, seeing the distress on her face. "Don't worry, you're going to be beautiful even if you get as big as Dodger Stadium. Now, come on. Let's go see a lady about a wedding."

Jordan wasn't appeased by his half-hearted compliment. In fact, she was worried. "You don't really think that I'm going to get huge, do you?"

Alex put his arm around her shoulder, steering her towards the front door. He gave her a squeeze and said, as reassuringly as possible, "No, of course I don't, honey." He said a silent prayer, asking God to bless her with good self-esteem, even when she could no longer reach her toes.

Blaine was happy to see them. She had met with Jordan on a few occasions after Paige's death, and she knew that Alex was having difficulty dealing with his grief. She also knew about the baby.

When Jordan and Alex were seated in her office, Blaine smiled at them reassuringly before she spoke. "Alex, you're looking better. How are you doing, really?"

Alex looked at her solemnly. "It's been hard, Blaine. I never knew that grief could hit so hard. I still miss her. I don't suppose I'll ever stop." He smiled at Jordan as she squeezed his hand.

Blaine answered him honestly, "No, you'll probably miss her for the rest of your life. But it hurts less as time goes by, and you'll be able to think of her with happy memories, and not just pain."

Alex liked Blaine. He appreciated the fact that she didn't offer him any platitudes about the blessings of faith or the promises of salvation. He needed to hear that grief was a real part of life. Blaine assured him that his pain was normal, that it would ease.

Blaine turned her attention to Jordan. "How are you feeling? Is everything okay with little Blaine?"

Jordan laughed at her. "Great, Alex swears this baby is a boy. And you already have it named."

"Of course. I wouldn't want you naming her anything stupid, like Hortense or Evangelina."

Alex looked from Blaine to Jordan, liking the smiles he saw on their faces. Yes, he thought, it's good to have laughter again.

"Don't worry, Blaine. I'd never let her pick out any stupid names." Then he looked back at Jordan. "We'd better tell her why we're here."

Slowly, Jordan explained their plans to marry. She

had told Blaine, at their last meeting, that Nick was marrying someone else, so Blaine knew that there was no hope of a reconciliation. But her heart ached for her friend's pain. Sometimes, God, she thought, I sure wish you would make peoples' lives easier for them.

When she spoke, she chose her words carefully. "I would be happy to do your wedding, if you're sure that's what you want. You're not kids. I'm sure you've thought this through completely. So, I'm not going to give you any advice, unless you ask for it."

"Alex and I would always listen to your advice, Blaine; but you're right. We have given this a great deal of thought. We think that this may be the perfect way to give this baby a happy home."

"You're sure that the child wouldn't be happy having a loving mother and a doting Uncle Alex?" Seeing their expressions, she waved her hand in the air. "I'm sorry. I have to ask."

Alex answered her this time. "We've talked about that, too. But, Blaine, I've always counted myself fortunate that my parents were happily married and that I was raised in a two parent home. Jordan feels the same way, and we have the advantage of not being swept away by hormones and emotions." He chuckled as Jordan and Blaine rolled their eyes at each other.

"Are you sure that hormones and emotions are such a bad thing?" Blaine asked.

For the first time that he remembered, Alex blushed. "No, but that will come. For now, we just know that we care about each other and we want to build a future of happiness and security with each other. That sounds pretty good to me."

Blaine nodded at him. "It sounds pretty good to me, too. Now, when do you want to get married?"

They scheduled the wedding for the following Saturday. It was important to Jordan and Alex to do it quietly, with only the necessary witnesses present. They decided that it would be easier for them to wait and tell their parents after the ceremony.

When they told Blaine of their plan, she mentioned that it sounded like they were cowards. When they didn't argue with her, she just laughed with them and agreed to their requests.

*

Saturday dawned, clothed in beauty. The surf outside the condo was quiet, the waves gently crawling up the beach. A lone seagull combed the sand, looking for breakfast. Three pigeons challenged him for a hotdog that had been dropped from someone's picnic basket the night before. The seagull won, and the pigeons moved on down the shoreline.

A jogger ran swiftly, silently down the beach, the music playing on her Walkman inspiring her movements. She smiled and waved at Jordan, sitting on the sand near the steps that led to the condo's balcony.

Jordan saw the sun's rays when they first crept over the buildings behind her, as they reached out to touch the waves. She watched the seagull and the pigeons. She didn't know that Alex stood in the doorway on the balcony behind her.

She heard him as he opened the door and walked down the steps towards her. "Cold feet?" he asked.

"No, cold fingers," she answered matter-of-factly, standing to face him.

"What?" Then, as she touched his arm with five of her ten icicles, "Oh, I get it. Jordan, are you all right?"

Jordan's eyes met his squarely. "Yes, I'm great. I just had to do some thinking. But, Alex, I think I'm really happy about this."

Alex groaned, "You think? I think I'm wounded." He pulled at her hand. "Come on, bride-to-be. Let's get you dressed and fed and to the chapel. Preferably on time!"

They met Blaine in the chapel of the church a few minutes before eleven.

"Blaine, it's beautiful. Is someone else having a wedding here later?" Jordan asked, looking around the chapel at the cream-colored candles, with pink roses draped around the base of the candelabras. Candles and roses were everywhere.

"It's my wedding present to the two of you. This may be a planned elopement, but you deserve to start your lives together in beauty."

Jordan grabbed the minister in a firm embrace and kissed her on her right cheek, Alex kissing her left.

"Thank you, Blaine. This is wonderful," he said.

"Well, you two, if you're ready... I see that the organist and her sister are out in the hallway. They can act as your witnesses. That is, if you didn't want someone else."

"No, they'll be perfect. And yes, we're ready," Jordan said.

Blaine looked her over and patted her belly. "I guess we'd better hurry. Little Blaine looks like she's starting to poof a little bit."

Jordan moaned, "Oh, no. I'm getting fat, and you have the nerve to tell me so right before my wedding. Some friend you are."

"Jordan, you're gorgeous." Seeing the doubt on the face in front of her, Blaine laughed. "I'm sorry I said anything about poofing tummies. I promise, you don't poof a bit. Let's get you two married before I get in any more trouble."

Jordan still looked skeptical, her fingers spreading

over her abdomen, measuring, feeling. "It does poof. Alex," she wailed.

He grabbed her arm and pulled her towards the chancel. "Blaine's right. You're gorgeous--and you're paranoid. Now, stop feeling sorry for yourself and marry me."

The ceremony had been written for them by Blaine. It was simple, beautiful, and everyone in the room cried. When Blaine said, "You may kiss the bride," Alex turned to look questioningly at Jordan.

"May I?" he asked softly.

Jordan, a tiny smile curving the edges of her mouth, nodded slightly, lifting her face to his. As Alex lowered his head, his lips meeting hers with gentleness, tears once again filled her eyes. She looked up at him, her smile tremulous, her hands shaking.

Alex blinked back his own tears, grabbed her hand in his, and led her down the aisle. The organist and her sister followed them out of the chapel. They hugged Alex and Jordan, congratulating the young couple and wishing them much happiness.

After thanking Blaine for the wonderful ceremony and the beautiful decorations, Jordan and Alex left the church.

"I suppose I should take you out for lunch or something," Alex sighed.

"Yeah, I suppose you should."

"What? You're not going to argue with me and offer to take me home so that you can slave over me?"

"Sure, Alex. I'll slave over you just as much as Paige did."

Finally, she was able to say Paige's name without feeling pain leap into her throat. This time, no tears sprang to her eyes as she thought of her friend. But Alex didn't answer immediately, and Jordan was afraid that she'd hurt him with her flippancy.

He pulled the car into the parking lot next to the Santa Monica Pier, climbed out and walked around to escort her to the stairway. "Great," he muttered, "Two women, cut from the same mold, and I had to marry both of them. I hope that next time around I can marry some sweet thing from the backwoods somewhere who wants nothing more than to serve her husband from morning 'til night."

Jordan was relieved, and she joined him in his laughter. "Sorry, mister, but this is it. You're stuck with me."

Out of respect for Jordan's highly sensitive sense of smell, they avoided the seafood restaurants. Jordan nodded appreciatively when Alex suggested hamburgers, and he steered her into the Crown and Anchor, a delightful little restaurant open to the sea air that swept over the pier.

They spent their afternoon walking together on the pier, watching the children ride the carnival rides that were set up for the summer months. They rode the carousel twice, with Jordan assuring Alex that a merry-go-round couldn't possibly be hazardous to the baby.

They went back to the condo early in the evening and had a simple dinner of cold roast beef sandwiches out on the balcony. They watched several children running in and out of the waves, their parents watching from a safe, dry distance. After an hour of playing in the water, the children left the encroaching tide and built an elaborate sand castle out of the reach of the waves.

Jordan and Alex enjoyed watching them. "Our kids will be down there playing like that someday, Jordan."

"Our kids," she repeated vaguely.

"Someday," he stressed. "I'm not naive enough to think that you're going to get over Nick right away, or that you'll fall madly in love with me, pick me up and carry me to your bed any time soon. But, Jordan, I'm willing to wait. I have some healing to do, too, remember? Let's just take our time, okay?"

Jordan looked at her husband. "You're a good man, Alexander Wyndham. Thank you for understanding."

They washed the dishes together that night. Dancing to music that blared from the stereo in the living room, they were careful not to break anything. Jordan almost doubled over in laughter when Alex jitterbugged to the cupboard, and the plate he was holding slipped from his hands. He juggled it from hand to hand to chest and back to the safety of his hands before he was able to put it on the shelf.

Jordan marched out to the living room, ceremoniously turning the stereo off. "I think that, for the safety of our dishes, you'd better not do any more dancing and drying at the same time," she told him.

They watched a movie together, munching on popcorn that was much too buttery, but Jordan was too polite to complain to the chef. They had started a second movie when Jordan, her eyelids feeling like wet cement, fell asleep, her head resting on the arm of the couch. Alex stood up and, thanking God for her small frame, picked her up and carried her into her bedroom. After he placed her on her bed, tucking the covers in around her, he kissed her forehead.

"Sleep well, Jordan. Sweet dreams," and he went to his room.

*

Jordan and Alex spent the next several months "putting their lives in order," as Jordan described it to Grady. He was surprised when she told him about the wedding. But when she explained everything to him, he agreed that she and Alex could build a life together.

"I wish you much happiness, Jordan. I've grieved

with you in your pain, and I'm happy that you're beginning to find joy again. There's something that I've been wanting to give you. I've been waiting for the right moment, and I guess that a marriage is a great time for presents."

Jordan was curious about Grady's words, but he made her wait for several days until he was ready to tell her. "You can invite me over for dinner," he told her. "I'll give you your present then."

That evening, after Grady finished every morsel on his plate, and Jordan plagued him endlessly about the surprise, he leaned back in his chair. "Well, Alex, I guess I've tormented her enough. Should I tell her now?"

"You know about this, Alex?"

Alex smiled at her, his eyes twinkling. "Yep. Grady told me a few weeks ago."

"A few weeks ago? Okay, men, my turn. What gives?"

"Well, I was going to do this in my will, but I decided that it would give me more pleasure to do it now."

"Your will? Grady, are you sick?"

"Jordan, you always jump to the wrong conclusion. No, I'm healthy as a horse...a very old horse, that is. But I want to give you McIntyre and Associates. I've had the papers all drawn up. All you have to do is sign them, and the entire business is yours."

Jordan was stunned. She blinked several times, her head held rigid. She had difficulty focusing on Grady. She cleared her throat and spoke hesitatingly. "No, Grady, you can't just give me your company. We're not even related."

"That's the stupidest reason I've ever heard not to give someone a gift."

"Okay, how about this one? It's too much. I'm just a partner. Why on earth would you give it to me?"

"Jordan, my dearest child, do you love me?"

"Of course I do."

"Well, I love you, too. You know Sarah and I could never have children. And when I lost her, I thought I'd never feel love again. But then this smart-aleck kid, fresh out of college, came along. She made me laugh, she inspired me to create beauty in my work, and she brought me love. If Sarah and I had ever had a daughter, I would have wanted her to be just like you. Of course, her skin wouldn't have been so pale," he laughed, "but other than that, she would have been like you."

Jordan leaned back in her chair, overwhelmed by her emotions. "Grady, you don't know how much that means to me. How much I wish I could have known Sarah. But Grady, I'm happy just to have your love. I certainly don't need your business. You've spent your life building it up."

Alex reached for her hand and squeezed it gently. "Jordan, this is what he wants to do. You spend more time trying to convince people that they shouldn't give you gifts than most people spend saying thank you and you're welcome."

"Well, it's not like you all give me little things. Alex, you bought this condo for me and now Grady, you're trying to give me your company."

"Jordan, I'm not *trying* to give it to you. I'm *giving* it to you, whether you argue or not, whether you say thank you or not. I have spent my life building it up, and I don't want it to disappear just because I'm retiring."

"You're retiring? Grady, I didn't think you ever wanted to retire."

"I didn't either. But I've been working for most of my years. I want to travel. I want to look at other people's buildings. I want to sit on the beach from sunrise to sunset and not worry about work. I'm old. I have a right to play for a few years. And," he said, waving a finger at her nose, "I'm old enough to know what I'm doing and to have my decisions respected. You will take McIntyre & Associates, and you'll be pretty darn happy about it!"

Jordan got out of her chair and wrapped her arms around Grady's neck. She kissed him several times, wetting his face with her tears. "Thank you, Grady. I accept. I will do everything I can to keep up your standards and make you proud."

*

Before Grady's "official" retirement, he ordered a new sign for the front of the office building along with matching letterhead stationary and business cards for Jordan and each of her employees. In beautiful Old English script, the elegant lettering read, "Blake & McIntyre, Architectural Firm." When Jordan arrived at the office the morning the sign was hung, tears poured down her cheeks once again.

"Oh, Grady, I still can't believe you're doing this for me. Why couldn't we keep the old name?"

"It's all yours now, Jordan. I only left you my name to give your clients some continuity. You can drop it later, if you like."

"I wouldn't drop your name for the world. This place wouldn't exist if it weren't for you. And part of it will always be yours. You know, Grady, if retirement is just a bit too boring for you, you'd always be welcome to return."

"I'll keep that in mind. However, Jenny might not appreciate that very much."

"Jenny? Who is Jenny?"

"She's my well-kept secret. She's a very wonderful woman I met a few weeks ago. She's very young, only sixty-seven," he paused and smiled at Jordan's muffled laughter.

"Well, she seems young to me!" he asserted.

"So, what are her credentials? Is she worthy of you?"

"You're going to fall madly in love with her, just like I did. I've asked her to marry me."

"Grady," Jordan sputtered, "I can't believe how secretive you've become. Why didn't you tell me about her?"

"I wanted to make sure."

"And now you are?"

"Absolutely. We've already planned our honeymoon. We're going to tour Europe. Sarah and I had always planned to do it, and I think it's time for me. Jenny's been there several times, so she's promised to be my personal tour guide."

"Oh, Grady, I'm so happy for you. And," she waved her hand toward the new sign, hanging outside the door, "for me, too. It seems that life is pretty good, after all."

Jordan and Alex were invited to Jenny's for dinner two nights later, and as Grady had predicted, they loved Jenny immediately. She was a small, plump woman, her skin almost as dark as Grady's. Her gray hair was cut short, allowing it to curl around her ears and on her forehead. She smiled almost constantly, and her laughter and sense of humor kept them smiling with her. She and Grady acted as if they'd known each other for years, and Jordan prayed that they would have many years of happiness to share with one another.

*

Jordan made repeated trips to see Suzanne, always begging her to cooperate with Ed Colson and Neil Larson.

"Help them catch the people responsible for what happened to you and Paige," she begged.

But, each time, Suzanne refused adamantly.

In frustration, Jordan finally went to see Ed Colson.

"I've reached a dead end. Suzanne absolutely will not cooperate with you." Jordan was determined not to let this defeat stop the investigation. "Mr. Colson, I want to help you. What can I do?"

Ed Colson watched her, his concern etched deeply on his face. "I've already lost a good agent, and now Paige Kendell. I won't endanger you. If you can get Suzanne to testify, that would put us miles ahead in this case. We can't pin anything on Derek Frank without her."

"What if she won't do it?"

"We'll pursue other avenues. But you can't help us any other way, Ms. Blake. I won't allow it."

Jordan became more determined than ever. She continued to pressure Suzanne, and at the girl's persistent refusals, she decided to work through other avenues. She contacted local counselors and psychiatrists, asking each one of them if they had any child clients who had been through situations like Suzanne's. She respected their privacy, but asked them to contact her if their clients were willing to talk.

After several months, the first telephone call came. Sandra Lee Chen, now seventeen, had worked with Derek Frank two years earlier. She had run away from home, and was living in the streets. Desperate, cold and hungry, when he offered her a job, she accepted. She worked for him until he told her she was too old, and put her in the streets again. Since that time she had reunited with her parents, and was in therapy.

Sandra Lee refused to speak to anyone but Jordan. She insisted that Derek had helped her at a desperate time in her life, and she wouldn't testify against him. But she knew that some of the children he used were not willing participants, and she wanted to see him stopped.

"Will you come with me to talk to Ed Colson?"

Jordan waited, breathlessly, as silence coursed through the telephone wires.

"I'll think about it."

Jordan told her that she'd call back in one week's time. As the week neared an end, Jordan became impatient. Talking with her mother one evening, she vented her frustration.

"I can't understand why these girls won't help. This man may be responsible for Paige's death. He's obviously responsible for the suffering of many children, and still no one will testify against him."

Celeste felt her daughter's dejection. "Honey, what you're doing is good, but you can't let it worry you. You have to be happy now, for the sake of the baby."

"I know that, Mom. But I think I would be so much happier if we got Paige's murderers behind bars."

Two days later, Jordan went to see Sandra Lee. The girl met her at the door, only opening it a few inches.

"Hello. Are you Sandra Lee Chen?"

The girl nodded.

"I'm Jordan Blake. Sandra Lee, I know you said you'd call me, but I was so afraid that you wouldn't help, I wanted to come talk to you in person."

The girl grasped the edge of the door firmly in her hand. "I can't talk to you any more. You have to go away."

Jordan was desperate for a different answer from this girl. "Why, Sandra Lee? When I spoke with you last week, you said you wanted to see Derek stopped. You could be instrumental in helping other children. Don't you want to do that?"

Sandra shook her head, tears slowly sliding down her face. "Please leave. I can't talk to you any more."

As she started to close the door, Jordan held it open. "Why? Has something happened to frighten you?"

Sandra slowly opened the door, wider this time. She nodded her head slightly and motioned for Jordan to enter. She led Jordan to a table inside of the front door and opened the center drawer. Her fingers wrapped around a crumpled piece of paper, which she smoothed out and handed to Jordan.

It read, "Keep your mouth shut. What's past is past."

"Where did you get this?" Jordan asked.

"It came through that window last night, tied to a rock," motioning to the window next to the door behind Jordan. Jordan looked at the window, noticing that the pane had been recently replaced, the molding still stripped away from the inside of the frame.

"Please leave now. I won't talk to you."

Jordan hesitated, then walked slowly to the door. "I'm sorry, Sandra Lee, if I've caused you any problems. I understand why you're afraid. But I'm sure that I could get some protection for you, if you'd come with me to talk to Ed Colson."

"No," the girl spoke firmly.

Jordan left, her emotions torn between concern for the girl's safety and frustration at her inability to convince Sandra Lee to help the investigation.

When she reached home, she was dismayed to find a police car in her driveway. Parking the Jeep quickly, she ran up the stairs into the condo. She found Alex in the kitchen, talking to an officer.

"Jordan, this is Sergeant Imes. You got a note today that I thought the police should see."

The police Sergeant handed a note, wrapped in a plastic bag, to Jordan. Written on the page in bold, dark scrawls were the words, "Leave it alone, Jordan. If you want a healthy baby, stop playing detective."

Alex watched Jordan while she read the note. As the blood drained from her face, he pulled her towards a kitchen chair, gently pushing her down onto the seat.

"Have you ever received anything like this before, Ms. Blake?"

"No, but the girl I just went to see got a threatening note last night."

When Jordan had given him the information about Sandra Lee and promised him that she would contact him if she received any more notes, he placed a phone call to Ed Colson.

After speaking with Colson for several minutes, the Sergeant excused himself and walked towards the door.

"I think, Ms. Blake, that you'd better do as the note says. Colson said the same thing. He doesn't want you in any danger."

"I don't either, Sergeant," Alex asserted. "I think her

142

investigating days are over. Yes," in response to Jordan's silent protest, "for the sake of this baby, they are. From now on, you are going to be safe. If anyone in this household is going to work with Colson, it'll be me."

After Sergeant Imes left, Alex followed Jordan to the living room. "I meant what I said, Jordan. This baby is too important. I don't want you involved in this any more."

Surprisingly, Jordan didn't argue with him. "I want a puppy for Christmas."

"Excuse me? What has that got to do with anything? It's not Christmas."

"I want a puppy that will grow up with this baby, and will protect her. A dog to be her playmate and her guardian."

"It's not a bad idea. Okay, what kind of dog?"

"I hadn't really thought about it. It can't be something that will just bond with one person. It has to like the whole family."

"What about a golden retriever?"

Jordan lowered her chin and looked at Alex questioningly from under her brows. "For a watchdog? It would probably try to lick a burglar to death."

"You're so picky," Alex grimaced at her, following her lead in her attempt to lighten the mood.

"I've got it. An Akita."

"A Japanese hunting dog? It would eat the baby for dinner."

"No way. If we train them right, they'd give their lives for him."

"Now it's them?"

"Sure. I even know a breeder. His son was one of my patients last week. He had his tonsils out, nothing serious, but his folks were so grateful for my fabulous care that they told me they'd give me my pick of dogs. I never seriously considered it before. But now it sounds like a pretty good idea."

The next day, loaded into Jordan's Jeep with a blanket in a box for the puppies, they drove to Claremont. As they drove up Indian Hill Boulevard, Jordan started to get nervous.

"Are you sure this is a good idea?"

"You're the one who said we needed a puppy."

"I know, but what if they're big and fierce?"

"Jordan, relax. Just wait until you see them, and if you're not convinced, we won't do it."

As they drove into the circular driveway of the Watsons' home, six large, furry beasts ran out to the Jeep, tails wagging. Jordan opened the door and jumped out, immediately feeling wet tongues on her hands.

"Oh, Alex, they're gorgeous."

"Yeah, great watch dogs, I see."

"Dr. Wyndham. I'm glad you came. What do you think of our puppies?" Lloyd Watson strode toward them quickly, his hand extended. He made his way through the pups, gently pushing on heads and shoulders to keep them from jumping on him, and greeted Alex and Jordan with enthusiasm. "Don't be fooled by their exuberance. They do make good watchdogs. These guys are still young, and I have to admit, we haven't worked with them much as far as training. My wife is too soft with them. She calls them all her babies."

Lloyd led them around the side of the house toward the small barn in back. "We've got a new litter ready to go. They've just been weaned, and they need good homes. Come on, I'll show you."

Jordan was enraptured. Tiny, bouncing balls of fur greeted them as they walked through the door. Sharp teeth gave love bites and excited tongues bathed her hands and ankles. She immediately dropped to her knees, and the puppies covered her face and ears with more kisses.

"They're marvelous. How can we ever choose?"

Despite her difficulty in making a selection, Jordan eventually settled on one puppy. Smaller than the rest, the young female was not strong. But her affection for Jordan captivated her immediately.

"Ma'am, I don't want to discourage you, but I can't make any guarantees on that one. She's the runt. Might never get real strong."

"Didn't you ever read Charlotte's Web? Sometimes the runt turns out to be the best," Jordan argued.

"Don't try to change her mind," Alex warned Lloyd. "It's impossible."

Alex wanted a playmate for the pup, and he quickly selected the largest, strongest-looking male. "Remember, we want a watch dog."

As they drove home, the puppies jumped back and forth from the front to the back of the Jeep, ably ignoring the box and blanket, Jordan handed Alex the list of names Lloyd had given her before they left. "Good Japanese names," he had told them.

Alex read them aloud as Jordan drove towards home. "I'm afraid I'm massacring the names, but how about Hiroko and Keiichi, or Sachiko and Yoshio, or Michiko and Tadashi?

"I like them all. What do they mean?"

As Alex read the meanings, they continued on the list, finally selecting Tatsumaki, meaning tornado, for the male and Tenshi, meaning angel, for his sister.

When they took the puppies into the condo, the formerly comfortable home seemed to shrink before their eyes.

"I don't think this is going to work," Jordan said, shaking her head. "They barely fit now. And they're not even half their adult size."

"We'll walk them on the beach morning and night. They'll be fine," Alex assured her.

"Are those famous last words?"

*

Jordan reached the end of her eighth month in good health, although she was dismayed at the proportions of her body. Her doctor assured her that all was well and that it was much better for the baby if she gained a little extra weight, rather than aiming for just ten or fifteen extra pounds as women in previous generations had often done.

The morning sickness she experienced in her first trimester was returning now in her third, though her bouts weren't as severe as in her first months. Soda crackers and peppermint candies soothed her queasiness easily.

Alex was delighted with her bulk. While Jordan alternately sulked and complained, Alex hugged her and kissed her belly. "Jordan, you're not turning into a beached whale for nothing. You're creating a life. Don't you know that some men think women are most sexy when they're pregnant?"

"Yeah? Well, introduce me to some of them," Jordan growled.

"Nope. This particular beached sea mammal belongs to me."

"Alex, I really don't like your descriptions of me. Couldn't you be a bit more sensitive? You know, you could tell me how beautiful I am. You could tell me that I'm not nearly as large as I think I am. You could be *nice* to me!"

"Why? Do you think I want your head to grow as big as your midriff?" He ducked quickly as a pillow went flying past his head. Suddenly sobering, he spoke again. "Jordan, I guess I should have asked you this a long time ago. I just wasn't ready to think about it. What is the status of Paige's and my house?"

She hesitated before answering, not wanting to remind him of his pain.

"It's all finished," she told him quietly. "I didn't want you to have to think about it until you were ready. The construction crew finished it a few months ago. Alex, I can arrange to have it sold if you'd like. You don't ever have to see it again."

Alex knew that he wanted to go to the house. "I wasn't ready to think about it for a long time. I meant the house to be for Paige. I planned it for her. I had you build it for her. And I've been afraid that if I went to it, all I would see was her. But I'm ready now. I think I can go there and see it with different eyes. I think that I can think of Paige with love now,

145

and not just pain. I want to see our house."

"I'll take you there, whenever you want to go."

"No, if you don't mind, I think I need to go by myself the first time. Would it be possible for me to get inside?"

"Of course. I have the keys in my bedroom. When would you like them?"

"Now, I guess. Do you mind?"

Jordan hugged him quickly. "Of course not, Alex. I just wish that I could help you do this."

"Why don't you meet me there in a couple of hours? That would give me some time to get my emotions in hand. Then we can decide together what we're going to do with it."

*

Alex stood on the threshold of the house, marveling at the beauty spread out before him. "Paige, she did it. Jordan built our dream home," he said in a low voice. "Can you see it, honey? Can you see any of this?"

Alex suddenly felt very lonely. He desperately wished that Paige could answer him. As Alex turned to go back through the door out to the front porch, he felt as if someone was breathing on the back of his neck. It was a warm feeling. He looked around and, seeing no windows or doors open, lifted his hands in the air to feel where the draft was coming from. Yet, he could find no draft.

He felt as if someone was pulling him into the front room. He followed the impulse and went into the empty room. The wooden beams in the ceiling were just as he had imagined they would be. The fieldstone fireplace was more massive than he had expected, but he was pleased with it. "We could have roasted marshmallows in there, Paige."

The warm feeling returned and a voice whispered in his ear, "Jordan."

Alex shook his head. "I'm going crazy," he thought. He looked around the empty room. "Paige, are you here?"

He walked to the hallway, telling himself that insanity had finally set in. Yet he felt strangely contented.

"Jordan," the voice spoke again.

Alex walked out to the front porch and sat on the top step, waiting for Jordan to arrive.

When she got there, Jordan pushed herself from behind the steering wheel of the Jeep, her growing stomach making it difficult to get in and out of the vehicle. She'd seen Alex sitting on the steps as she drove up, and she now walked towards him. It wasn't until she stood at the foot of the stairs that she saw his tears.

Jordan ran up the steps, sitting at his side. "Alex, what's wrong? Oh, I knew you shouldn't come here. I knew it was too soon."

Alex shook his head at her and took her hands in his. "No, Jordan. This is good. It's right. I just realized that I needed you with me to go through the house." He stopped, wondering just how much he should tell her. "I did go in, but something really strange happened. You're going to think I'm looney-tunes, but I'd swear that Paige spoke to me."

He looked at her out of the corner of his eyes, waiting for her to leave his side. But she didn't move. He turned his head to look at her directly. "Jordan?"

"I don't think you're crazy. I felt her, too, the first time I came in here after she died. It was like she was walking through the rooms with me. I felt better, like her spirit was somehow touching me and comforting me. But I thought you'd think I was crazy if I told you!"

Alex stood up, laughing, pulling her up with him. "I have a feeling that Paige was trying to tell me something when I was in here before. Let's go find out what it was."

Alex and Jordan walked through the house room by room, hand in hand. At one point in the tour Alex stopped. "She's here, Jory. It's like she's blessing this house. I think she wants us here."

Jordan looked at him, wondering what could be going through his mind this time. She didn't wonder long.

"Let's move in here. Jordan, this would be a wonderful place to raise a child. Look out there," he said, waving towards the back yard. "Just think of the wonderful playground we could make for him out there. He could have a dozen pets. Besides, we've got to get Tatsu and Tenshi out of that condo."

The puppies had quickly demolished the couch, the railing on the balcony, and a kitchen chair during their bored, lonely hours alone. Alex knew that this argument was a sure-fire winner, but he continued for good measure. "We could build the baby a basketball court and a swimming pool and a tennis court and..."

"Stop! Okay, I'm convinced. But I think just a nice lawn will keep her happy for a long time to come." She thought for a moment. "Alex, I'm due in three and a half weeks. You're not considering moving before the baby's born, are you?"

"Why not? Would you rather settle into a new house with a big belly, or a crying baby?"

"I really resent your implication that this baby will cry, Alex. You should know by now that any child of mine will be perfect." Jordan winked at the face he made at her. "All right. Point well taken. Let's do it now."

Moving was much simpler than Jordan expected. Alex insisted on hiring movers to do everything for them. Whenever he caught Jordan moving a box or a piece of furniture, he pounced on her immediately and made her sit down.

"Your job is to be the supervisor. If you lift one more thing, I'm going to tie you up. Now, stay put."

Jordan didn't stay put for long, but she became more cautious...she only moved things around when Alex was out of sight.

The puppies remained underfoot, but the movers were so taken w!ith them that they were fed cold French fries and part of a cheeseburger that were retrieved from the cab of the moving van. One of the men got Lloyd's name and number from Alex, mentioning that his kids needed a puppy of their own.

Jordan decided to keep the condo on the beach. She still loved it, and she thought it would either make a wonderful weekend home or they could rent it to college students.

They brought their favorite furniture with them from the condo, but did most of the decorating with new furniture purchased specifically for the house. They had already gotten everything they would need for the baby, and that was moved into the room across the hall from the room that was to be Jordan's bedroom. Alex's room would be next to the baby's. "That way," Alex had told her, "when you're in the middle of your new mommy blues and you're exhausted, I can get up with the baby in the middle of the night. I'll change his diapers and everything."

"Are you going to nurse her, too?"

"Well, I might have to wake you for that, but then I'll take him back to bed when you're done. How's that?"

Their plans and their excitement grew, and their thoughts of grief diminished more and more with each sunrise that greeted them.

One evening, as they were clearing their dessert dishes from the table, Jordan's knuckles suddenly whitened as her grip tightened around the plates she carried. She grabbed at her belly, sinking back into her chair.

Alex was on his feet immediately. He ran around the table and knelt down beside her. "Jordan, what's wrong?"

"Goodness, that's a new one. She's never hurt me that much before."

Fifteen minutes later, as they were leaving the kitchen, the pain returned and Jordan knew that little Paige Alexandra Blaine Blake-Wyndham wanted to enter her world.

"Alex." She leaned against the wall. "I think you're going to be able to take your turn carrying the baby for a while."

Alex looked perplexed for a moment. Then, as the realization of what she was telling him hit, he jumped into the air, let out a loud, "Yahoo," and ran towards the stairs. He got halfway up, turned around and came back to Jordan's side. He led her to the antique parson's bench in the entryway and directed her to sit while he retrieved the bag from her room.

148

When he returned to her side, she was again holding her belly and had begun her breathing exercises. "This isn't fun any more, Alex. Let's not do this," she whispered.

"Sorry, love. I don't think you can chicken out of this."

They made it to the hospital in just under seven minutes, although on their trial runs it had taken them a minimum of thirteen. Jordan wasn't sure if she was more frightened of the impending birth or her husband's driving.

They had filled out the necessary papers at the hospital a few days earlier, and were led to the birthing room a few minutes after their arrival at the hospital. The room was painted light blue, with a wallpaper border of "forest babies" circling the room. Jordan selected the raccoon as her focal point as soon as the nurse helped her into the bed.

Her labor was much easier than either she or Alex had expected. She didn't once yell an obscenity at him. She did try to convince the doctor that drugs might be a good idea, but Dr. Landis calmly smiled and told her that if she could deliver three babies, each over nine pounds, without drugs, then Jordan could make it through one who must surely be smaller.

As Dr. Landis grasped the baby's shoulders and began to pull gently, Alex could stand it no longer. He had been at Jordan's side through her entire seven and a half hours of labor, and now he wanted to welcome his son. He watched, a dim-witted smile on his face, as the baby entered the world.

"It's a boy," he cried joyously.

"Alex, how could you tease me like that at a time like this?" Jordan asked in exhaustion.

Dr. Landis, with great joy on her face, presented Jordan with her son. "I think you'd better take a look, Jordan."

Jordan didn't care. The months of preparing for a girl meant nothing. The tiny little boy in her arms was the most perfect, wonderful being in the entire world. She touched his tiny, purple fingers. She touched his nose and his toes. She ran her hands over his soft back and bottom. Then she kissed him, and was lost.

"Oh, my precious little child. I've been waiting a long time to hold you like this. So, you're the little one who's been kicking my bladder. I guess I can forgive you."

She was reluctant to give him up, but Alex insisted on holding him before he was taken away to be measured and examined.

"Alex, you have the silliest look on your face. Are you okay?"

"Jory." He spoke quietly. "I'm so amazed. I never in my life imagined that I could have feelings like this. He's so beautiful, so wonderful. Thank you for letting me be a part of this. This is the best moment of my life." As the nurse took the baby, Alex moved over to Jordan's side, holding her hand firmly in his. He leaned over and gently kissed her lips. "Thank you, Jory. Thank you."

When Joshua was two weeks old, Alex suggested to Jordan that they hire someone to help with child care and housework.

"I don't want someone else to raise my son, Alex," Jordan insisted.

Laughing softly, running his finger under her chin as she sat in the rocking chair in the nursery, Alex knelt beside her.

"I don't either, Jordan. But we both plan to keep working. I can't keep him at the hospital with me, and you can't drag him all over town with you." Seeing the confusion on her face, Alex gently caressed the nursing baby's head. "Haven't you thought about this before?"

Jordan shook her head, looking at him in despair. "I thought I'd convert a room at work into a nursery."

"That would be fine for now, but what about when he's older and needs room to run?"

"I'll work at home. I'll move my office here and let Quentin take care of things there. He's a new man since he and Barbara got married. I know he'd do a good job."

"Jordan, think this through completely. You'd still need to go to building sites and that's no place for Joshua."

Jordan closed her eyes and leaned her head on the back of the chair, gently stroking Joshua's fingers as they curled around her thumb.

"You're right. I know you are. Okay, if we decide to do this, where do we start?"

"How did Neil and Celia find their nanny?"

"They called an agency. But that seems so cold. How will we know if she's reliable or trustworthy? I'm still going to work at home." Seeing the grin on Alex's face, Jordan smiled reluctantly. "I know, I'm already one of those over-protective mothers."

"No, you just love your son. Besides, it's your job to watch out for him. Okay, you can work at home and if we can't hire Mary Poppins, we'll get the next best thing."

When Nancy showed up on their doorstep, complete with a carpet bag, Jordan's prayers were answered. Nancy was in her early sixties, with smile lines etched into her plump face. Her own children were grown and starting families of their own, but her daughter was in Florida and her two sons were in Minnesota. Her six grandchildren only visited once a year, and Nancy couldn't afford to visit them except at Christmas, when they all got together in Florida. She missed her family and had often considered moving to Miami to be closer to Melinda and her family, but she'd lived in Los Angeles all her life and told them she wasn't ready to leave yet.

Now she had little Joshua and his folks. Nancy felt needed once again. Despite Jordan and Alex's best efforts, they really were not good cooks. Nancy believed that that fact alone was God's message to her that she should take care of them. Along with her sumptuous cooking, she demanded an immaculate house and insisted that all her free time be spent in entertaining Joshua. Nancy's favorite thing to do was to sit on a blanket beneath the eucalyptus tree, and read Dr. Seuss books to her favorite little boy, insisting that no child is too young for reading.

Shortly after Jordan and Alex moved into the house, Alex insisted that they build a guest house across the gardens. After having the rent raised three times in eight months in her apartment building, Nancy set up residency in the guest house.

When Jordan had offered her the use of the house, Nancy was appalled. "Oh, no, Ms. Blake. I could never live in such a beautiful place. Besides, you need to save that for your company."

"Nancy, it would be a blessing to have you right here. We could have you watch Joshua for us during the evenings, and we wouldn't feel guilty about you driving home alone afterwards. When I get a craving for your molasses cookies, I can have you come bake them for me. We have so much room in the house, our company will never need to use the guest house. I don't know what Alex was thinking when he suggested building it."

They argued for some time, but Jordan won. Nancy had the idea that Jordan rarely lost her arguments. On the day that she moved in, she called each of her children, raving about her new, luxurious accommodations. She marveled at the sunken bathtub in the master bath that opened onto a tiny, private garden.

Her new bedroom was larger than her entire studio apartment had been, and the light, peach-colored paint and the delicate plaid wallpaper were an incredible improvement over her old dirty, pink paint.

Nancy had helped Jordan decorate the bedroom, the simple but elegantly-styled brass bed reminding her of the one her grandmother had had when Nancy was little. Jordan asked her opinion on every piece of furniture that went into the house, even before they knew Nancy would be moving in. Realizing that Jordan could have very easily and tastefully made all the decisions herself, Nancy loved her all the more for including her in the process.

Joshua's proud grandparents came for his six month birthday party. They were so delighted with their grandson that they each swore he was the most perfect child ever born. Their own offspring were not thrilled about being excluded from the list of perfect children, but they were mollified by Joshua's coos and gurgles.

151

As Jordan carried the coffee cups into the kitchen, Celeste and Marguerite followed her.

"Darling," her mother said, "there's something we'd like to ask you about Joshua."

Jordan felt herself growing rigid. "What is it, Mom?"

"If it's none of our business, you can say so, but who is Joshua's father?"

Jordan blinked rapidly, clearing the tears away. She looked from one concerned, loving face to the other. "Alex is his father now, okay?"

Marguerite and Celeste watched her, noting the tears and the way the blood drained from her face.

Marguerite reached for her daughter-in-law. "It's all right, dear. We want you and Alex to be very happy. We've all recovered from our surprise about your wedding, and we want to be as supportive of you as we can."

Jordan had never felt that their love and support was absent. They had gone to see the Blakes on the day after their wedding, and their news was greeted with smiles and hugs. The reception at the Wyndhams' had been the same. None of the parents questioned the wisdom of their hurried marriage. They had silently wondered, but showed none of their concern.

Jordan put her arms around the shoulders of the two mothers. "We're going to be very happy, and we're going to try to be the kind of parents that you've been to us. We're trying to do our very best to make a happy and secure home for Joshua."

"We'll help in any way we can," Celeste told her.

"I know you will, Mom. Alex and I appreciate it. But, for right now, we need to depend on each other. We've got to build our own future. It's easier than I expected. I grow to love him more each day. He lifts my spirits when I most need it, and makes me laugh even when I don't think I can. And I think I do the same for him. He's been wonderful to me, and now to Joshua. I think we're going to have a good life together."

Marguerite studied Jordan carefully, "Have you told Alex any of this?"

"Little bits, I guess."

"I don't mean to pry, Jordan, but my son is very concerned about you. He doesn't say much, but he has mentioned that he's afraid you'll never be able to fully accept him as your husband."

Jordan blushed, thinking with guilt about their separate bedrooms. Alex had never pushed her into a sexual relationship. She assumed that he was still grieving over Paige. Now, she wondered if he was ready for more from her.

Marguerite squeezed her shoulder. "Just talk to him, Jordan."

That night, after Joshua had been put to bed and the doting grandparents had gone home, Jordan told Alex. She was shy, hesitant, afraid, but Alex listened, encouraging her to tell him everything.

"It's all so confusing for me, Alex," she told him. "Our relationship has taken some strange turns. I certainly never expected to care for you as more than a dear friend."

"Nor I, you. But Jordan, we've been through more together than most 'friends' ever go through. I've learned a new respect for you. I admire you. And, I do love you. Jordan, my love is growing. I can't think of you just as Paige's friend any more. I think of you as my wife, in every sense of the word," he concluded meaningfully.

"I guess I feel the same way. It's just taken me a long time to realize it. I've been afraid that any feelings I might have for you would be a betrayal to Paige."

"But Jordan, Paige would want us to find happiness. Now, come over here and sit by me. I want to start courting you."

CHAPTER TEN

I have been feasting with mine enemy;
Where, on a sudden, one hath wounded me.
-Romeo and Juliet

Over the next several days, Alex did his very best to woo his wife. He bought her flowers. He fixed her gourmet meals, destroying the kitchen in the process, relying on newly purchased cookbooks for directions. He had chocolates delivered to her office, and sexy lingerie delivered to the house. When the lingerie arrived, Alex laid it out on Jordan's bed, planning for her to find it when she got home after work. He took the afternoon off, telling the nurses that he needed some quality family time and to call him only in case of *extreme* emergency.

Alex got home, surprising Nancy. He explained that he was planning a romantic evening for Jordan, and he wanted to beat her home.

Nancy had often wondered about the young couple she worked for. They seemed to care about one another. They laughed together and respected each other. Together with Joshua, they seemed like the perfect family. And yet, Nancy knew that Alex and Jordan slept in separate bedrooms.

When Alex announced that he wanted a romantic evening with his wife, she felt that her prayers had been answered. She had grown to love this family, and she wanted great happiness for them.

As Alex stood bashfully in front of her, telling her that he wanted to court his wife and to entice her into a romantic evening, Nancy's mind raced. Jordan deserved more than the typical flowers and candlelight supper, but how could she plan something better?

She sat Alex down at the kitchen table and began to verbalize her thoughts. "Okay, the first thing we need to do is plan your supper. We'll never get Jordan to eat veal or lamb, but I think she'll go for Italian, don't you?" She barely paused in her brainstorming to get his reaction.

"Let's see, you'll need an aperitif, an appetizer wine before dinner. I think a campari, served with soda over ice will do nicely. Then, we'll start you off with some Shitake mushrooms." Seeing Alex's amused smile, Nancy paused. "I know, they're not Italian, but they're elegant. Now then, where was I? We'll want a light wine to go with those, then a nice bolognese meat sauce over pasta and a sweet rosé to go with that. Then, my Italian bread--you'll love it--with some sautéed broccoli with garlic, and how about some chestnut-stuffed pork tenderloins? Yes, that will do nicely. Now, for dessert. For a romantic evening, I think we'd better stick with a nice fruit dish, rather than something heavy. I've got it. We'll go with macaroon-stuffed peaches, and a sweet dessert wine to go with that. You don't think that's too much wine, do you, dear? No," answering herself once again, "for an evening of romance it should be just fine. Then we'll top it all off with a cup of espresso. That sounds fine, doesn't it?

"We'll set it all up out on the patio near the pool, and should you decide to take a little dip sometime after dinner, we'll have your towels out there, ready for you. But," her eyes twinkling, "I don't think you'll need swimming suits. You couldn't be shy with only the light of the stars and the candles, could you?"

She finally stopped, looked at Alex, and waited for a reply.

Alex got to his feet, kissed her on the top of her head and said, "Nancy, you are a godsend. I leave it all in your capable and creative hands. I don't think I'd ever be able to plan something like this." Then he clapped his hand to his forehead. "Oh, no, what about Joshua? Maybe I could take him to my parents'."

"Don't you worry about that little boy for a minute. He'll come spend the night with me. I can have all this ready for you beforehand, and I'll show you how to serve everything. Then, I'll take Joshua back to meet my new stuffed animals and the Fisher Price Farm I just got for him." She winked at Alex. "With my drapes closed, and those beautiful junipers that Jordan planted, you'll have absolute privacy."

*

When Jordan got back to her office at five o'clock, she was ready to leave for the day. But Barbara had left a message on her desk, saying that Alex wanted her to arrive home at precisely seven o'clock. Not before, not after. He had told Barbara explicitly that Jordan was to come at seven.

Jordan tried to question Barbara, wondering what Alex was up to, but Barbara merely smiled and said, "Just wait until seven." She had grilled Alex unceasingly, wanting to know what he had planned, and she now happily refused to spoil the surprise.

With two hours to kill, Jordan decided to go shopping. She drove to the nearest toy store and spent an hour and a half planning Joshua's birthday presents for the next twelve years. She got him an elephant slide, which she arranged to have delivered to the house, as well as kit for a playhouse, to replace the one that Alex had tried to build.

She giggled as she glanced over the instructions of the playhouse, remembering Alex's eager but disastrous attempts at building.

"You'd better leave the house building to me, Alex," she'd told him. "You can stick with patching people up."

Alex pretended to be wounded by her remarks, but seeing his completed project, he had to agree with her. "Maybe you could hire one of your contractors to come build a good playhouse for Joshua," he suggested.

Jordan thought the kit would be just as useful to her little explorer. Following the suggestions of the over-eager clerk, she ordered the largest kit.

When she got home, she found the porch light on and a note on the door. "Follow the lights, follow your heart."

Smiling, Jordan stepped into the entryway. Noticing the darkness of the living room, she walked up the well-lit stairway. All the doors were closed on the second floor except for her own bedroom, and she could tell from the flickering of the light coming from her doorway that it was only lit by candles.

Jordan went into her room, gasping when she saw the beautiful, dark green negligee that Alex had left on her bed. It was a low-cut, spaghetti strap, form-fitting, full-length gown, with a sheer lace matching robe.

Jordan slipped out of her clothes, took a quick shower, and dressed in the lovely green satin. As she stepped out of the bedroom, she realized that the light in the hallway had been turned out. She went back for the candle and used it to light her path to the stairs. As she reached the tops of the stairs, the light overhead went out and she held the candle out before her as she descended. At the foot of the stairs, the light in the entryway went out. As she proceeded through the house, each light was turned off as she walked toward it. Finally, the only light she could see came from the French doors at the back of the house. She walked through the doors, gasping in delight at the scene before her.

Alex, who had preceded her into every room turning off light switches before she could see him, now stood, dressed elegantly in a black tuxedo, with one hand on the back of a chair, the other hand held out to her.

The table was covered with a beautiful, antique lace tablecloth, and decorated with candles and flowers. Jordan's china was set out, and next to the table was a cart with chilled wine and covered dishes.

Jordan reached out for Alex's hand, trembling as her fingertips touched his. "Alex," she said softly, "it's so beautiful. Thank you," she said, motioning to her negligee.

Alex touched his forefinger to her lips, pulled her into his arms and, as the music started, danced with her.

His lips caressed her hair, her earlobe, her neck. When the music ended, he led her to her chair, motioning for her to be seated. He served her exactly as Nancy had instructed him, pleased that he was doing so well.

Jordan was enthralled. The dinner was divine, the wine made her feel warm and Alex's constant attention kept a blush on her cheeks.

When they finished eating, Alex led her to the side of the pool. "We can swim, if you like. Nancy left these for us." He motioned to the towels.

"No suits?"

"She didn't think we'd need them."

Alex gently lifted the robe from her shoulders, kissing the skin that he'd exposed. He slipped the straps of her gown from her shoulders, and visibly shook as it fell to the ground. He was out of his clothes in moments and pulled her down the steps, into the cool water.

From friendship, this relationship had grown. They had never expected passion. They had never planned it. Now, as they reveled in the glory of it, they knew that God had blessed them.

*

Three months later, Nicholas Wyndham moved back to Los Angeles. His interest in his personal life was nonexistent, his every waking moment dedicated to his research. He often found convenient excuses to be out of town for each holiday when the family gathered together.

Lianna hovered over him as often as he would tolerate her. He sometimes escorted her to various plays and social functions, always at her insistence. She had proposed to him a total of sixteen times, and intended to keep doing so until he gave in to her. But Nick never gave in. He had no interest in marriage.

When Nick first learned of Alex and Jordan's marriage, he immediately volunteered to teach another class at St. Bartholomew's. His disbelief at their marriage shielded his heart for several weeks. But as the reality of it penetrated his mind, his anger renewed his mistrust in all women. Lianna had hurt him once before and he would not trust her again, despite her declarations of love and nearly constant proposals. Furthermore, he didn't love her.

He was never rude to Lianna. Just firm. He had no intention of marrying her. His mother loved her, and she was always welcome in their home, but not in his personal life.

On the rare occasions when Nick was home during Alex and Jordan's visits, he focused his attention on Joshua. He was instantaneously captivated by his handsome young nephew. He often wished that he and Jordan could have built a future together; that this child was theirs. He and Joshua played together frequently, feeding the ducks in the Wyndhams' pond, taking trips to the park, playing hide and seek in the gardens. But whenever Nick found himself

157

wishing, he chastised himself and decided that this wonderful nephew was enough to satisfy any paternal needs he might have.

Jordan often watched Nick and Joshua as they frolicked and laughed together. One afternoon, as she saw Nick sitting on the ground near the duck pond, holding a giggling Joshua on his lap, her eyes filled with tears.

"Are you going to tell him?" Alex's voice spoke at her shoulder.

Jordan's voice shook. "I know I need to. It's just so hard."

Alex reached up to massage the tightening muscles in the back of her neck. "You know, Jordan, I really don't think he's going to marry Lianna. I think he still loves you. If you want a divorce, I'll give you one."

Startled, her eyes widening, Jordan whirled around to face her husband. "Alex. No. Oh, Alex, no I don't want that." She reached up to run her fingers down the side of his face, her hand stopping on his shoulder. Wrapping her arms around him, she pulled him into a powerful embrace. "Alex, what we have is beautiful. I have no intention of throwing it away."

Relieved, Alex pulled back just enough to look into her eyes. "I'm glad," he spoke softly. "Will you tell Nick about Joshua?"

"Yes. But not yet. I just can't do it yet. Do you think that's awful?"

Alex looked at her tenderly. He took in the pale cheeks, the trembling lips, the tearful eyes. "No, honey. I understand completely. But don't wait too long, okay?"

Nick intentionally avoided any close contact with Jordan. He remained cordial, but cool. He knew Lianna had been right on some counts. Jordan had made a fool of him. She'd made him fall in love with her, and then turned away from him without even an explanation. He wouldn't trust her again. He'd be polite. She was, after all, his sister-in-law. But he needed to hide his growing hatred of her. His mother would be very displeased if she saw him treating Jordan badly.

Nick didn't know that Marguerite was much more astute than he realized, nor that she suspected he had been disconsolate when Jordan married Alex. He had no idea how she prayed for him and his happiness, and how angry she was with him for sending that telegram announcing his engagement--a move for which he still made no explanations.

He never questioned Alex and Jordan's sudden marriage. Lianna had explained it all to him. They had been such good friends for so many years, they'd probably fallen in love earlier, and now that Paige was gone, decided to make a more solid commitment. Nick believed her.

When his parents finally asked him about his

engagement to Lianna, Nick merely laughed. "What engagement?" he asked.

"Why, dear, you sent us a telegram to tell us that you were getting married."

When Nick heard these words, he said nothing to his mother and drove directly to Lianna's apartment. He didn't wait for her to answer his loud knock. He shoved the door open, the thud echoing as it swung open, hitting the wall behind it.

"Lianna," he bellowed.

Lianna, who had been curled up on the couch for a mid-afternoon snooze, pouted at him as he glared down at her. "Why, Nicky, what brings you here? What's put you in such a foul temper?"

"I believe you have some news for me."

"News? What news?"

"Something about our engagement?"

"Oh, Nicky, you heard about the telegrams. I was just helping you save face."

"Telegrams? Plural? You didn't by any chance send one to Jordan, did you?"

"Well, of course I did. I mean, there she was, your special lady, and then she practically spit in your face by dating that man from her office, and *then* she had the nerve to marry your own brother." As always, Lianna twisted history to suit her own interests. "I couldn't let her make a fool of you like that, Nicky. I had to show her that you didn't need her. That you had someone else."

As Nick sank down to the cushion next to her, Lianna leaned over. Putting her arm around his waist, she rested her face on his shoulder.

"Oh, Nicky, you will forgive me, won't you? I do love you, and I just couldn't stand what that woman did to you. I know you cared about her."

Nick leaned forward, his face in his hands. Lianna kissed him on the fingertips. "Nicholas?" her voice was light and seductive. "I still love you. Marry me, Nicky, and we'll put all of this behind us."

Nick stood up quickly, turning to look down at her. "Lianna, get this through your head. I don't want you in my bed, even though you have offered yourself up repeatedly. I don't want to marry you. Now, if you don't want your precious little ego bruised, stop asking. And stop interfering in my life. I don't want you to take any more matters into your pretty little hands. Leave my life to me."

*

Alex sat in Ed Colson's office, demanding that he be

updated on the case. "You've shut me out for too long. Paige has been gone for almost three years, and you still haven't caught the people responsible for her death. Doesn't that seem ridiculous to you? Three years is an incredibly long time. I've been patient. I've trusted you to conduct the investigation, and then to come up with some answers. But I'm out of patience. I want to know what's happening. I want to know who killed Paige."

"We never closed the case, Alex. It's been an ongoing investigation. But these people are slippery. While we keep arresting and prosecuting the little people, we just can't seem to get to the top. We know that Derek Frank was working for someone else, but he never gave us a clue who it was."

"So, you're just giving up?"

Ed stood up, walked to the door of his office, leaned through the doorway, and said, "Send Griffin in here, okay, Meg?"

A few moments later, the door opened and Alex stared, open-mouthed, at the blond giant entering the room. He clamped his jaw shut, leapt to his feet, and extended his hand. "Luke Griffin, geez, it's been years. It's good to see you, man. What are you doing here?"

"It's good to see you, too, Alex. I've been sorry that we lost touch with each other after high school." Luke turned to Ed and explained, "This little twerp almost broke my leg in football practice one day. Landed right on the side of my knee. He was more upset about it than I was. I was in a brace for two weeks, and he waited on me hand and foot the whole time. We were best friends after that."

Luke and Alex walked back to the chairs placed opposite Ed's desk. Alex smiled at his friend, curiosity lighting his eyes.

"You still haven't told me why you're here. You're not an agent, are you?"

"He's one of our best, Alex," Ed answered for Luke. "He's just asked to be transferred to this case."

"I've been living in D.C. for the past several years, so I didn't know anything about this. I'm awful sorry for your loss, Alex."

Alex rubbed his chin thoughtfully with his hand. "It's been the worst time of my life, Luke. And, the best, too. I'm married again, and I have a wonderful little boy. He's got hair the color of yours. Say, you know," he teased, "you don't happen to know my wife, do you? We've never quite been able to figure out where that blond hair came from."

Luke laughed, waving his hands protectively in front of him. "I promise, I never met her. Must've been the milkman."

The men sobered, remembering why they were sitting in this office. Alex looked around the room, noting the many citations and awards hanging on the walls. He ran his gaze over the bulletin board, solidly covered with newspaper clippings of the many cases the bureau had worked on. Some cases solved, others not.

"Luke, I'm glad you'll be working on our case. It's been hell not knowing who was responsible for Suzanne's kidnapping and Paige's death. Knowing that those people are still out there, possibly prostituting and defiling more young kids, rips my heart out. We've got to stop them."

"The way I hear it, they closed up shop and disappeared again just after your wife was killed. Word has it that Derek Frank, who kept Suzanne--the one she saw before the shooting--spends more time behind bars than roaming free. But he's never cooperated with us. He's been convicted of producing child pornography, and he serves his time without a whimper. His fines and legal fees are always paid. We know he couldn't have that kind of money. Last time he was sentenced to two years, and over a hundred thousand dollars. We figure that someone's buying his silence, and if we could find out who it is, I think we'd have the person behind the whole operation, as well as Paige's death.

"I'm not going to let this drop, Alex. Derek disappeared for a while, but one of our agents spotted him a few weeks back. He's got to be working with someone in the area, or he wouldn't keep coming back here. This time, I promise you, we're going to trail him like a shark going after the scent of blood."

Alex was reassured by Luke's presence. He knew his friend to be intelligent and loyal, and he believed that if anyone could crack this case, it was Luke Griffin.

Luke asked Alex to keep his presence a secret. He explained that the fewer people who knew of his involvement, the better chance he'd have of getting information. He knew that he'd have to go undercover soon, and not knowing where he would direct his attentions, he wanted anonymity.

Colson, Luke, and Alex talked for an hour and a half, Alex's hopes rising. In the past, when he he'd talked with Ed Colson, Alex had been frustrated by the lack of progress in the case. Several people were arrested in connection with child pornography, but most of them were individuals making the films in their own basements and garages. They couldn't be connected to Derek's organization.

With Luke's reassurances ringing in his ears, Alex left the office. Since Paige's death, he'd continued with the research that Suzanne had begun years earlier, and he'd worked with the Anti-Pornography Coalition in their attempts to gain stronger legislation against pornographers. While a convicted pornographer could be sentenced to ten years in prison and two hundred and fifty thousand dollars in fines, the pornography continued. The Coalition worked to make the penalties stiffer, in the hopes that it would put an end to the atrocious crimes being committed against children.

Alex began to feel that he hadn't done enough. Suzanne's abductor was dead. But Derek, the man who had filmed her and then threatened her family when she was released, was still at large. Derek, who had seen her again years later and tried to seduce her into working with him, was walking the streets. Just possibly, this Derek had somehow known that Suzanne and Paige had gone to the authorities. Just possibly, he had been behind Paige's murder. Or, if not, he must surely know who was.

Luke told Alex that Derek had been seen entering an abandoned store on Laurel Canyon Boulevard in Pacoima. When the building was searched, all the agents found was two video cameras and a set of satin sheets, tucked in a box in the corner of the building.

Without having the workforce to watch the place day and night, they occasionally drove by, but the judge who gave them the original search warrant to the building refused to issue another one until they had proof that something illegal was taking place on the premises.

Something told Alex that this was the place to start. Two days after his meeting with Luke and Ed, he called in sick to the hospital and told Jordan he needed to do some thinking.

He had told her about his meeting with Colson. He assured her that progress was being made, but that the meeting had ignited old memories and he thought he might spend the day on the beach.

After Jordan left for her construction site, Alex yanked an old, torn, paint-spattered sweatshirt out of the bottom drawer of his dresser and pulled it on over his head. He climbed into a pair of jeans with holes in the knees and the seat. He smiled as he remembered Paige's innumerable threats to reduce them to scrub rags. These will be perfect, he thought. He completed the ensemble with a pair of Nikes that he had purchased his senior year in high school. They were still comfortable, so he refused to throw them away though they were worn beyond recognition.

He sneaked out of the house, not wanting Nancy to see how he was dressed. With his throat constricting, Alex drove away from his home, got onto the Hollywood Freeway, and drove toward Pacoima.

The drive only took a few minutes. Alex's heart beat faster as he exited the freeway at Tierra Bella Street and turned onto Laurel Canyon Boulevard. He drove slowly, not knowing which side of the street he'd find the store on, nor which block. He searched for forty-five minutes before he drove past a store he hadn't noticed the first time by. The windows were boarded up, the glass missing from several of them. In the lower right hand corner of the window nearest the front door was a "For

Rent" sign.

Alex kept driving, thinking quickly about what he would do next. He found a liquor store a few blocks away and, parking around the corner, he walked to the store. He bought a bottle of cheap wine, making sure the clerk put it in the stereotypical brown paper bag. He hadn't showered after he'd gone jogging that morning, so he knew he didn't smell good. He drank some of the wine, allowing it to drip down his chin and all over the front of his sweatshirt.

His hair was sweaty and dirty, and now he messed it up as he walked toward the empty store. He ran his hand over his whiskers, glad that he hadn't shaved that morning, and that his beard grew so quickly. If Jordan saw me now, he thought, she'd never go to bed with me again.

When he got to the block where the store sat, he paused on the corner. Seeing no one on the street, he turned and walked toward the alley. He knew that the store was the third from the end, so he walked through the alley, staggering now, stopping at the door that he thought must belong to the third store down.

Alex tried the door, and began pounding on it when he found it locked. He kept pounding for a full five minutes, alternating fists when one would get tired or sore.

He finally sat down next to the door to wait. If there were children inside, someone would come sooner or later. The kids wouldn't be left alone for long.

He'd been there for six hours, wishing that he'd brought a sandwich to munch on. The day grew hotter and hotter, and he regretted choosing the sweatshirt. Thirsty but afraid to leave his post, he drank the wine, cursing the cheap stuff.

Finally, he was rewarded. A van drove up and a teenager climbed out. The boy wore a black leather jacket, tight blue jeans, and black leather boots with a chain around each ankle. His black hair was shaped into a long, curving mohawk, the rest of the hair cut shorter, nearer the scalp. He wore a nose ring, and Alex wondered if it caused him problems when he had a cold. Chuckling to himself, he stood up, stiff from his hours of sitting on the cold concrete.

"Who are you?" the boy asked.

"Lookin' for a job," Alex slurred. "Just need a couple bucks."

The boy thought about all the groceries and supplies in the back of the van. He thought about how much he hated carrying them inside. He looked at Alex, thinking that there must be muscles underneath the baggy sweatshirt.

"How drunk are you? Can you carry stuff without dumping it?"

Alex pulled himself up to his full height, wanting to impress the kid with the size of his frame. "I can carry anythin'.

163

Whatcha want me to do?"

The boy opened the side door of the van and then walked to the back door of the building, unlocking it with a large silver key.

"Grab an arm load of bags, and follow me."

Alex grabbed a couple of bags, much less than he could carry, wanting to spend as much time inside as possible. If this was the right place, he might find something useful inside that door.

He followed the boy into the dark building. Only one dim bulb was lit overhead. They walked to a counter where a cash register had been in an earlier time. Alex was careful to look around only when the boy's back was to him.

He was dismayed to see a heavyset, balding man in an ill-fitting suit walking toward them. He was adjusting his belt and checking the fly of his pants, as if he had just left the restroom.

"Kenny," he growled, "who is this?"

"Just some bum, Robert. He wants to earn a couple of bucks. I figured he could carry the stuff in for us."

"You're so lazy. Can't figure out for the life of me why Derek keeps you on the payroll."

Derek? Alex outwardly showed no interest, but his eyes darted furtively around the room. On the counter, next to the groceries he had already deposited, sat a microwave. There were opened packages of napkins, plastic dinnerware, and paper cups. Pushed up against the counter was an old, extremely dirty refrigerator, an orange extension cord wrapped around the base of the counter and plugged into the outlet on the floor.

"All right, mister. Go out to the van and get the rest of the stuff," Kenny muttered to him. "Hurry up about it. If you take too long, I won't pay ya."

Alex walked back toward the door, making sure that he staggered occasionally. He kept his shoulders hunched over, his head bent, but his eyes explored the large, empty room.

He could see marks on the floor where the shelving had stood. Lined up against the wall at the north end of the store was a long wall of plywood. It stood eight feet high, and ran the length of the store. It was punctuated with doors, each of which had numbers painted on them with spray paint.

The wall was poorly constructed, greatly resembling the playhouse he'd attempted to build in the back yard for Joshua. Alex didn't think it could be too sturdy, and wondered if he'd ever have a chance to try to break through one of those doors.

On the opposite side of the room was a sight that made Alex's heart stop. The end of the room had been divided into two sections, each open to the rest of the larger room. In each section there was a bed. One section was painted to look like the inside of a log cabin, the bed a rustic pine frame with old, worn-out furniture scattered about. The second section was lavishly furnished with red velvet draperies, a white canopy bed, and a hot tub set up in the corner.

That end of the store was very dark, and as Alex looked at it, he realized that the darkness had kept him from noticing it before. His steps faltered as he realized that he was exactly where he had wanted to be, and now didn't know what to do about it. He'd have to get Luke here immediately.

"Hey, mister, you gonna carry my stuff or not?"

"Yeah. Sure is a pretty little spot you got over there," he said, nodding his head toward the beds.

Kenny coughed nervously. "Don't you pay any attention to that."

"Sure would like to sleep in a bed like that pretty one there," Alex sighed. "Is this gonna be a sheet store?"

"Yeah, something like that. Now, go get my stuff."

As Alex brought in the last load of bags and boxes, he heard Robert warning the boy, "You shouldn't be bringing strangers in here, kid. Derek would have a fit if he knew you'd done it."

"He's just a bum, Robert. He's not gonna cause any trouble."

"Well, I hope not. We just found this place, the rent's cheap, and we're almost ready. Don't foul it up, boy."

Alex had reached them and he paused, running his fingers through his greasy hair, looking down at his feet. "Anything else you'd like me to do?"

Kenny handed him two dollars. "No, that's all, but thanks for helping. Stay away from the booze, okay? Your money'll last longer."

"Yeah, that's what they tell me at the shelter."

"That's what I tell my folks all the time, but they don't listen much," Kenny said softly. "Oh, well, you can go now. Thanks."

Alex couldn't think of a reason to stay longer. With all the frozen dinners he'd carried in, all the cases of soda, he knew that if there were no children behind those doors now, there soon would be. Where would they come from? Would they come off school playgrounds like Suzanne? Would they be runaways and unwanted children, like Josie and Melanie?

His stomach churned as he left the building. When he climbed into his car, he reached into the glove compartment for an antacid tablet.

*

Alex parked in the carport and went around the back of the house. He intended to take a quick shower in the pool

165

house before going inside. He'd left a change of clothes there early that morning, and wanted to get changed before he went into the house.

He was deep in thought, and didn't see Jordan until she said his name. He looked up and saw her climbing out of the pool. As she walked toward him, he tried to step into the shadows, not wanting her to see how he looked.

She ran to his side, wrapped her arms around him and gave him a hug. "Alex, I've been so worried about you. Are you all right? Did you have a good day at the beach?"

He couldn't lie to this woman. What could he say?

Jordan backed away from him. "Ooh, Alex, you need a shower." She sniffed. "Alex, you don't smell like you've been to the beach." She stepped towards him and, standing on her toes, gently touched the tip of her tongue to his cheek. "No salt spray, Alex. You haven't been to the beach. Where have you been all day?"

He didn't have an answer for her. "I've been out walking and driving."

Jordan grabbed his hand, and pulled him toward the light at the side of the pool. "Alex, you're filthy. You look like a homeless person. What have you been doing?"

When he still wouldn't answer, she knew that something was wrong. "Alex, you're not drinking again, are you? You smell like cheap, stale wine."

"I only had a little bit. Just for effect."

"Effect?" Realization struck her with furious strength. "No," she whispered. "You can't be playing detective, can you? I just wanted you to help the F.B.I., not do their work for them."

"Jordan," he groaned, "I have to. Don't you see? The cops and the agents are all tied up with their rules and codes of honor. They've got their hands tied. I can snoop around and get information that they might never be able to get."

"That's faulty rationalization, Alex. You could get yourself killed. You'd never let me do anything like this."

Alex pulled her into his arms, hugging her fiercely. "I'll be careful, Jordan. I just had to check something out today."

"Alex, please don't do this again. I want to catch the people who killed Paige, too, but I've lost too many people that I loved. I can't lose you, too."

"You're not going to lose me," he whispered into her hair. "I promise."

Jordan pushed away from him and looked up into his eyes, eyes that mockingly reminded her of Nick. "Don't make promises that you can't keep. You're not going to stop this, are you?"

When he didn't answer, Jordan turned and ran to the

house, her fear and anger strangling her.

*

Luke was not in the office the next morning when Alex called. Neither was Ed Colson. Alex left a message that they were to call him immediately upon their return.

What Alex didn't know was that Luke and Ed were interrogating two men: nineteen year old Kenny Johns and forty-seven year old Robert Weems.

Luke's conscience had been plaguing him since his meeting with Alex. He had to do more to investigate this case. Okay, so we can't get another search warrant--we can still watch the place.

When he got to the store the night before, he didn't see Alex leave by the back door but he noticed lights flickering inside as the evening grew dark. Luke got out of the car, walked quickly around to the alley, and saw Robert entering the back of the building.

Well, he wondered, what kind of information has he got to share? He returned to his car, called Ed, and the two of them met Kenny and Robert when they left the building two hours later.

They took them to an old office building that they frequently used in Burbank, and began their questioning. They continued throughout the night.

At first, Robert and Kenny remained silent, refusing to answer any questions. For Robert, it was a game. Derek had warned them about interrogations like this and Robert knew that these men had no evidence against them. They were just trying to get information. And he had every intention of giving false information, but he couldn't look too willing.

Luke felt like they were playing freeze tag. As soon as he felt they were getting somewhere, Robert and Kenny would help each other and they'd be back where they started.

But Luke was a patient man. He'd had several cups of coffee early in the evening, and was prepared to question them for as long as was needed.

Luke saw the warning glances Robert gave the boy. He heard him whisper, "Remember, be careful."

As the hours wore on and the sun rose high in the sky, Kenny was running out of determination and reason. He was also becoming intimidated by Luke. Luke hovered above him, growling at him, scowling down into the young man's face.

"Just tell me, Kenny. I know you're working with Derek Frank. I know that you do despicable things to innocent little kids. If you don't tell me who's in charge of it all, I'm going to lock you up for a long time.

"Tell me where the money comes from, Kenny. Tell me who bankrolls you. Who bails Derek out of jail and pays his

167

fines when he's sentenced? Who pays the bills and buys the equipment and keeps your whole operation one step ahead of us? Come on, Kenny, just tell me."

Robert was glad that Kenny didn't know much. He figured that the boy would break soon, and he was relieved. He'd had enough of this. He wanted to go home.

Finally, Kenny had had enough. Every time Luke's face came close to his, he shook a little more. Now, as Luke leaned over him, his large hands gripping the arms of the chair Kenny cowered in, Kenny exploded.

"All right, I'll tell you. His name is Wyndham. Some big, rich guy. Okay? That's all I know. Wyndham. Now, let me go. I can't help you any more than that."

The name was not one that Ed Colson and Luke Griffin expected to hear. They looked at one another in disbelief.

Luke glared at Kenny. "You're feeding me rotten eggs here, son. I want the truth, or I swear you're going to prison, and all those horrible things you've been doing to those kids are going to happen to you. Would you like that?"

Terror blanched Kenny's face. "Really, Mr. Griffin. Derek called him Wyndham. Samson, or something like that."

An hour later, Kenny and Robert were gone. Luke and Ed still sat quietly in the office.

"It doesn't make any sense, Luke. Why would Samuel Wyndham be involved in anything like this? He certainly doesn't need the money."

"I don't believe it either, Ed, but Kenny sure did. Did you see the look on his face? He's scared to death of me," he chuckled. "Didn't know I was so intimidating."

Ed silently appraised the young agent, noting the broad shoulders, the rippling muscles that made the women stare, the incredible height that made basketball coaches drool, the face that, when angry, reminded one of a charging bull. "I wouldn't be surprised if poor little Kenny didn't need to change his britches when he gets home. Yeah, I agree. He was telling you everything that he knew. So, you think they planted that information on him?"

"I wouldn't be surprised at all. Weems was cool as a cucumber. He almost smiled when Kenny named Wyndham. Like he'd been waiting for that to happen."

"We still have to check it out, you know?"

"I know. But I don't like this, and Alex isn't going to like it, either."

"Don't tell him. You don't want to tell him that you're going to investigate his father."

"I'll think about it. I have an idea. Do you suppose Alex could get his parents to hire me to work on their estate? I'd make a great butler, don't you think?"

"I think a bouncer is more up your alley. What do

168

you hope to accomplish by working for the Wyndhams?"

"You can investigate him from the outside, while I get in and find out the intimate details of his life. Alex will want me to do it. He'll want me to prove that his father is innocent."

*

Late that afternoon, Alex returned to the house. He sat at the desk in his den, writing a letter to Jordan. He wanted to let her know, should anything happen to him, how he felt about her. How she'd brought laughter and joy into his life when he didn't think the sun would ever shine again. How she and Joshua were the most important, precious people in the world to him. How grateful he was to her for allowing him to be a part of their lives.

Alex also made notes about every detail he could remember from the case, from the moment Suzanne was abducted. He included all that she had told him and Paige, and he included his meeting with Luke and his excursion to Pacoima. If anything were to happen to him, he wanted Jordan to go directly to Luke. He would help her.

Now, where could he put the papers, where Jordan would be sure to find them, but only in the event of his death? He ruled out hanging them on the back of a picture or taping them to the bottom of a drawer. She'd only find them there if she were to move. He didn't think that was too likely.

No, he'd have to put them somewhere else. Someplace she'd be sure to find them at the appropriate time.

*

Upon investigation, Ed discovered large deposits in several bank accounts in various cities around the country. Samuel Wyndham's name was on each account. The deposits were always made in cash, with no connection to any of his legal business deals. Ed was convinced that they had found the accounts too easily.

"It looks really fishy," he explained to Luke. "Unfortunately, we've got to follow up on this."

Alex's impatience with the investigation had grown beyond his control. At Luke's request, he had encouraged his parents to hire him. Alex was furious when Luke told him that Samuel was under investigation. He refused to believe, even for a moment, that his father was the head of a porn ring.

"There's just no way, Luke. My father thinks all children are sacred. When he found out what happened to Suzanne Kendell, he wanted to deal with the pornographers himself. He suggested an old-fashioned lynching party. I will not believe that he's involved in this."

Even when Luke told him that further investigation

169

had revealed large deposits in a Swiss bank account, none of which were associated with any of his legitimate businesses, Alex would not believe him. But, just as Luke had expected, Alex agreed to help him get a job on the Wyndham estate.

"You'll never find proof against my father, but maybe you can prove that he's innocent."

Shortly after Kenny and Robert had been questioned by Luke and Ed, the store on Laurel Canyon Boulevard was deserted. They packed up the equipment and left sometime in the night, when no one in the neighborhood was awake to see.

Alex was determined to find their new location. He became a regular visitor to the porn shops in the area, always asking proprietors about videos with kids in them. He'd been given names of people to contact only after he convinced the store managers and owners that he wasn't a cop.

He met with one man who made videos at home, using neighborhood children. It took all of Alex's resolve to keep from smashing the man's face in, and it took every bit of acting skill he could summon to show an interest in the business. He suggested to the man that he'd like to get started, and had heard that a man named Derek Frank could help him out.

The man knew Derek and he told Alex where to find him. Alex thanked him profusely, and immediately gave his name and telephone number to Ed Colson. He did not, however, reveal the fact that he had a lead to Derek Frank.

Now, as Alex stood at the far end of an alley, watching the entrance to a warehouse in San Fernando, his anger and frustration boiled over. They were trying to pin this on his father? If they couldn't find the person who was really the head of this organization, he'd do it himself. He'd do it if he had to stand in this alley for the rest of his life.

He'd been here for two days, always evading Jordan's questions when he returned home late each night. He'd seen Kenny and Robert enter and exit the warehouse several times each day. He'd also seen the man he guessed to be Derek Frank.

From his hiding place behind a trash dumpster, he knew they couldn't see him; but he had a good view of the cars that parked by the door and the people who went into the building.

From the amount of food that went into the place, he figured that the children were now in place, that the operation had begun. He was torn between his desire to help the children, and the need to find out who was the man in charge-- the man undoubtedly responsible for Paige's death.

His heart ached as the days slipped by. Was he doing the right thing? What was happening behind those walls? How old were the children that were being kept inside?

As he watched the building, he prayed that the man

who had given him the tip about this building wouldn't tell Ed Colson about it until he had some kind of evidence. As Alex waited, his legs cramping from his crouched position, another car drove up and parked outside of the warehouse.

Alex watched the driver emerge from the car. "No," he whispered to himself. "Not you. Dear God, there must be a mistake. It can't be him." But even as he watched, as he saw the way the driver greeted Derek, he knew that at last he had the truth.

Alex wiped the tears from his eyes, carelessly standing up, his shock outweighing his common sense. He didn't see the eyes that were turned in his direction. Nor did he see Robert, who followed him down the street. He didn't see Robert copying down his license plate number as he drove back toward the freeway.

Not a cop, Robert thought. The car's too nice. But definitely worth checking out.

*

Alex began his mourning the moment he left the dumpster and walked toward his car. Torn between his loyalties and the fact that he now knew the truth, he felt he and Jordan couldn't survive any more heartbreak. He knew he'd have to tell Luke what he'd seen, but he didn't know how to do it. How could he admit that a man he'd admired and trusted was the head of a child pornography ring, that he'd probably been responsible for the death of his beloved Paige?

For the next two days, Alex wanted nothing more than to get stinking drunk. But after Paige died, booze had nearly destroyed him. Instead, he went to the park for a run. Running always helped him clear his head. It relieved the stress, and helped him deal with the pain in a positive way.

He loved to run in the park. He liked to watch people walking their dogs, or pushing their babies in strollers. He liked to hear the laughter of children on the playground, and see young love blossoming on park benches. He especially loved to be outside, where there was lush, green beauty all around him.

Today, he saw none of that. As he ran, he saw drug dealers behind the restroom. He saw gang members glaring at one another, touching the weapons hidden in their pockets, their graffiti covering every wall and fence within view.

He saw a father strike his little girl across the face. He saw two ten-year-olds trying cigarettes. He saw a man and a woman screaming at each other. Permeating all the evil before him was the memory of the face he'd seen in the alley outside the warehouse.

Alex finished his run, sweat and tears mingling on his face. He still needed a drink, but he'd settle for juice. He

171

stepped up to a juice bar across the street from the park and ordered a large glass of grapefruit and orange juice mixed together.

Lost in his grief and his agony, he failed to see the stranger walk past his table, casually flipping a pill into his juice. Consumed by his torment, he didn't notice a difference in the flavor, and the odd metallic taste.

Alex's last thoughts, as he fell to the ground, clutching his chest, were for Jordan. He looked up into the cold eyes of the stranger and realized that she had been right. He should have been more careful. But his notes were complete. She'd find them--and she'd take them to Luke.

CHAPTER ELEVEN

Poison, I see, hath been his timeless end.
-Romeo and Juliet

Nancy answered the doorbell on the third ring, wondering why the visitor allowed no more than a few seconds to pass between rings. When she opened the door and saw two police officers standing before her, she thought they surely must be at the wrong house.

"May I help you?"

One of the officers, a tall, thin, tired-looking man, said, "We'd like to speak to Mrs. Wyndham." Fifty-ish, with graying temples, Officer Morrow had made too many of these calls. They were no easier now than they had been thirty years ago.

"Her name is Ms. Blake. If you had any real business with her, you'd know that. What do you want?" Nancy felt protective of her young family, and she didn't want these people to waste Jordan's time. Yet, as she looked at their faces, fear began to penetrate her. She knew they weren't here to sell tickets to the police officers' ball.

The second officer, a pretty woman who appeared to be in her thirties, smiled gently at Nancy. "Please, ma'am. This is very important."

Nancy hesitated, "Could I see your identification? Anyone can get one of those uniforms, you know."

Officers Morrow and Connoly held their badges for Nancy to see, patiently waiting as she studied them intently. She raised her eyes to theirs, and backed up into the entryway. "Would you please step in? You can wait here while I get Ms. Blake."

As Nancy walked towards the office, her heart began to beat faster. She sensed the worst. Had something happened to Jordan's parents? Or, to Alex's? No--if that were true, then Alex would be here to tell her. "Please," she whispered, "don't let it be Alex."

She leaned through the open door of the office. "Jordan?"

Seeing the concern on Nancy's face, Jordan stood and walked toward her. "Nancy, what's wrong?"

"There are two police officers here to see you."

"What do they want?"

"They didn't say. Just said it was important." Nancy reached back to lay a reassuring hand on Jordan's arm. "Don't worry, dear. Someone probably just ran over a neighborhood dog, and they want you to tell the owners."

Jordan didn't mention that this explanation seemed

highly unlikely. As she approached the officers, Nancy's fear now showed on Jordan's face. Commanding herself to stay calm, she invited them into the front room.

"Please, won't you sit down?" As they did, she seated herself on the front edge of a couch cushion, tension permeating her body. "Now, what can I do for you?"

Slowly, with well-practiced gentleness and well-controlled sorrow, Officer Morrow told her.

Jordan listened, willing herself to remain conscious. Blackness threatened to envelop her and she gripped the cushion, her eyes focused on the wall behind the officers. "How did it happen?"

Officer Connoly, the daughter of a funeral director, knew the importance of each and every word. She watched the blood drain from Jordan's face, her whitened knuckles tightening fiercely on the couch cushion. "Witnesses saw him running in the park earlier this afternoon. It appears that he suffered a heart attack. I know it seems unlikely. He seems to have been in good physical condition, but sometimes hearts just aren't as strong as we'd like them to be."

Jordan's eyes blinked several times, two tears escaping. She quickly wiped them away. "He had a heart defect. He never liked to admit it, but he did. He was born with it. But he's always been so athletic. Why would it give out now?"

The two officers looked at each other, their own sorrow in evidence. Officer Morrow shrugged his shoulders and shook his head sadly. It was Allie Connoly who answered.

"Maybe it just ran out of strength. Ms. Blake, we are terribly sorry. I wish we could go to people's homes and give them good news, but the truth is, these things happen. The human body has its limits, and apparently your husband's body reached its limit. I am sorry."

"Where is he?" Jordan's voice was almost imperceptible.

"He's been taken to the county coroner's office. Since it appears that he died of natural causes, you can have him transferred to a mortuary." Officer Morrow almost made it through the entire explanation without his voice breaking, but he seemed to choke on his last words. No, he thought, this never gets easier.

They stood to leave, wishing fervently that they could comfort this young woman. Wiping away her own tears, Nancy led them to the door in silence, only speaking as they stepped outside.

"Thank you for telling her so nicely. When my husband was killed in a car crash, they weren't nearly so kind to me." She patted each of them on the shoulder. "You seem to care about people. I'm glad they sent you to tell her."

After they had gone, Nancy returned to Jordan.

174

"Honey, is there anything I can do for you?"

Jordan roused herself from her torpidity. "I've got to call his parents." As Jordan reached for the telephone on the end table, she looked up at Nancy. "Where's Joshua? I have to tell him, too."

"He's taking his nap now, dear. I'll let him sleep a little later today, to give you some time to absorb this."

"Thank you, Nancy. You're a good friend." She picked up the telephone receiver and began to dial.

Nancy walked quietly from the room, torn between her desire to help this young woman, and the knowledge that Jordan needed to find her own strength to deal with this new tragedy. She knew from experience that sometimes the deepest agony could quell tears, but she also knew that tears could be healing and she wished that Jordan could find that release.

As Jordan dialed the phone number for the Wyndham Estate, Nick sat, reading quietly, in the den. He picked up after the first ring.

"Wyndhams'."

"Hello. Nick?" Jordan's voice shook.

He knew immediately that something was wrong. He dropped the book in his lap, swung his feet off of the footstool in front of his chair, and sat upright.

"Jordan?"

"Nick, it's Alex. The police were just here. They say he had a heart attack." Jordan paused, swallowing hard. "Nick, I'm so sorry. He's gone."

Nick couldn't speak. Alex dead? Alex, whom he'd been angry with for so long. Alex, whom he'd been jealous of and whom he'd never really forgiven. Alex, whom he'd loved since the day he'd entered this world.

"I'll tell my parents. We'll be right there."

Jordan didn't notice the minutes passing as she waited for the Wyndhams to arrive. She sat in her numbness, wondering how she could have lost so much. Wondering how she would cope. And grieving over how she could possibly explain to a not quite three-year-old that Daddy couldn't come home any more.

She didn't hear the doorbell ring, or hear Nancy as she led Marguerite, Samuel, and Nick down the hall into the darkened room where she sat, leaning wearily against the arm of the couch.

"Jordan?" Marguerite spoke softly.

No answer.

Marguerite strode into the room, reaching for a lamp switch, her men following in silence. As the light came on, she gasped at the sight of her daughter-in-law.

Jordan's eyes were full of unshed tears, her face bloodless. She sat in the dark, quiet and still, absorbed in her thoughts and her pain.

Marguerite went to her side, sitting next to her, reaching for Jordan's hands. As she massaged the cold fingers, she spoke quietly.

"I know this is painful, dear. I don't know what it would be like to lose a husband. But I now know what it's like to lose a child. And as much as I grieve, I know we can get through this."

Jordan sat up, nodding her head, turning to face Marguerite. She grasped the older woman's hands in her own, unaware of the men who watched the scene before them.

"I know, Mother. It's just that, right now, it seems like too much to bear. It hurts so much I can't even cry." She choked on her words. "And Joshua--how can I possibly explain this to him?"

"You'll tell him the truth. You'll tell him just what you need to, and you'll love him through his own sorrow."

Jordan smiled weakly. "Yes, I can do that." Suddenly she looked up at Nick, more pain crossing her features.

Nick caught her glance, his own agony matching hers. His confusion wreaked havoc with his reason. Lianna always painted a dismal picture of Jordan. He had grown to believe that Jordan couldn't feel real, solid love for anyone; that, having married her best friend's husband shortly after her death, having betrayed both Paige's memory and Nick's love, she was incapable of faithfulness.

Yet here she sat, seemingly crushed by her grief. Nick paced the floor, fighting his feelings of sympathy. He masked his sorrow with anger, always able to shield himself with his distrust.

Jordan, watching Nick pace the floor, turned back to Marguerite. "I've never thought of myself as a helpless person. I've survived a lot, you know. But suddenly, I feel helpless."

"This is very fresh, Jordan. Give yourself a little time. You'll face it better in the morning. You know he didn't have a good heart. This wasn't completely unexpected. That reality will help you."

"Mama?" Joshua's voice spoke from the door. He ran across the room, throwing himself into Jordan's lap. Snuggling his head under her chin, he smiled at his grandparents and Nick. "Hi," he said, sticking his finger into his mouth.

"Hello, darling." Marguerite leaned over to kiss her grandson. "Mama needs to talk to you for a bit. Would you like to go walk around the garden with her?"

In response to his nod, Jordan stood, gently standing Joshua on the floor in front of her. He placed his hand in hers and they walked toward the dining room. She stopped momentarily next to Nick, who now stood with his arm resting on the mantle above the fireplace. She wanted the tension of the past years to be put behind them. She needed his support now. But as he turned cold eyes towards hers, she swallowed hard and turned from him, leading Joshua outside.

Jordan and Joshua walked over to the Mr. Lincoln rosebush Alex had given her for her last birthday. Jordan leaned over, smelling a newly-opened bud.

"Me too, Mama."

Jordan smiled, lifting Joshua up to smell the flower. Setting him down again, she knelt beside him.

"Joshua, Mama has to tell you something that's very sad. Honey, you know that Daddy loves you very much, don't you?"

Joshua, sensing his mother's sorrow, nodded solemnly. "I love Daddy."

"I know you do, precious." She grasped his hands in hers. "Daddy's love will always be with you. But, Joshua, Daddy can't come home to us any more."

"Why? Mama, I want Daddy." Joshua's bottom lip quivered, tears forming in his brown eyes.

"Joshua, inside here," Jordan touched his chest, "you have a heart. It makes everything in your body work. Well, Daddy didn't have a good, strong heart like we do, honey. His heart had to work really hard for a long time, and it got tired. It couldn't work any more."

"He can have my heart, Mama."

The tears that had been stopped before, now cascaded down Jordan's face. She grabbed Joshua to her chest, crushing him in her arms. Releasing him, she ran her hand over his soft, damp cheek.

"You are a wonderful boy, Joshua, and I know your Daddy is very proud of you. But honey, he doesn't need your heart. You see, he's gone to live with God. We're going to miss him a lot, but God's going to make him feel all better in heaven."

"Will his heart work there?"

"I think so, sweetheart. I think Daddy will be really happy there. He's with Aunt Paige now. You remember we've talked about her?"

Joshua nodded. "I want to see him. Can we go there?"

"Not for a very long time, Joshua. Not until we're very old, and our bodies are too tired to work any more. So, we're just going to have to give each other extra bunches of love, okay?"

"Okay, Mama," Joshua wrapped his arms around her neck. "Can you carry me now, Mama?"

Jordan picked him up gently, walked to the garden swing and sat quietly, cradling her precious bundle in her arms.

Marguerite stood at the windows, watching mother

and child, Samuel's arms wrapped around her. She wiped her tears. "Oh, Samuel, they are going to make it, aren't they?"

"Yes, dear, they'll be fine. And," in response to her unspoken fear, "you will, too. We've lost our boy, but we've got each other. And we'll make it."

Nick, still at the fireplace, listened to his parents. "I wouldn't worry too much about Jordan if I were you, Mother. I'm sure she'll make out just fine."

Pulling from her husband's grasp, Marguerite frowned at her son. "Her pain is very real, Nicholas. She loved Alex very much. It was a special kind of love. One that grew out of shared sorrows, good friendship, and mutual caring and respect. I hope that someday you'll be able to understand all of that."

"You're very gullible, Mother."

"And you're very cynical, Son."

*

The next morning, Jordan and Marguerite met with Blaine to make arrangements for the funeral.

"I think he would have preferred a memorial service," Jordan told Blaine. "He never wanted an open casket. I'd like him to be buried next to Paige." She raised questioning eyes to Marguerite. As Marguerite nodded, Jordan continued. "I think he would like that."

That afternoon, a note was delivered to the Wyndham Estate by a private messenger service. It was addressed to Samuel Wyndham and marked, "URGENT."

When Samuel read the contents of the note, he tightened his hold on the page so that it crumpled in his hand. Marguerite, seeing her husband's reaction, pulled it from his fingers and sank into her chair as she read. "If you'd like to know more about your son's death, you might ask Jordan Blake. She knows much more about this than she's telling you. If you're smart, you'll keep your grandson safely at your side." Not unexpectedly, there was no signature, nor a return address.

"Samuel," Marguerite spoke breathlessly, "what does this mean? Didn't Alex have a heart attack?"

"I don't know, but I mean to find out."

"But, Samuel, this is nonsense. How could Jordan possibly know anything about this? She's been devastated by his death."

"Maybe not. Maybe Nick's right, and she just puts on a good show for you. By George, if she had anything to do with this, I'll see her in prison for the rest of her life. And she'll not lay one finger on my grandson."

"Samuel." Marguerite stood, her initial shock receding as she began to comprehend what her husband was

178

thinking. "You can't possibly believe what this infers. If Alex didn't die of natural causes, we'll find out. But I will never believe that Jordan had anything to do with it. If you think for one moment that she'd ever harm Joshua, then you're certainly not the man I married."

Marguerite left the room and headed for the garage. I need to go for a drive, she thought. Just to calm myself down. Imagine, Samuel believing that note. It's just maliciousness.

As she entered the garage, she smiled at the sight of their chauffeur. "Luke, would you be a dear and pull my Mercedes out for me? I'd like to go for a drive."

"Sure, Mrs. Wyndham. Would you like me to take you someplace?"

"Yes, I think I'd like that. I'd like to bend your ear for a bit, if you don't mind."

Luke, still reeling from the news of Alex's death, was more determined than ever to solve this case. He'd known about Alex's heart defect. That was old news to him, Alex having confided in him during their football days. But it seemed too coincidental that Alex should be investigating the pornographers' ring, and suddenly drop dead.

He helped Marguerite into the front seat, as she insisted that it would be difficult to talk to him if she were in the back. He went around the car, climbed into the driver's seat, and carefully backed out of the garage.

Marguerite told him about the note Samuel had received. "Luke, you and Alex were good friends. You were around here enough as a boy that I feel like you're part of the family. But if you don't want to talk about this, please tell me."

Luke did want to talk about it. As carefully as he could, he asked her about her impressions of the note. Could it be a hoax? Could it have any basis in fact?

If this was a case of murder, Luke thought, agonizing over the possibility, I intend to find out who's responsible for his death. Luke's guilt consumed him. I should have anticipated that his life would be in danger, he told himself. Good God, he thought, could I have prevented this?

As Luke listened to Marguerite, he was convinced that her judgment was ruled by her emotions, her love for Jordan, and he began to wonder. Paige was killed almost immediately after she returned to California to help Suzanne in her pursuit of Derek Frank. How many people knew that Paige was back? And who, of those people, knew why she had returned? Jordan Blake had known.

Who knew that Alex was working with the F.B.I. to find the pornographers? Who knew that he had been looking for Derek Frank, in the hopes of finding out the identity of the person running the organization? Jordan Blake knew it all.

When Luke returned Marguerite to the estate, he told her he needed some personal time. Never one to deny her employees any request, Marguerite assured him that they could manage without him.

Luke went directly to Ed Colson's office, and there he came face to face with Jordan Blake.

*

After leaving the church and saying good-bye to Marguerite, Jordan found herself pacing the floor in her front room. Alex, she thought, why did you die now? You've survived harsh physical activity, traveling, stress, sorrow, even medical school and an internship and residency. Why would your heart give out now? Just when you promised me that you'd be careful and not endanger yourself with your stupid sleuthing, now your heart quits and you die.

The sleuthing. He had never really promised that he'd stop. He'd promised that he wouldn't get hurt. But who could make a promise like that? Alex, you didn't stop, did you? You disappeared for hours and hours on end, with few logical explanations for your absences.

And then, a sudden thought: Alex, did they get to you?

Jordan raced for the telephone, quickly dialing the number of Alex's doctor. Explaining to the nurse that it was an emergency, she was quickly patched through to Dr. Lowenstein.

"Doctor, I need you to tell me something. Could Alex have been murdered? Could someone have given him something that would make it look like he had a heart attack?"

"Jordan, what are you asking me? Is there some reason you think this is a possibility?"

"Yes, please, Dr. Lowenstein. I don't have time to explain now, but I need to know. Is it possible?"

"Well, given his medical problems, yes. A simple nitroglycerin pill could do it. For all intents and purposes, it would look like a heart attack."

"Would that show up in an autopsy?"

"Absolutely."

"Thank you, doctor. I may be calling you back."

As she hung up the phone, fear and adrenaline coursing through her body, she hollered at Nancy, "I have to go out. Please kiss Joshua for me when he gets up from his nap."

Driving to Ed's office, her mind raced as quickly as her heart pounded. Murder? First, Paige. Now, Alex? Was it possible? Or could she just be a grieving widow, confused by her emotions? No, she told herself. She'd been closing her eyes to the real situation for too long. When the Kendells had refused to tell her about Suzanne so long ago, she'd steeled herself against asking too many questions. When Joshua was born, she'd blinded herself to facing any real danger. She

180

wanted an ideal, safe world for her son. She'd ignored any possible threat to her picture-perfect scenario.

Jordan had known that Alex was entering dangerous waters. She knew he should leave the detective work to the professionals, but when he died, she was all too ready to believe that it was of natural causes. Why hadn't she considered murder before now?

*

By the time Luke got to Ed's office, he was ready to tear Jordan's head from her shoulders. All throughout his drive there, his grief and guilt expanded like milk boiling over on the stove. Was Alex murdered? Was Jordan responsible? And could Luke have saved his friend's life?

When he saw Jordan sitting in front of Ed's desk, he struggled with the raging monster who so often intimidated the people he investigated. His anger barely held in check, his voice carefully controlled, he glared down at Jordan.

"So, Ms. Blake, what can you tell me about Alexander Wyndham's death? Samuel Wyndham received a note today that inferred you might know a great deal about it."

Jordan looked confused. "I think I might be learning more about it, but I don't know much right now. That's why I'm here."

"Sit down, Griffin," Ed ordered. "Jordan just talked to Alex's doctor, and she believes that he might have been murdered."

Luke continued to stand, well accustomed to using his height to unnerve people. "Oh, she believes that, does she? My guess is, she knows that for a fact. So, Ed, are you going to order an autopsy?"

"Already done, Luke. But I believe you owe Jordan an apology."

Luke glared at Jordan's white face. "No, I don't believe I do. I believe that I owe Alex an apology. For not looking a little closer to home. It's just possible that the note Samuel Wyndham received today spoke the truth."

Jordan stood up and faced Luke, not frightened of him as he had intended. "How dare you? Someone out there may have murdered my husband, and you stupidly try to blame me? Are you too lazy, or too much of an idiot to try to find out who's really behind this?" Her voice grew louder and stronger as she spoke. "If my husband was killed, then you will find out who did it. You will not mock my grief, nor will you insult me like this."

"Insult you? If I find out that you were responsible for Alex's death, I'll do more than insult you."

"Griffin," Colson roared, "Sit down. Now. That is enough. I warned you not to let your personal feelings interfere

181

with this case. You're acting like a fool and you're being extremely unprofessional. You have no reason to lay this all in Jordan's lap. You have nothing more than an anonymous note to lead you to think she might have anything to do with her husband's death. I expected much more from you, Griffin. Shut your mouth until your reason returns."

Luke's reason did not return that day. By the time Jordan left, she was deeply shaken. Luke had surprised her, more with his anger than his suspicions.

She knew that in a murder investigation, all possible suspects had to be considered carefully. It didn't bother her that he would think of her. After all, she was very close to both Paige and Alex. But surely no one would seriously believe she had killed them.

*

Jordan awoke late the next morning. She snuggled with Joshua, who had climbed in bed with her at about three o'clock after his nightmares woke him. She pulled him into her arms, kissing his eyelids, his forehead, and his cheeks.

"Sweet darlin', wake up."

Joshua stretched, smacking Jordan's forehead with his fist as he spread out in the bed.

"Good morning, Mama."

"Good morning, precious. Do you think we should get up now?"

"Will Nancy make us pancakes?"

"I suppose she might if we ask her."

Joshua was up and down the stairs in moments. Jordan showered, dressed quickly and ran to the kitchen, not surprised to smell pancakes cooking on the griddle.

"Nancy, you spoil him."

"I intend to. He deserves it. So do you. Here, have some coffee. I put chocolate in it, just for you."

"Nancy, you could just buy it this way at the store."

"Mine's better. Now, sit down and eat. Your pancakes are ready."

After breakfast, Nancy took Joshua to the park, telling Jordan to sit and relax. "You need to take care of yourself. You're looking a bit peaked."

Jordan sat in the front room, moving restlessly from chair to chair. The television didn't interest her. No book or magazine enticed her. Her thoughts were flooded with memories of yesterday's encounter with Luke, and her conversation with Dr. Lowenstein.

The doorbell rang, and Jordan was surprised to find Ed Colson at the door.

"Ed, please, come in. What brings you here?"

Following Jordan to the front room, Ed seated

182

himself on the love seat opposite Jordan, who sat on the couch.

"We got the results of the autopsy, Jordan."

Jordan closed her eyes, taking a slow, deep breath. She said, in a low tone, "Already? I thought it would take longer."

"I had them working on it all night. Jordan, Alex was murdered."

Her lips compressed and a frown creasing her forehead, she nodded at him. "I think I knew it." Then, shaking her head slowly, disbelieving, "All he ever wanted to do was save people's lives. And now, someone's taken his. It's so hard for me to understand. He never hurt anyone. Neither did Paige. But someone was so afraid of them that they killed them."

"Someday we're going to have all the answers for you, Jordan. I promise you that. In the meantime, you are to stay completely away from this investigation. We've made too many mistakes, and Paige and Alex became targets. I don't understand about Paige's murder, either. She had only talked to us. She didn't know anything yet. But I think Alex knew much more than he was telling anyone. Did he ever mention any notes he might be making?"

"You mean about the case? No, why?"

"He told me once that he thought it might be a good idea to keep complete records of his questions, and any answers he might come up with. Said that it might help him understand all this better. I just wondered if he'd said anything like that to you."

"No, he didn't. If he was keeping notes of some kind, could they be around here somewhere?"

"It's entirely possible. Could you look around for them?"

"Of course. You know I'd do anything to help with this. Despite what Luke thinks, I didn't have anything to do with Alex's death."

"I know that, Jordan. Deep inside, I think Griffin does, too. He's just angry and a bit guilt-ridden right now. Still, he had no right to treat you as he did, and I'm sorry."

"It's all right. We're all hurting right now. But if he tears into me again, I'll have his head on a platter."

"If he tears into you again, I'll serve it to you."

*

Two days later, on the morning of the memorial service, Jordan's mother called, apologizing. "Honey, I'm so sorry. I wanted to be with you today, to support you, but you're father's feeling quite ill. I don't think it's anything too serious, just a severe case of the flu, but he's asked me to stay with him. He must be feeling really poorly to expect me to miss

Alex's service."

When she was assured that Jordan would be all right, Celeste reminded her daughter to tell Joshua, "Happy Birthday."

"I don't understand why you would schedule the services for his birthday. Couldn't you have postponed the funeral?"

"Mom, it was Joshua's idea. He wanted to know if he could have a Going to Heaven Party for his Daddy, instead of a birthday party. I figured this might be the best way to help him understand about Alex's death, and may be a positive way to deal with his grief. I think he'll be all right, Mom. Sometimes I think he's wiser than I am."

"Jordan, how are you holding up? I'm so worried about you. Just knowing that Alex was killed because he tried to find out about Paige's death frightens me. What if someone tries to hurt you? Or Joshua?"

"Mom, Alex took some risks that I would never take. He was following these people around. I won't do that. But I do intend to help the F.B.I. in any way I can. Ed Colson thinks that Alex may have left some notes around here somewhere. Something that details everything he knew about the case. So, after the funeral today, I plan to come home and tear this place apart. If there are notes here, I intend to find them."

"If there are notes there, Jordan Marie, you'd better let the authorities find them while you get out of the house. I don't want to come to your funeral next."

"I've got the dogs here, Mom. You know they'd never let anyone hurt us."

"Tatsu and Tenshi can't open doors and let themselves in the house. You'd better keep them inside with you. I want you safe."

"Okay; they'll love you for it. I'll let them sleep in Joshua's bedroom with him. Will that make you happier?"

"Much. Oh, dear, I hear your father calling. I'd better go see what he wants. Jordan, I love you, sweetheart. I am so sorry that I can't be with you today. Just know that my love is with you."

"I know that, Mom. Take care of Dad, and don't catch whatever he's got. And don't worry about me. I'll be fine."

But as Jordan hung up the telephone, doubts assailed her. I'll be just fine, she reminded herself. I'm going to bury my husband next to my best friend. Luke thinks I'm responsible for their deaths. Nick hates me. I'm now a single mother. The real murderer is lurking out there somewhere. And I tell myself I'll be fine? I wonder.

Jordan turned, facing the mirror, and adjusted her collar. Pinching her white cheeks to put color in them, she went to help Joshua get dressed.

Jordan looked at her friends as they gathered around her, greeting one another with handshakes, embraces, and quiet words. The sun shone on Joshua's little blond head and she thought, "This should have been a day of celebration for him. Birthdays are supposed to be special."

She thought of the birthdays of her childhood. The favorite meals and special outings that she had planned so carefully. The "best chocolate cake in the world," baked lovingly by Milly, her parents' cook.

Jordan glanced down at her son and her heart ached for him. Together, they had planned this day. As she watched him, he turned and smiled bravely at her as if he knew her thoughts. "It's sunny, just like we wanted, Mommy. So we can smile, okay?"

The weather was exactly what she had ordered for the day. Warm, but not too hot. Just the slightest hint of a breeze to stir the air around them. A beautiful day for a third birthday, she thought sadly, but not a good day for a funeral.

Funeral days should be dreary and cold. No sunshine, just clouds darkening a stormy sky. Jordan glanced at her husband's coffin, barely hearing the condolences offered by those nearest her, not seeing the hundreds of flowers placed carefully near the casket. "Your last days were so full of darkness," she whispered. "Perhaps you deserve a final day of glorious sunshine to honor your memory."

She watched Blaine as people shook her hand and gave the usual, expected praises. "Good message, Reverend." Most people at funeral services are lost in their own thoughts and more likely than not had heard little of the message. But, with her usual grace, Blaine accepted their compliments. She slowly extracted her hands from theirs and made her way purposely towards Jordan.

Marguerite Wyndham reached Jordan's side first. Her grief was apparent, but this was a woman who rarely lost her composure. She and Jordan stood silently, arms around one another.

"I've lost my child. He may have been a grown man, but to me he'll always be my little boy."

Jordan squeezed the older woman's shoulders. "I'm so sorry, Mother. I'll do anything I can to help ease your pain."

"Only time can do that, my dear. Only time."

Jordan nodded knowingly, but made no comment. Her mother-in-law hesitated a few moments before continuing. "I think that it might do you good to have some time to deal with all of this. I have a request to make."

"Of course, Mother. What is it?"

"I'd like to take Joshua home with me. The only

185

thing that will bring me out of my despair is the presence of my grandson."

Torn between her own need for her son's presence and the reality of the many "arrangements" still to be dealt with, Jordan felt weighed down by more than she was ready to bear. She feared for Joshua's safety more than ever, and she knew he'd be safer within the confines of the Wyndham Estate than at home. Even with the dogs, Jordan wasn't entirely sure she felt safe at home.

"Yes," she finally answered. "I think that would be a good idea. It would be good for him to spend some time in his Daddy's childhood home. And if he can bring you any comfort, then he must stay with you."

"I'm sorry, Jordan. I must seem terribly selfish to you." Marguerite's voice broke. "You have your own grief to deal with, and with your parents unable to be here..."

"I have many details to take care of over the next few days," Jordan interrupted her reassuringly. "It would help me to have you caring for Joshua. I know he couldn't be in more loving hands. Mom and Dad will come as soon as he's feeling better."

Blaine, who had inevitably been detained again and again, finally reached the two women. She clasped Marguerite's hand. "Thank you, Mrs. Wyndham, for your help with the service. It makes it so much more personal and meaningful to have the family help with the planning."

Marguerite shook Blaine's hand gently. "Thank you, Reverend Michaels. It was beautiful. I know that the three of you," she nodded at Jordan, "were close friends. The family is quite pleased that you were able to conduct his service."

"If there's anything else I can do..." Blaine began.

"I'll be sure to let you know. Samuel and I must be going. I'll send Joshua over to say his good-byes." Joshua had scampered over to his grandfather's side and was clinging to the large, comforting hand. "I'll have Luke drop by your home this evening, Jordan, to pick up some of his things." She walked away slowly, pausing only for an instant at the side of the casket. "Good-bye, my son. I love you."

Jordan and Blaine watched as the woman spoke to her grandson. The boy she spoke with was tall for his age, like his father and grandfather had been. He had inherited his mother's large brown eyes, and his father's long curly eyelashes. For the first time in several days, Jordan smiled as she watched him coming toward them.

They talked briefly, then she gave him enough hugs and kisses to last several days. "I'm sorry to leave you, Mommy. But I need to take care of Grandma," he said in his most grown-up tone. Then, reverting to his three years, he said solemnly, "Could you please send Billy?" When he was reassured that his beloved teddy bear would be safely delivered, he turned to rejoin his grandparents. "Bye, Mommy. Bye, Blaine. See you later, okay?"

"You betcha, babe." Jordan blew him a kiss, which he caught mid-air and rubbed on his chest, in the area he thought his heart might be located.

Jordan spoke with each of the people still remaining at the grave site, but lingered behind as they walked to their respective cars and drove away. Blaine allowed her several minutes of solitude and thought, glancing occasionally at the slender woman standing beside her.

The young widow wore a simple forest-green dress which accentuated her dark eyes and beautiful complexion. She had explained to Blaine earlier, "He hated black, you know. Said it was morbid." The minister had replied, "You look lovely. Don't worry, people wear all kinds of things to funerals these days."

Blaine put her hand on Jordan's shoulder, "Come on. I'm taking you home. I think after all this you could stand a little pampering and a stiff drink."

Jordan laughed softly. "Of Diet Coke?"

"You betcha, babe." Blaine echoed Jordan's words to Joshua. "Diet Coke it is."

*

As Joshua climbed into the limousine behind his grandfather, he turned to look back at his mother.

"She's really sad, isn't she, Grandpa?"

Samuel picked up his grandson, pulling him into his lap. "You don't worry about her, Joshua. Your mommy can take care of herself. But I need your help to make Grandma happy again. Will you help me with that?"

Joshua nodded his head solemnly. "Do you think if I give her kisses she'll be happy?"

"I can almost guarantee it."

Nick helped his mother into the car and followed her in, smiling at Joshua's question. "I think we could all use some of your kisses today, Joshua. Do you have any to spare?"

Joshua climbed off of his grandfather's lap, seating himself next to his beloved Uncle Nick. Reaching for Nick's hand, he rubbed the fingers over his lips.

"I've got kisses for everyone, Uncle Nick."

*

As Jordan got into Blaine's car, Blaine asked, "Where's Nancy? Does she need a ride?"

"She rode with the neighbors. They're going to stop for lunch before they go home. I told Nancy that she might as well take a trip to see her grandchildren. With Joshua staying at his grandparents', I won't need much attention. I think she'll try to get a flight out tonight."

"Jordan, are you sure you want to be in that great big house all by yourself? That'll be quite an adjustment to make. Why don't you come stay with me for a while? Or go back to the condo, where you can remember happier times."

"Thanks, but the house is home now. I've got Tatsu and Tenshi. I promised my mother I'd let them stay inside with me, so they'll probably follow me everywhere."

When they got to the house, Jordan opened the front door. "Come on in. I'll run up and change while you go fix me that Diet Coke you promised."

Jordan was halfway up the stairs when she heard Blaine call her. "Jordan, you'd better come here."

Walking towards the dining room, she felt a slight breeze.

"Jordan, did you leave these doors open?"

Jordan looked up to see the back doors standing open. One panel of the French doors had been broken out next to the lock. Broken glass was scattered on the carpet.

Jordan turned to look at Blaine. "I don't like this. Someone could still be in here. Do we look for them or do we call 911? Where are the dogs?"

"Your son just lost his father. He doesn't need to lose his mother. We call 911. When the police get here, we'll worry about the dogs."

Pulling the portable phone off of the wall, they walked out the back door. They called for the dogs as they walked around to the front of the house, and sat down on the curb. The police arrived in three minutes. Telling Jordan and Blaine to wait outside, they went into the house.

"I can't stand this waiting," Jordan said impatiently, pacing up and down the driveway. "They've been in there forever."

"It's only been a couple of minutes. Look, here they come."

"Ms. Blake, you can come in now, but I don't think you're going to like what you see. We found your dogs, but they seem to be unconscious. I've called our animal control officers--they're only a couple of blocks from here. They were after a stray, but they're on their way over here instead. They can check out your dogs and take them to the animal hospital for you, if you like."

Jordan followed the officers through the house and out to the pool house. There, just inside the door, lay two very still dogs.

"What's wrong with them?" Jordan asked, falling on her knees between the two dogs, ignoring her tears as she caressed their ears.

The officer who had led her to the dogs, a young

man of about twenty-five, was the first to speak.

"There's some meat over there in the corner. I assume it's poisoned."

As he spoke, the two animal control officers came through the door. They were followed by Jordan's neighbor, Felicia, a veterinarian.

"Jordan, I saw their truck," Felicia spoke, nodding her head at the animal control officers. "What's going on?" As she spoke, she knelt to check the dogs. "What did they eat?"

When the police officer nodded towards the meat in the corner, Felicia walked over to pick up the butcher wrap. She fingered the hamburger. Finding chunks of white tablets, she looked at Jordan. "Their breathing is fine. Their heart rates are a bit slow, but it looks like they've just been given some kind of sleeping pills. I'll take them in and pump their stomachs, then keep an eye on them for a few days. I'm sure they'll be fine. You can come in and check on them any time you want."

Without waiting for Jordan's assent, she nodded to the two animal control people, who carefully lifted the dogs onto a stretcher and carried them through the door.

Jordan, still kneeling on the floor, sat as if in shock. "I don't think I can take any more, Blaine."

Blaine, standing next to her, put her hand on Jordan's shoulder. "I'll be with you every step of the way. Now, let's go look at the house."

The police officer who seemed to do most of the talking again led the way. As they walked towards the house, he said, "You'll have to let us know if anything is missing. I doubt it. You've got a lot of valuable stuff still in here. It looks more like they were looking for something. I understand that your husband was killed recently, and that the F.B.I. is involved in this case. I just called in, and an Ed Colson is on his way over here to take a look around. You can look around now, if you like, but please don't touch anything. We'll need to check for fingerprints."

Jordan, her arms folded in front of her waist, walked through the house. Pictures had been taken from their places on the walls. Drawers were pulled out and overturned on the floor, the contents obviously rifled through. Furniture was pulled away from the wall and the lighter pieces tipped over, revealing the manufacturers' warning tags still on the bottoms. Clothing had been pulled from closets, the boxes normally stored on the upper shelves pulled down, sweaters and shoes added to the piles of shirts and blouses. Even the hatch to the attic was open, a step stool from the kitchen positioned directly beneath it.

A message was scrawled with lipstick across the mirror over the dresser in her bedroom. "You can't hide them forever. We'll get what we want."

189

"I don't know what that means, Ms. Blake, but I suppose Mr. Colson will have an idea. I know this seems really awful," the young officer said, leading Jordan back downstairs. "But, most of the damage is superficial. They trashed the place pretty good, but it doesn't look like they broke much. There's one room they didn't get to--that's the office back here. You may have come home and surprised them."

Two hours later the police left, black fingerprinting dust covering every flat surface of the house. As Jordan surveyed the damage caused by the intruders and the investigators, the telephone rang.

Celeste was calling to check on Jordan. "I've had you in my prayers all day, honey. How are you holding up?"

Jordan tried to assure her mother that she was doing well. But when she explained about the break-in, Celeste became frantic.

"You can't stay there now, Jordan. If you don't want to stay here with us, go stay with Blaine, or with the Wyndhams."

"They've taken everything away from me that matters, Mom. They will not take away my freedom and my sanity. I'm staying here. I'm going to find whatever it was they were looking for. This battle is not over. If I have to take up where Alex left off, I will."

"You're an architect. You are not a cop or a detective. You're just a civilian. I know that in the movies regular citizens take on all the bad guys, but it doesn't always work that way in real life. Jordan, Paige and Alex both lost their lives because they somehow crossed these people. Now you want to do the same thing?"

"No, Mom, of course I don't," Jordan sighed wearily. "I just want all of this to stop. I want the murderers to go to prison. I want the pornographers to be put permanently out of business. I want my son to grow up and live happily ever after, but that's not always how real life works, either. I will be careful, that's all I can promise you. I'm not going to let them completely destroy my life."

When Jordan finished talking to her mother, she went to join Blaine in the dining room. Suddenly feeling as if weights had been tied to her shoulders, Jordan's strength gave way. She sat down heavily, her head buried in her hands.

"You know, Blaine, anger can make a person feel invincible. Grief can make you lose common sense. I guess I'm just as susceptible to that as anyone else." She lifted her head, meeting Blaine's worried gaze with her own. "I know that I have to be careful. I don't want Joshua to grow up without a mother. But what I said to my mother is true. I want a happy ending, and I don't think that's going to happen if we don't put an end to this nightmare."

"Jordan, at least go stay someplace safe for a while.

Go stay at the Wyndhams. Then you can be with Joshua."

"All right. I hate it, but I know you're right." She waved toward the destruction that surrounded them. "I don't think I can face this today, anyway, but this is just for tonight. I'll be back tomorrow."

"Fine. In the meantime, Nancy and I can start cleaning up this mess. If her plane doesn't leave for a while, we can get lots of this straightened up."

"I can't ask you to do that. Blaine, you're a minister, not a janitor."

"Yeah, well, I've done plenty of janitorial work in my day. And sometimes it's a more important ministry than going to meetings and preaching great sermons. Besides, you're not asking. I'm offering."

                              *

As Jordan turned the corner nearing the Wyndham Estate, she was surprised to find the gates closed. In all the times she'd visited their home, she had never seen the gates closed. She pulled her car next to the post, and pushed the button between the mailbox and the intercom speaker.

"Hello?" Jordan knew the voice belonged to Noreen, the Wyndhams' housekeeper.

"Noreen, this is Jordan. Could you let me in?"

The silence stretched so long Jordan wondered if Noreen had heard her. "Noreen?"

"I'm sorry, Ms. Blake, but Mr. Samuel left instructions that you are not to be allowed in."

"Why? Noreen, you must have misunderstood him."

"No, Ms. Blake. He was very clear. He said that you are not to be allowed in, and you are not to see Joshua."

"Please call Mr. Wyndham to the intercom, Noreen. This makes no sense."

"She doesn't need to call me, Jordan. I'm right here. And the order stands."

Jordan heard Marguerite's voice, farther from the intercom. "No, Samuel. You can't do this."

"Jordan," Samuel continued, "I received a note warning me about you. It intimated that you had something to do with Alexander's death. Marguerite insists that it was a hoax. But until we find out the truth, you will not enter those gates. You will not attempt to see Joshua. You will stay away from our home."

As he spoke, Jordan climbed out of the car. With her hands on the immovable gates, she yelled back into the intercom. "Samuel, no, you can't believe that note! Marguerite is right. Please, my house has been broken into, the dogs have been poisoned, and I just can't face it all tonight. Let me see my son. Samuel, please. Don't do this."

Samuel Wyndham was not easily swayed. As much as she pulled on the iron gate before her, it could not be moved. Dejectedly, Jordan returned to her car and drove to her parents' home.

She called the Wyndhams' several times that night, and again the next day. Each time, Samuel intercepted her calls and refused to see her. Refused to let her see her son.

Marguerite knew what her husband was doing. She grew more impatient and more furious with him as each hour passed.

"Samuel, you've always been an obstinate man, but this time you've gone too far. You're wrong about Jordan. I'm living in a household of stubborn men. Nick thinks that Jordan betrayed him. You and Luke actually think she's capable of murder. And poor little Joshua is the one to suffer. You can't keep him away from his mother. Go talk to the F.B.I. or the police. Do anything. But don't interfere like this. It's wrong.

"Just promise me one thing, Samuel. Promise me that you won't let Joshua or Nick know anything about this. Joshua loves his mother. Nick is already confused by his feelings for her. If you poison either of their minds, I promise you that I will leave you."

"Marguerite, you're being ridiculous. After thirty-six years of marriage, you'd leave me?"

Marguerite turned to face her husband, her chin lifted stubbornly. "You're wrong this time, Samuel. What you're doing is wrong. I will not stand by and watch you ruin three lives."

Standing directly in front of him, within arm's reach, she looked up at the man she had loved for nearly forty years. The man who had been everything to her. "Yes, Samuel," she said quietly, "I would leave."

The following day, Jordan returned to her home. She was relieved to see that Nancy and Blaine had removed most of the fine, sticky black dust that the police had left behind. As she walked through the house, she found that clothes were once again hanging in closets, pictures on the walls. Furniture was standing upright, and dresser drawers had been returned to their rightful places.

Traces of the chaos remained. The black powder could still be seen in the corners of the pictures. New scratches glared from the surfaces of the parquet floor in the entryway. One lamp, broken but still functioning, was askew, the break turned towards the wall in the front room. Books from the bookshelves were out of order, several of the torn jackets now removed and in the trash. There was a piece of cardboard taped over the broken windowpane in the back door, the handles of the two doors chained together securely. The lipstick had been hurriedly wiped from the mirror in her bedroom but the tube of lipstick, her favorite color, was in the trash, the lipstick crushed.

On the bulletin board in the kitchen was a note from Blaine. "We tried to do as much as possible. Nancy took a later flight, so we had a little extra time. Sorry we couldn't work miracles. Preacher power only goes so far. Call me if you need me, okay?"

I need an awful lot right now, Jordan thought. But most of all, I need to feel my son in my arms. Holding Blaine's note in her hands, she turned her back to the wall. Leaning heavily against it, she slid down to sit on the floor.

Crossing her arms over her knees and resting her forehead on her arms, Jordan began to plan. If they're still here, I've got to find Alex's notes. Okay, Alex. Where would you hide important papers? Where would you put something that even the intruders couldn't find?

I'll find them, Alex. I'll help Ed Colson. And I will give Joshua a happily-ever-after life. That I promise.

CHAPTER TWELVE

Lo, here upon thy cheek the stain doth sit
Of an old tear that is not wash'd off yet.
-Romeo and Juliet

"Do you know Lauren and Grant, Uncle Nick?"

Nick and Joshua were walking hand in hand through the garden, a bag of stale bread crusts hanging at Joshua's side, saved lovingly by Noreen so that he could feed the ducks in the Wyndhams' pond. Nick had a suspicion that Noreen donated not-yet-stale bread to the cause. She endlessly pampered Joshua and now, as Nick looked down at the beautiful child at his side, he silently praised her for doing so.

Where was Jordan? How could she stand to be away from this precious child? He knew that Joshua missed his mother. Didn't she have any maternal instinct whatsoever?

Yes, he thought. Noreen can spoil you as much as she likes.

"Do you, Uncle Nick?" Joshua's query brought him back to the present.

"No, Joshua, I don't."

"I do. They're my friends. My mommy takes me to their house sometimes. They made me a playroom there. Lauren and Mommy bought me toys for the room. And we go there and play with the toys and play on the beach. Will you take me there?"

"Maybe we'll find another special place I could take you to, Joshua. Would you like that?"

"Could Mommy come with us?"

Nick stopped and knelt down to face Joshua. "Do you love your mommy, Joshua?"

Joshua nodded his head, his lower lip sticking out. "This much," he said, stretching his arms out, dropping the bag of bread. "I want to see my mommy. Can we go see her?"

Nick wanted to make this little boy smile. But he wanted the smile to light his heart, not just his face. He picked up the bag of bread and lifted Joshua into his arms. Gently kissing the child on the forehead, he gave him a hug.

"Would that make you happy?"

"Uh huh."

"Then I'll talk to your mommy and see if we can come see her."

"You don't like Mommy, do you?"

"What do you mean? Of course I like her."

"No, you don't. She told Daddy you're hospital to her."

"Hospital?" Nick thought for a few moments. "You

mean hostile?"

"Yeah. That. Are you hospital?"

Nick gave Joshua another kiss. "Yeah, sweet stuff, I guess I am hospital."

*

Jordan became a regular visitor to Ed Colson's office. She learned that Derek Frank had been arrested again. This time Robert and Kenny were arrested with him, and seven children and adolescents were found in the warehouse they rented. Three were teenagers who were accepted into a halfway house for former prostitutes. The program was run by a local church. It helped them return to school, and encouraged them to build better futures for themselves. Two were runaways who were very happy to be returned home. The final two were runaways who had come from abusive homes. They happily went into foster homes, one with a family who had already raised sixteen adopted and foster children; the other, at Suzanne's insistence, went to live with the Kendells.

Along with her parents, Suzanne intended to give eight year old Christie a happy life. Christie began seeing a psychiatrist twice a week, and the family met with Dr. Williams each Saturday afternoon. The healing that took place touched four lives: hurting, angry parents, a physically and emotionally scarred young woman, and a frightened child who needed to learn about the power of love.

Ed Colson shared his news and his frustrations with Jordan. He knew that Samuel Wyndham still tried to keep her from seeing her son.

"You know, Jordan, what he's doing is illegal. You could bring charges against him."

"I think that would be more damaging to Joshua than our being separated. And, Marguerite's been wonderful through all of this. She sneaks Joshua over to see me several times a week. She tells him that it's their secret adventure, and so far he hasn't mentioned it to his grandfather. He thinks it's great fun.

"Marguerite dotes on him. She fills him up with chocolate chip cookies and love, and tells him how much she loves having him stay with her.

"I know that he misses me, and he misses being at home. But I'm still afraid that whoever had my house torn apart will come back. I don't want Joshua there when they do."

"Jordan, have you had any luck looking for Alex's notes? If they exist, they've got to be there somewhere."

"I've looked in with his will. I've looked through the pockets of every article of clothing he had. I've looked through his dresser drawers, and through his keepsake boxes. I can't find anything that resembles a file on this case. Isn't it possible that he put them somewhere else?"

"Luke's looked everywhere he's had access to at the Wyndhams', and we've checked through his medical records thoroughly. Nothing. That only leaves the house. Don't give up. Alex was a very organized person. I can't imagine that he wouldn't have written everything down. Keep looking. They've got to be there somewhere."

Later that afternoon, as Jordan spoke with her mother on the phone, her frustration surfaced.

"Mom, I don't know what else to do. I've looked everywhere I can think of. I haven't gotten rid of a single thing of Alex's, because I've been afraid that I'd inadvertently throw out his notes."

"Just be patient, dear. I'm sure you'll find them eventually." Then, her mouth away from the receiver, "What's that, Emerson? Oh, Jordan, your father says to tell you not to worry about them. He says to let the professionals take care of things, and you just go back to being an architect." Lowering her voice, she continued, "Don't pay attention to him, sweetheart. You do what you think is best."

*

Jordan stood up to greet the small man who was walking into her office. She held out her hand to shake his and smiled, more at the obvious nervousness of the man than out of greeting. She wondered why he was nervous, but determined to make him feel at ease.

"Hello, Mr. Smith. I'm happy to meet you. What can I do for you? My secretary was a little vague about your phone call."

"You have a very good reputation, Ms. Blake, and I'd like to hire you to work on a house."

Jordan laughed softly. "That certainly doesn't sound very mysterious, although Estelle hinted that you might be hiding from the law or something."

Mr. Smith relaxed a bit in his chair and looked directly at Jordan. He liked the look of this straightforward young woman. He returned her smile. "No, nothing that exciting. It's just that this house is to be a secret. My wife knows nothing about it."

Jordan thought the man looked a little too much like a faithful puppy to be pulling anything underhanded. "I see," she began.

"Oh, no. It's nothing like that, Ms. Blake. Cross my heart," he said, doing just that. "But this house is to be a surprise. That's why I've come to you. I've heard that when you are interested, you'll go beyond the duties of an architect, and that you'll actually help out with the decorating."

"Well, I'll admit I do enjoy that aspect of the work, but

no, I don't generally take that on as part of the project."

"Let's not worry about that right now. Perhaps I'll be able to convince you later. For now, let me tell you a little bit about what I'm looking for. The house is to be built above Malibu Cove. Are you familiar with the area?

"Yes, of course."

"We'd...uh, I'd like the house to be similar to the Palmer house; in fact, it will be on half of their property. Do you know the home?"

"Well, yes, Mr. Smith. I'm surprised that since you know of my reputation, and that you know their home, you don't know that I drew up the plans for that house. The Palmers are close friends of mine."

Mr. Smith flushed slightly, his discomfort returning. He didn't want this young woman to know the full story, and he'd have to be very careful. Drat, he thought, I'm just not good at this cloak and dagger stuff. Aloud he said, "I will admit that I did know that. I'm just so anxious for you to take on my project that I guess I'm a little nervous."

Jordan wondered why she had taken a liking to this funny little man who so obviously wasn't telling her the whole story. She wondered if he were with some sort of witness protection program, but she chastised herself for her vivid imagination. He's come here for business reasons, not for me to question him about his life, she told herself. She looked into the pale eyes that had no specific color, and the hair that he combed across the top of his balding head.

"All right, Mr. Smith. Why don't you tell me a little more about what you're looking for?"

Mr. Smith explained to her that he wanted the basic floor plan to be the same as that of the Palmers' home, but certain dimensions needed to be changed. "I hope you won't feel that I'm criticizing the work you did on their home. It's just that there are some things that will work better for my own situation."

Jordan, not at all offended, was eager to hear his ideas. She listened in amazement as he outlined his plan to her. "Mr. Smith, those are the exact changes I would make if I were to build the home for myself. In fact, if I'd thought of it sooner, I'd have tried to purchase that property before you ever found it. Yes, I'd be delighted to work on your plans for you. Between the two of us, we'll build the most wonderful house ever put on that beach. When would you like to begin?"

Mr. Smith congratulated himself on his success. "I'd like to begin as soon as possible, so would now be too soon?"

He liked the sound of her laughter as she answered him. "Well, this takes me a bit by surprise, but yes, today is fine. I do appreciate enthusiasm in a client. People like you are much easier to work with."

"I am quite anxious to get this house built. I hope we

can have it completed in a few months."

"I don't want to discourage you, Mr. Smith, but you do realize that there are numerous details to take care of before we can even break ground?"

"No, I just assumed that you could draw up the plans and we could start building."

"I wish it were that simple. It generally takes a minimum of a month to draw up the plans. Then they have to be submitted to the planning and building department for the city of Malibu. It could take them up to six weeks, maybe more, to check them and note any corrections that need to be made. The city's plan check may take another six weeks. The city may require a site plan review, which could add on another three months."

"Good heavens." Mr. Smith was visibly dismayed. "I had really hoped that we could have this completed in a few months."

"We might be lucky. If all goes well, we could break ground within three months. But, I don't want you to get your hopes up. It's my job to make sure you understand the realities."

"Just do the best you can. I'm sure that we...uh, I will understand."

*

As Mr. Smith had hoped, they were lucky. The plans were familiar to Jordan and required fairly uncomplicated changes. It took a total of six weeks for them to get everything planned, approved, and prepared. Jordan and Mr. Smith stood side by side as the construction crew broke ground.

Jordan watched in disbelief. "You must have used a magic wand for this to go so smoothly, Mr. Smith. I've never had things go through so quickly."

"Thank you for sticking with this faithfully, Ms. Blake. I know you've been through some hard times in your personal life, and I want you to know that I appreciate your efforts." Then, in response to her inquisitive glance, "The Palmers explained a little bit about your situation. I'm sorry for monopolizing so much of your time, when perhaps you should have had more time for grieving." Mr. Smith knew that he had needed to pursue this building project, but he felt guilty.

Jordan felt a stabbing pain in her chest, but she tried to answer him lightly, "You know what they say about keeping busy, Mr. Smith. It doesn't allow time for the hurt. I've been working like a demon lately for exactly that reason."

"Perhaps this isn't the right time to ask you, but I still hope that you'll consider helping me with the decorating. You did such a beautiful job with the Palmers' home."

"Mr. Smith, what you really need is an interior

decorator. I have fun doing that sort of thing, but I'm really not trained. Grant and Lauren and I just chose our favorite things and put them together the way we thought they should be."

"But they're so perfect! I would appreciate it if you'd at least consider my request. After all, how would I, a businessman with no flare for decorating, make a home beautiful enough to please my wife?" He hoped that this last plea would be the one to entice her. For good measure he added, "I would pay you generously for your time, and I wouldn't interfere at all. In fact, I wish you'd just do everything as if you were decorating for your own home. I'd trust you completely to do a lovely job."

Jordan's thoughts strayed to her recent, devastating loss, and to the son she missed so incredibly. She was at a stand-still with Ed Colson and the investigation, and she knew she needed something to keep her mind busy.

"Okay, Mr. Smith, I'll accept your offer. You certainly don't need to pay me. I really need something to keep my mind occupied, and this may be just the thing. You have to promise me that if you don't like something, you'll tell me straight out."

"I promise; but I'm sure I'll love it all."

"Couldn't you at least give me an idea of the color scheme you prefer?"

Mr. Smith looked bewildered. He stammered in response, "I trust you and your taste."

Jordan laughed at the expression on his face and promised, "Don't worry, Mr. Smith. I'll bring you samples of things, and you can choose from those."

Mr. Smith agreed, although somewhat reluctantly. Good heavens, thought Jordan, this man needs to develop some opinions of his own. She wondered if Mrs. Smith was the kind to walk all over her spouse. Perhaps she knocks the opinions right out of him. Jordan began to feel sorry for poor Mr. Smith, and she resolved to help him as much as she could.

*

A week later, as Jordan went to make a routine inspection of the Smith home, she noticed that the foundation looked wrong. She borrowed a tape measure from one of the men on the construction crew and took him with her to measure the rooms. With a copy of the plans tucked under her arm, she began to make notations of the errors that had been made. When she had completed her task, she immediately found the general contractor whom she had worked with on previous occasions.

"Hello, Ms. Blake, it's nice to see you here today," but the expression on his face seemed to deny his words. Jordan knew that he was aware of the mistakes.

"Mr. Mason, this foundation is completely wrong.

Several of the rooms are even the wrong dimensions."

"No, Ma'am. We built it just like you drew it."

Jordan was not in a mood to argue with this man. "Freddy," she called to the construction worker, "could I borrow your tape measure again?"

Tape measure in hand, Jordan asked Mr. Mason to accompany her. Together they measured each room, and Jordan pointed out the differences to him. "You see, Mr. Mason, this building has not been built according to the plans I drew up."

"We always follow the plans completely."

"Mr. Mason, let me see your specs." As Jordan looked over the papers he handed her, she realized the mistake immediately. "Mr. Mason, these are the plans from the Palmers' house. How could you possibly have gotten them confused?"

"I guess there was a mix-up in the office." Mason seemed impatient. "This is close enough."

Jordan had had enough stress and pain in her life of late to keep her hanging on the edge of her sanity. Now, her anger took the place of her pain. "This most certainly is not 'close enough,' Mr. Mason. Those studs will have to come down. The foundation will be extended and rooms will be made according to the plans for *this* house."

"Come on, Ms. Blake. Old Smith will never know the difference. Let's just leave it."

"When you and I are hired to build someone's home, we do it the way they want it, not however our whims or mistakes lead us. Please have the changes made by the end of the week."

"You'll have to pay us for the overtime."

"We will stay with your original bid. I can't ask my client to pay extra for careless mistakes."

"I want to see your superior, Ms. Blake. What you are asking is preposterous."

"I am the superior, Mr. Mason. If you are unwilling to work with me, perhaps I'd better find another contractor."

"Nobody's ever fired Bill Mason."

"And I won't now, as long as you do as I ask."

Mason walked away from her without further words. He appeared to be extremely angry. But Jordan's anger equaled his, and she was not daunted. She turned to return to her car, and found Freddy at her side.

"Ms. Blake, I'm sorry about all that. I should have called you to let you know what was going on."

"You mean you knew all along?"

"Yes. We couldn't not know. It said "PALMER HOME" right on the specs, with the address right by the name. But when I asked Mason about it, he threatened to fire me if I didn't keep my mouth shut. I really need this job, Ms. Blake. I've got two kids, and my wife's expecting our third. She's had a difficult pregnancy, and she had to quit her job."

"I understand, Freddy. I don't blame you a bit. If Mason asks you what we were talking about, tell him I was asking after your family. But what I don't understand is why he would do such a stupid thing. He knows that I always inspect my building sites. The changes are so obvious, he must have known that I would realize what was happening."

"I don't know, either. I wish I could tell you."

"Freddy, I have a strange request for you. Do you suppose you could be my eyes and ears around here? I'd like to hire you to do a little spying for me."

"Heck, Ms. Blake. You don't have to hire me. I'd be happy to do it for you."

"Nope, I'll pay you. After all, if Mason found out, you might lose your job with him. I want to keep my conscience clear."

Freddy thought about how helpful a little extra money would be for his family. "You got yourself a deal, Ms. Blake. Just call me 'Bond. James Bond'," he said in his best Sean Connery impression.

"I hope it won't be that drastic, Freddy. But do let me know if you see or hear anything."

Jordan was shaken by her encounter at the building site. She wondered why Bill Mason had suddenly become so antagonistic. They'd worked well together in the past, and his lack of professionalism was unexpected. She tried to place a call to Ed Colson on her car phone, hoping that he could give her an update on the case, but was told that he was out of the office for the day.

*

Bill Mason hid his smile well as he walked back towards his trailer. Jordan Blake would be easy to distract. The man on the phone would be pleased, and Mason would be well paid. The man had told him to cause her problems, to keep her occupied. Well, he was certainly doing that.

Mason felt a bit of remorse as he remembered the previous times he had worked for Jordan. She's a nice enough lady, he thought; maybe I shouldn't have agreed to do this.

Then he thought of his daughter's orthodontia and his son's college expenses, and his guilt disappeared. After all, he wasn't causing her any harm. Just a bit of inconvenience.

When the man called next time, he'd have a good report to make. Yes, the money would make it all worthwhile.

*

Jordan drove toward home, wishing that she could see Joshua. She knew there would be a battle if Samuel saw her on the estate, and she didn't want Joshua to witness any difficulties between his mother and his grandfather. She decided that she would drive by the estate, park outside the gates, and watch to see if she could see him out near the pond where she knew he spent a great deal of time.

As she neared the gates, she noticed Samuel's limousine nosing slowly down the drive from the house. She pulled to the side of the street and watched the limo. She was relieved to see Luke turn the car to head in the opposite direction. She felt her heart leap as she saw Joshua's head through the side window at the back of the car. She knew that she would follow.

She drove several yards behind the limo, hoping that they wouldn't see her. Luke drove to the large park located a mile from the Wyndham estate. He parked in the parking lot closest to the playground, and helped Joshua and Samuel out of the back seat. Jordan watched as they walked towards the swings, Joshua's favorite ride, but was frustrated by the trees which blocked her view. She climbed out of the car, now grateful for the cover of the trees.

Jordan walked towards the playground quickly, steadfastly keeping to the shadows and the cover of the mighty oaks. She felt a bit foolish, thinking of western movie heroes, half expecting to hear gunshots at any moment.

Her heart thudded in her ears and tears swelled in her throat as she crept closer to where Joshua sat on a swing. He sat, barely moving. He was more interested in the dirt he pushed with the toe of his sneaker than in the activity of the other children around him.

Vivid memories sprang into her mind. Memories of a happy child swinging. "Higher, Mommy, higher." Again she saw the glorious smiles that made Joshua's face light up. She heard the laughter which could make her heart sing. Precious memories.

But as she watched him now, there were no smiles or laughter, only downcast eyes. Again she felt incredible doubt. "Am I doing the right thing? There must be a better way." Resolve filled her heart, and she whispered quietly, "You must be in a safe place. You need to get to know your daddy now, but I won't let you lose your mommy in the process."

She watched as Samuel rose from the green-speckled park bench and walked toward his grandson. She was so intent on watching the two figures before her that she failed to hear the leaves crushed under heavy footsteps behind her. She wasn't aware of anyone's presence until the man grabbed her shoulder and swung her around.

CHAPTER THIRTEEN

Methinks, he looks as though he were in love.
-Taming of the Shrew

Jordan turned, startled by the sudden action, yet ready to do battle. She swallowed her words as she looked up into the large face of the F.B.I. agent/driver.

"Luke. I didn't hear you," she said, as if those words could explain everything.

"Obviously," he returned. But the curt response seemed to carry more concern than accusation. Indeed, his face was full of compassion, and his eyes shone with sorrow.

"Luke? What is it?"

"I'm sorry for the way I treated you in Colson's office. I had no right to jump to the conclusion that you were responsible for Alex's death. There has never even been any evidence to point to you. Anyway, Ed and Marguerite have been on my case, and I'm ready to beg your forgiveness. I understand a little more about your relationship with Alex now. And Marguerite reminded me, none too gently, that Alex loved you and he trusted you completely."

"It's all right, Luke. I guess sometimes we all jump to conclusions." As she spoke, her eyes strayed to look at the elderly man playing with her son.

"I want you to know that I'm on your side, Jordan. I want to help you."

"If only you could. If only you knew..." Jordan's voice trailed off.

"I know a bit more than you might think. Tomorrow's Tuesday," he paused. When she didn't respond, he continued, "My day off. Will you be home?"

"Yes, of course. I have my office there now, you know."

"I'll be there. You'd best be going now. I'll draw their attention the other way so that you can leave without skulking."

Jordan noticed the twinkle in his eyes, and she began to wonder about this man. As he turned to leave, he glanced back at her. "Don't lose hope," he said. The twinkle had disappeared, replaced with kindness.

"Take care of him, Luke. He looks so sad."

"He misses you, Jordan. But Samuel is adamant that you not be allowed to come visit. He's still threatening to tell Joshua that you hurt Alex, if you try to see him." Seeing the pain on her face, he said, "I'm sorry, Jordan. This will all work out. Don't worry about Joshua. We've become quite good buddies--he likes to help me take care of the cars. He's a smart little boy. He asks lots of questions about what makes

203

cars go, and which ones are the fastest. He misses you, but he's okay. As hard-hearted as Samuel is toward you, he's as soft as cotton candy to that boy. He and Marguerite shower him with love."

"I'm glad. I was afraid that Samuel would transfer his anger from me to Joshua."

"Joshua's his grandson, Jordan, and he loves him."

"I'll trust that he'll be well cared for. I don't want him caught in the middle of this misunderstanding between Samuel and myself." Jordan wanted to ask about Nick. She wanted to know how he felt about Joshua, and she wondered if he ever spent any time with the boy. But she couldn't ask. Not yet.

Jordan watched as Luke led Joshua towards the waiting limousine, Samuel following the two silently. The boy reached out and placed his small hand within that of the giant walking next to him. Luke lifted the boy's hand in the air as if to say, "Here's the winner." Jordan knew it was a message for her.

"Don't lose hope," he had said. Joshua trusts him, she thought, and for some reason, so do I.

She blew a kiss at Joshua as he walked with Luke, deep in conversation with his newly acquired friend. "Soon, precious, soon," she whispered.

*

The telephone was ringing as Jordan walked in the front door. "Nancy," she called, "I'm home. Is that for me?"

Nancy, still suntanned from her days of leisure on the Miami beaches, stuck her head around the kitchen doorway. "Yes, it's someone named Freddy. He says it's really important."

Jordan ran into the front room, throwing herself into the dark blue wingback chair.

"Yes, Freddy," she spoke breathlessly, "what is it?"

"I've been following Mason, just like you said, Ms. Blake. I heard him on the phone just a little while ago. You've got to be careful, ma'am. Something real weird is going on around here."

"What did you hear, Freddy?"

"Well, it was real loud out there--you know how it is on a building site--and I couldn't hear everything. But I heard Mason say that he's distracting you real good, and that he'll keep you busy as long as whoever he was talking to wants. And," he paused, swallowing hard, "Ms. Blake, he promised the person that he'd do his best to scare you. I don't know if he's gonna hurt you or nothin', but be careful, okay?"

Scare me? I've already been scared more than I ever thought possible. What else can they possibly do to me? Jordan wondered.

"I'll be careful, Freddy. Thank you. If you hear anything else, you let me know. Okay?"

After Jordan hung up, she had a great desire to call her mother. Somehow, in the worst of times, it was nice to turn to a familiar soul. She tried several times, but the line remained busy.

Oh well, she thought, I'll try again later.

As she went to find Nancy, she suddenly became concerned for her housekeeper's safety. If Nancy stayed here, would she be in danger?

"Why are you scowling, dear?" Nancy asked when she saw Jordan standing in the hallway, frowning contemplatively.

Jordan knew that if she told Nancy of her fears, she would brush them away unheeded. "Nancy, didn't you mention that you have a cousin in San Diego?"

Nancy's face brightened immediately. "Oh yes. My cousin, Mary. She's a delightful woman. Even chubbier than I am," she said, giggling. "You'd just love Mary. And Joshua would love her pancakes. She has a secret recipe, you know."

Jordan smiled back at her. "I've been thinking. With Joshua staying with his grandparents, there's really not much for you to do around here. Would you like to go visit Mary for a while?"

The prospect immediately appealed to Nancy. But even as she began to accept the offer, she thought about Jordan. "Oh, sweetheart, I couldn't leave you here alone."

Jordan hugged her friend. "I appreciate that, Nancy, but I'll be fine. You deserve to get away for a while. You've taken such good care of all of us."

"I just got back from Miami. I certainly don't deserve any more vacation time."

"Nancy, I promise to call you if I need anything. Would that appease your conscience?"

Nancy considered the possibility. "Well, I haven't seen Mary in some time. Yes, I think I would like that."

Jordan kissed Nancy on the cheek. "Good. You can leave in the morning if you like. I want you to have a good time."

*

The next morning Jordan was up at six, exercised, showered, and dressed by seven, and working in the office with a new excitement and energy. Her visit to the park the previous day had rejuvenated her. Seeing her son was like a magic potion to her aching soul.

She reached for the plans she was working on for a new client. "This is going to be one gorgeous house," she said to herself. "Maybe I'll build one for me and Joshua someday."

Jordan worked for an hour without looking up. Then the ache in her neck dictated that she take a break. She stood up and stretched luxuriously, and walked to the kitchen to fix a mug of hot chocolate. She thought about Luke and their encounter in the park. She wanted to like the man who had befriended her son, the man who had been such a loyal friend to Alex. She remembered Alex's description of Luke at the time he was hired by the Wyndhams: "...driver, bodyguard, all-around good guy and personal, true and loyal friend and companion of yours truly."

She went back into her office, determined to complete the first phase of the plans she was working on. She hummed to herself, determined to be cheerful and optimistic about the future.

"Well, well, if it isn't little Mary Sunshine," said a steel-cold voice from the doorway.

Jordan felt as if someone had grabbed her heart and twisted fiercely. She dropped the mug she had been toying with and turned around to face him. It had been several weeks since they had spoken. He had been at Alex's funeral, but had refused to come near her. She didn't know that the reason he hadn't spoken to her at the funeral was that he was afraid he'd lose his temper and upset his mother. She also didn't know that, unaware of her secret rendezvous with Marguerite and Joshua, he now considered her to be a neglectful mother since she had relinquished the care of her own son.

Jordan marveled at the coldness in the voice that had once been so warm and tender. She turned to look at him.

"Hello, Nick."

"Surprised to see me? Didn't think I'd pay a call on my sister-in-law, the grieving widow?"

The sarcasm in his voice and the way he spat out the word, "grieving," made her wince.

But she said none of this. She merely said, "It's nice to see you, Nick. How's Joshua?"

"Oh, you mean you care? When's the last time you came to see him? It looks like I'm going to have to be the one to give my brother's boy a decent family life. It didn't take you long to dump him on our doorstep, did it?"

"That's enough, Nick," Luke growled as he walked through the open door. "You shouldn't speak so much when you know so little."

Nick turned to meet the angry man who stood glaring down at him, but his words were for the pale young woman behind him. "Going for the chauffeur now, Jordan? Kind of lowering your sights a bit, aren't you? Watch out for this one, Luke. She seems to lack scruples," he paused, "and loyalty." The final two words were barely audible as he left the house, the door slamming shut behind him.

Jordan made an attempt at composure, knowing that

206

Luke was watching her. "Well, Luke, can I talk you into some of my world-famous hot chocolate?" Her tone was light, her smile almost convincing.

Luke responded in the same vein. "Of course. I can't think of anything that would suit me better this morning." Then, "Why did he come?"

"I suppose to wish me a happy Tuesday." Seeing Luke's smirk, she shook her head, "No, he came to let me know how awful he thinks I am. And I can't say I blame him."

"He doesn't know much of the story, Jordan. He doesn't even know that he's Joshua's father, does he?"

Jordan's astonishment played across her face. "How on earth did you know? Alex was the only one who knew. And, of course, my mother and Marguerite."

"Alex told me. He was afraid that something might happen to him, and he wanted to make sure that you would have an ally. Someone who knew all the facts." He accepted Jordan's questioning look with a smile. "I know, I wasn't the world's greatest ally. I hereby vow to do better, if you'll have me."

"Alex spoke highly of you. He could read people very well. With Alex and Joshua as references, I can't think of anyone I'd rather have as a friend right now."

"Good. Then let's get down to work."

"Work?"

"It's time for me to fill you in on some things you may not be aware of. You knew I worked with the Bureau?" Jordan nodded her head and he continued. "Shortly after Paige was killed--actually, just after Joshua was born, I had a long meeting with Ed Colson. I met with him and Alex, and they told me everything. All about Suzanne, the kidnapping, the porn ring, Suzanne and Paige's involvement in the investigation. After I heard it all, I asked to be assigned to the case. I knew that Alex wasn't about to back down. After Paige was killed, he was more determined than ever to protect his loved ones, and to find out who was behind everything. I understand that you were aware of his involvement with us."

"Yes."

"You need to understand that Alex never officially worked with us. Ed wouldn't allow a civilian to work under the auspices of the Bureau. But, knowing Alex's determination, he considered it a blessing that someone in the family could help. That's about the time that evidence started to point to Samuel Wyndham."

"Alex told me a little bit of that. He couldn't believe that his father was responsible for the child pornography, or for Paige's death. He never accepted that theory."

"That's why I went to work for the Wyndhams. It was fortunate that their driver had retired, and that cars have always been a hobby of mine. With Alex vouching for me, I was almost assured that they would hire me."

"Alex told me that you were an old school buddy of his."

"I was. We knew each other from way back. It's just that the sob-story he gave his parents wasn't quite true."

"You mean about you being a down-on-your-luck college drop-out who couldn't find meaningful employment?"

Luke smiled appreciatively at her. "Yeah, that story. I finished college. At the top of my class, no less."

"I figured that much out for myself. But I was still surprised that he helped to install you in his parents house."

"He believed in his father completely. He thought that if I were there, I'd end up clearing Samuel of all suspicion. He was right. We've found out that Samuel had no connection to the bank accounts. They were made by a man who had been hired to impersonate him. The men who had implicated him recently recanted when they were threatened with perjury charges."

"Did they give you any other names?"

"Not one. They're too scared. They said that they were paid to implicate Wyndham, but they wouldn't say who paid them."

"Luke, why are you telling me all of this, now?"

"Because, I think you have something of Alex's that may put you in danger."

"Alex's notes. I know, Ed told me. But I don't think they're here. I've looked everywhere."

"I know they exist, Jordan. I think he was working on a lead, but he didn't tell us. We questioned him, but all he'd tell us was that he didn't know enough yet. We were afraid that he was in danger. In fact, we had two of our best men taking turns following him, to protect him. They began tailing him two days before he was killed. That's why we can't figure out how he was murdered. Our men were watching him all the time. Neither one can figure out how anyone got to him."

Jordan's eyes filled with tears, the memories too fresh. She sat in silence while Luke averted his eyes.

Jordan looked at Luke. "We will find out what happened, won't we? We will catch the people who did this?"

Luke wanted to assure her that they would, but he was beginning to have some doubts. He decided to change the subject. "Tell you what, Jordan, you need a day away from it all. How about joining me for a day of relaxation and good old-fashioned fun? I've got a couple of days off coming to me. Why don't we go to the beach or to a movie or something?"

Jordan thought about the days since Alex had died. No laughter. Nothing lighthearted. Only pain, tears, worry. Except for the trip to the park, she hadn't seen Joshua for three weeks. Samuel had found out about the visits, and when he threatened to tell Joshua about Jordan, Marguerite temporarily halted their trips. "I'd like nothing more than to bring Joshua here to be with you permanently, Jordan, but I know how you feel about his safety."

Yes, Jordan thought, I need some laughter. She turned to look at Luke. "I can't think of anything I'd like better. Let's do it."

*

Jordan spent most of the morning getting ready. She wasn't sure where they were going, but Luke had warned her to be ready for anything. She heard the car and hurried out to greet Luke. She didn't realize just how much she was looking forward to a day of diversion.

The car had barely stopped at the curb when the back door opened and Joshua scrambled out. The heavy door was almost impossible for him to push open, but his excitement gave him added strength. He was out of the car and running toward Jordan before she realized he was there.

"Mommy, Mommy," he yelled joyously as he ran toward her. Jordan's heart slammed into her lungs, and breathing was impossible. She stopped on the bottom step, quick tears springing to her eyes. "Joshua," she whispered. Then, as she raced to her son, enveloping him in her arms and burying her face in his hair, "Oh, Joshua, my precious baby. I've missed you so." Luke was at her side before she could say more. She stood and faced him, her tears and gratitude shining in her eyes. "Thank you, Luke. This is the most wonderful surprise in the world."

Luke smiled at her, swallowing the lump in his own throat. This boy should never have been separated from her, he thought, and I'm going to do everything in my power to convince Samuel Wyndham of that and make it safe for him to come home. Aloud, he said, "Don't thank me yet, Jordan."

Luke took Jordan's bag from her shoulder as Joshua pulled her impatiently to the back door of the limousine. The door stood open, just as he had left it, but the darkened windows and the angle of the opened door kept her from seeing the man waiting inside.

In the back of the limousine, Nick had watched the scene play out before him with disbelief and anger. He was furious with Luke for conning him into coming on this excursion. He was even more furious with Jordan, his fury at her went beyond explanation. As he watched her pull Joshua into a fierce embrace, as the tears escaped her eyes and cascaded down her cheeks, as she looked up to thank Luke, Nick couldn't help but think that all of this was sincere. But he couldn't imagine that a loving mother would desert her son, dumping him in the laps of her in-laws.

Marguerite tried to soften her husband's harsh

209

words whenever he spoke of Jordan. But despite her best efforts, Nick knew that his father didn't trust Jordan. A sentiment which he shared.

Nick didn't know that Marguerite and Luke had engineered this outing, telling Samuel that the child needed a day of fun, and since he and Luke had developed such a special friendship, she asked him to take Joshua out for the day. Samuel agreed, much to his wife's relief, and gave Luke his blessings on their outing.

It had been Marguerite who suggested to Luke that he coerce Nicholas into accompanying them. "If you tell him that Jordan is going, he'll never agree to it," she told Luke. "But, if you just tell him that his nephew needs to get to know him better and a day away would be good for him, I'm certain that he'll agree to go."

"And how do I explain it when I drive towards Jordan's house to pick her up? He knows the way there, and I know he'll object."

"Yes, he'll be most vocal about it, and he'll be very angry with both of us. But it's time for him to see Jordan as he once saw her. As I see her now, not as his father sees her." Marguerite was heartbroken about the pain that Samuel was causing for Jordan. She knew that her daughter-in-law had loved Alex with a gentle, comfortable love, and she knew that Jordan had had nothing to do with his death. It had been Jordan who had reintroduced him to life when Paige was killed; Jordan who had brought joy to him once again.

Marguerite looked at Luke, wondering how much he actually knew about their family. "Thank you, Luke, for helping me in my little conspiracies. I'm forever trying to work magic for my loved ones, and I know this is right." She didn't want to explain that she knew Nicholas and Jordan belonged together, but somehow when she felt Luke's intense gaze, she knew that he needed no explanations.

Luke invited Nick to join him and Joshua when Marguerite and Nick were walking through the gardens early that morning. Nick, looking over at his nephew feeding the ducks in the pond, felt an unidentifiable tug at his heart.

This was Alex's son. Nick was amazed that Alex could have gotten involved with Jordan after Paige's death, and that they would have had a child so quickly. He still experienced the pain and jealousy he'd first felt when he heard that they had married. Much as he loved his nephew, there were times when he looked at Joshua, that he buried his pain and allowed his anger toward Jordan to grow.

But the child was his nephew, and he needed the love of his uncle. "All right, Luke, I'll go. What are the plans for the day?"

"Well, Mrs. Wyndham, if you've no objections, I'd like to take Joshua to Disneyland. I've never met a three year

210

old who didn't love the place."

Marguerite smiled at him. "I think that's an excellent idea."

Neither she nor Luke mentioned anything about Jordan earlier that day. Luke hadn't figured out a way to tell Nick and decided that he'd just drive to her house, letting Nick make the discovery on his own.

The discovery was made quickly. "Luke, where are you going?"

"I've got to stop at Jordan's for a bit."

"Jordan? Mommy?" Joshua's face glowed, and he would have bounced in his seat if the car seat had not held him firmly in place.

Luke looked at the boy's face in the rear view mirror, carefully avoiding Nick's angry eyes as they glared at his reflection. Quickly deciding on the tack he would take, Luke said, "Yes, Joshua. That's part of the special surprise for today. Your mommy is going to go with us. Do you like that idea?"

Luke knew that anything he had to say would be powerless against Nick's apparent anger, but one look at the three year old in the back seat would melt the coldest heart.

"Oh, Luke, thank you. Uncle Nick, I get to see my Mommy! Will you be nice to her today? She laughs real pretty, and she lets me get ice cream at Disneyland, and she carries me when I get tired, and she lets me ride the Dumbo ride five times and the tea cup ride seven times, and she lets me sit on her lap to watch the parade 'cause the ground is too cold for my bottom. Oh, Luke, are we there yet? I want to see my Mommy."

Nick said nothing. How could Jordan abandon such a wonderful child? A child who obviously adored her? Had she no heart?

As they pulled up in front of Jordan's house, Nick reluctantly glanced at the beautiful home. He hadn't really looked at it when he'd been there a few days earlier, and he had to admit that it was marvelous. But as he saw her emerge, hatred consumed his thoughts.

He watched as Joshua pulled her toward the car, watched as she helped Joshua step up into the car. Then he cringed when she leaned further in and, seeing him inside, backed away, a look of fear on her face.

"Oh, no, Luke, I can't do this," Nick heard her say quietly, trying to lower her voice so that Joshua wouldn't hear.

"Mommy, come on, get in. Luke and Uncle Nick are taking us to Disneyland. Won't we have fun? Can I have ice cream?"

Jordan still stood outside of the car, her heart hammering in her chest. Her throat tightened until she couldn't speak. She felt Luke's large hand grasp her shoulder firmly and reassuringly.

Nick saw the gesture and felt his jealousy rise. Stupid, he chastised himself. She's a fickle, unfaithful, unreliable woman. But he still wished that Luke wouldn't look at her with that adoring and protective expression on his face.

Luke looked at Nick, almost in warning, and turned to Jordan. "Come on, Jordan, don't disappoint Joshua. He's missed you horribly. I promise that everything will be okay. I'll make sure of it." Once again he glared at Nick.

Jordan looked at her son. "For Joshua," she murmured, and climbed in over Nick's immovable knees. Sitting next to Joshua, she faced the man she most didn't want to face. She determined that she wouldn't look at him. She'd focus all of her love and attention on Joshua, and she'd work with Luke to make this a special day for him. He deserves it, she thought, but she wished that Nick would stop glaring at her.

Almost the moment she made the wish, Nick turned to look out the window. He'd watched her as she carefully buckled Joshua's seatbelt, before she did her own. He'd seen her gently brush a strand of hair out of her son's face, and now the two of them sat hand-in-hand, as if they could communicate all their thoughts through a simple touch.

Nick felt himself relenting. He remembered the time he had burst into her apartment when she was living with Alex and Paige, the time he had accused Paige of being a gold-digger. He remembered the way Jordan had defended her friend, and how Paige had swayed his opinion of her so easily. Briefly, he wondered if he could again be mistaken about Jordan. But he remembered his father's words, spoken the day of Alex's funeral--words that had been chosen carefully, and said only when Marguerite was out of earshot.

"Don't trust her, Nick. She knows much more about Alex's death that she's telling us. And she's much more involved in all of these tragedies that we would have ever guessed."

As Nick watched her, he felt himself softening. Ridiculous, he told himself. I turn hot and cold. I can't seem to control my feelings for this woman. Dad's right. It doesn't matter how Joshua feels about her, or how Alex did, or even how I did. It doesn't matter how she can thaw my heart. She can't be trusted.

Luke watched Nick's face in the rearview mirror. Throughout his childhood he'd heard his mother complaining about men. Men's stubbornness. Men's pride. Men's impossible blindness to reality. Luke was beginning to wish he couldn't be categorized with the rest of the members of his gender. As he watched Nick, his thoughts echoed his mother's repeated cries. "Men!"

The four people riding in the limo were consumed with their own thoughts. Even Joshua sat quietly, merely content to have his mother at his side. Every few minutes he squeezed her hand, as if to reassure himself that she really sat beside him. Just as often, she leaned over to kiss the top of his head.

Nick felt his resolve weakening again. She really seems to love him, he thought as they pulled into the parking lot. But then he reminded himself that she hadn't even tried to take her son home with her.

As Nick watched Jordan and Joshua walking hand in hand towards the ticket booth, he tried to keep his hurt from clouding his judgment. Alex had trusted her, and Alex had always been a good judge of character. He had proven that, first with Lianna, and later with Paige. But Nick wasn't ready to relent. Jordan had married his brother only days after they had buried his wife. His mother's phone call to tell him the news had filled him with anger and grief such as he had never known.

"No," he muttered fiercely to himself, "she's not to be trusted."

Luke, hearing his words, whispered harshly, "I wouldn't bet on that if I were you."

Jordan felt Nick's eyes on her frequently throughout the day. She felt extremely self-conscious, and wished he hadn't come. But she was so overjoyed to be with Joshua again that she pushed aside her feelings of uneasiness, and just delighted in her son's pleasure.

Just as Joshua had predicted, Jordan took him on his favorite rides as often as he wanted. Several times, as Nick and Luke stood watching them on the rides, Luke felt impelled to speak in Jordan's defense. But, seeing the myriad of emotions that crossed the other man's face, he limited his conversation to brief remarks such as, "She sure loves that boy," as they circled overhead on the Dumbo ride. And, "I think she'd do anything for Josh," as Jordan bought her son the Goofy hat with the long ears and Goofy's long snout forming the bill of the hat. As the four of them emerged from Big Thunder Mountain, a pale Jordan walked next to Joshua, again holding his hand. This time Luke addressed her, his voice rising for Nick's benefit. "I'll bet you'd walk through fire for that kid, wouldn't you, Jory?"

Nick glowered at Luke, annoyed at his familiar use of her nickname. As Luke led her to a bench and brought her a drink of water, teasing her about being frightened of an amusement park ride, Nick wished that he was the one to help her and laugh with her.

Good Lord, I'm doing it again, he chastised himself. He didn't notice that this time, as he was lost in his thoughts, Jordan was watching him, incredible sadness filling her eyes. But Joshua saw it.

"What's wrong Mommy? Are you going to cry? We

won't take you on any more scary rides, okay? Luke will take me, right, Luke?"

"Sure, buddy, what's next?" Luke asked, holding his hand out to Joshua.

But Jordan wasn't sure which would be worse, waiting with Nick, or riding the scary rides. "Don't be silly, darling, I'll go with you."

"Don't you be silly, Jordan," Nick finally addressed her. "If you can't handle Big Thunder Mountain, you'll never survive Splash Mountain or Space Mountain. Let Luke take Joshua. The boy won't have any fun if he's worrying about you."

Joshua took her silence as assent, and quickly led Luke off to their next adventure. Nick and Jordan followed them without speaking.

Luke and Joshua went on several rides together. The crowds were sparse that day, the lines short, and they were able to get through quickly. But as Jordan stood with Nick, waiting for them to emerge from each ride, the time seemed interminable. She excused herself frequently to take pictures of Luke and Joshua, and stood several steps away from Nick whenever possible.

*

During the ride back to Jordan's house, Joshua fell asleep leaning into her lap, her hand caressing his head and shoulders. Jordan, no longer caring that Nick watched her, reveled in the nearness of her son. She leaned her head against the back of the seat and closed her eyes. She hadn't meant to sleep, but was startled when Nick placed his hand over hers.

"Jordan, we're here."

Luke quietly opened the door and waited for Jordan to climb out. Talk to her nicely. Tell her you enjoyed the day, he silently willed the man in the back seat. Come on, Wyndham, see her for what she is. But his will was not strong enough. Nick said nothing.

Jordan gently unbuckled Joshua's seatbelt and lifted him over her lap. She settled his car seat in carefully next to Nick, fastened him in securely, and leaned him against Nick's side. She softly ran her fingers over Joshua's cheek, kissed him on the forehead and climbed out quickly, before her tears could fall.

She took Luke's hand as he helped her from the car, gaining strength from his firm grasp. She looked back in at the sleeping child and then at Nick, unaware that the dome light in the car accentuated the glistening tears that now escaped. "Please, take care of him," she said softly, and turned to go.

Nick's eyes had been fastened on her all day, and

214

this was no exception. He watched as she walked toward the house, Luke's arm draped around her shoulders. Nick wondered what they talked about, and he wished mightily that Luke would remove his arm. She *is* going for the chauffeur now, he thought in disgust.

Jordan felt too weary to walk to her house. Her despair at once again saying good-bye to her son drained away her remaining energy. She felt Luke's arm go around her shoulder, and knew that he could feel her pain.

"You are a good friend, Luke. Alex was very right to trust you so much."

"He was right to trust you too, Jory." He turned her to face him as they stood at her door. "I couldn't save Alex. I still don't know exactly why he and Paige were killed, or who is responsible for their deaths, but please know that we're getting closer."

Jordan nodded at him slowly. "Thank you for your perseverance, Luke. I know that Alex and Paige are together again and that helps my hurt, but knowing that they had to suffer so much will always make me grieve. And knowing that Joshua and I might still be in danger scares me to death. I don't know anything, but someone thinks I do. I can't have my son live with me for fear of his safety, I can't sleep at night, and I have to have you help me steal away so I can be a real person again and have some joy. Help me, Luke," she said, her tears choking her. "I can't take much more. I need my son."

"Jordan, I'm going to fix this for you. I'm not sure how yet, but Alex asked me to take care of you, and I'm going to do it."

Jordan impulsively stood on tiptoe to kiss Luke's cheek. "Thank you, Luke. Thank you for being such a good friend to Joshua and to me. And thank you for today. It really was wonderful. I only hope it doesn't get you in trouble with Samuel."

Luke chuckled. "Don't you worry about that. Marguerite's got everything under control." With that, he turned to go. "Good night, Jordan."

Luke returned to the driver's seat of the car, hoping that the anger he could see on Nick's face was put there by jealousy this time. He knew that Nick had watched them as they stood on the porch, and much as he had enjoyed Jordan's kiss for its own merits, his enjoyment was heightened by the fact that Nick could see it. He glanced back at Nick several times on the drive back to the Wyndham estate. Yes, Jordan, he promised silently, I'm going to help you.

As they drove up to the house, Marguerite met them on the steps. She smiled as Nick carefully carried Joshua from the car. She walked toward him, pausing as Luke put his hand on Nick's arm. "Nick, I need to talk to you."

Nick, too angry to speak, muttered, "Tomorrow."

Marguerite reached for her grandson. "No, son. If Luke needs to talk to you, you go now." She didn't know all that Luke had to say to her son, but she could guess most of it, and she knew that the time had come. "I'll take Joshua and put him to bed. You go and have your talk."

Nick looked at his mother's determined face. It was a look he had learned not to argue with. She was small and she was easy-going, but when she looked like that, he didn't argue.

"All right, Luke, what is it?"

Luke led him around to the garage. "I'll put the limo away later. Right now, why don't you come up to my apartment with me? We have some important things to talk about."

Nick followed Luke up the stairs on the outside of the garage to the apartment overhead. He hadn't been in this apartment since he was a child, and he marveled at it once again. His mother had designed it with both comfort and beauty in mind. It was extremely large, as its expanse reached over the entire garage, which had been built to house a minimum of a dozen cars at one time.

The apartment was decorated in shades of green and brown, and Nick recognized his mother's touch everywhere. Luke followed Nick's gaze. "Your mother is a generous lady with her money and with her love. You know, she loves Jordan very much."

"I know that, but just why are you involved in any of this? Why did you take Alex's son to Disneyland? Why did you arrange for Jordan and me to go with you? And why," Nick's voice was growing louder, "why in the devil are you seeing Jordan?"

Luke was calm, liking what he saw in the man facing him. Jordan still loves him, he thought. Alex had been right. When Alex first told him about Jordan, he explained about their relationship. But Alex knew that at least a part of Jordan's heart still belonged to his brother. Luke asked him if that didn't bother him, now that she was his wife. Alex admitted to a bit of jealousy. "Sure, Luke. Every man would like to have his wife go ga-ga over him," he'd joked. But then he grew serious.

"She's a good woman, Luke. I do love her, just as she loves me. We have a bond that's been strengthened by the years and even by the tragedies. It was my brother who brought her heartache. The hurt he caused her was more than she should ever have had to experience, and now I'm pledging my life to making her happy.

"She saved me after Paige died. She brought me happiness again, and that's exactly what I'm going to do for her."

Several weeks before Alex was killed, he and Luke had spoken again. This time, Alex sensed the danger he was

216

in. He refused to tell Luke of the new evidence he had uncovered, telling him that he needed more information. "But, Luke, promise me that if anything happens to me, you'll take care of Jordan and Joshua."

Luke tried to reassure his friend, tried to tell him that they could all live happily ever after, but Alex refused to listen. "Just promise me," he demanded. Luke promised.

Now, as Luke stood before Nick, he resolved to take care of Jordan in the best way he knew how. And he knew that the best way to end her pain was to make this stubborn man before him open his heart to her again.

"Your brother asked me to take care of Jordan," he began, "and I will do everything in my power to keep my promises to him."

"Why would Alex ask you to do that?" Nick's suspicions were aroused immediately.

Luke didn't answer directly. "Nick, what do you know about the deaths of your brother and his wife?"

Nick was astonished. "They were murdered," he said bluntly. "Paige in a drive-by, Alex by poison. Why are you asking me about that?"

Luke walked over to the jacket he had lain on the back of the sofa when they entered the apartment. He reached into the pocket and pulled out a black leather wallet. Without speaking, he walked to Nick and flipped the wallet open, revealing the badge inside.

Nick gasped, "F.B.I? I think you'd better explain everything."

Luke began with the story of Suzanne's abduction. Nick had known small portions of the story, but had never been told about the terrors she had experienced, the horrors that had been inflicted upon her young body and mind. He sat in silence, his disgust and rage evident. Luke didn't stop. He told Nick that Paige and Suzanne had been working with both the local police and the Bureau when Paige was killed.

"We knew that it was a warning to the family not to dig any further, but we couldn't figure out who was sending the warning. We knew that Suzi must be close to making some discovery, and someone wanted to stop her. It worked. After Paige was killed, Suzi went into shock, blaming herself for her sister's death. She said that if she'd never involved Paige, she'd never have been killed.

"Jordan wasn't ready to give up. As soon as she learned about the secrets behind Suzanne's kidnapping, she became determined to find out if Paige's murder was connected. We believed that it was, and that made her more determined. But when Alex found out she was pregnant," he paused and looked at Nick, waiting for a reaction. Nick's glare was reaction enough for him, and he continued, "when he realized she was pregnant, he forbade her to have anything more to do with the investigation. She argued with him at first. Told him in no uncertain terms that Paige was her best friend, and she owed it to her to find out who had killed her and hurt Suzanne. But your brother was a stubborn man. He told her that she owed it to the baby to keep him safe." Luke chuckled. "Alex always knew it would be a boy.

"Anyway," Luke continued, "Alex promised her that he'd pick up where she was leaving off. We couldn't have him working with the Bureau officially, but we figured we could have him keep his eyes and ears open and report anything he learned back to us. We'd already lost one of our agents when his identity was discovered, and we were a little leery about sending anyone new in."

"So you sent in my brother, an untrained civilian?" Nick's voice was loud enough to wake the cat now sleeping on Luke's coat. She lifted her head, glared at Nick, stood, turned around a few times, and settled back in to sleep.

"We didn't exactly send him in. In fact, we warned him to stay out of it. When Jordan found out that he was trailing the pornographers, she begged him to stop. But, like I said, he was a stubborn man. He said he owed it to Paige. He started spreading the word in the streets that he was interested in buying some movies. The illegal, illicit kind. He never used his real name. Called himself Dexter Drexler. Yeah, I know, pretty goofy. He thought it sounded like a good pervert's name. I kind of thought it sounded like a cartoon character. But his reputation spread to the right places. Without our knowledge, he wormed his way into a local pornography ring. He kept detailed records of everything he learned, but he refused to turn it over to us. Said he didn't like what he was finding, and he needed more info. That's when we really cracked down on him. We told him that if he wanted to live to see the baby grow up, he'd better tell us what he knew. He said that some of the people had indicated that the top dog, financier of the organization was a man named Samuel Wyndham."

"Samuel Wyndham?" Nick stood up abruptly, slamming his fist on the table. This time the cat left the room, giving him a disdainful look.

"Sit down, Nick, and hear me out. We'd also been following up on that lead. Some of the jerks we'd arrested earlier had named him as the head honcho. Well, Alex never believed for a minute that your father would do anything like that. The man worships children, and we were a little suspect. We'd been given his name too easily. So, that's when I came up with the idea that I'd move in here. My boss wanted me to find the evidence to convict your father; your brother wanted me to clear his name.

"Here comes the hard part. Alex kept up with his investigations. Jordan kept begging him to stop. With Joshua to protect, she wanted to ensure that her family would be safe.

Nick, she received a note, before Joshua was even born, threatening his safety. That did it for Jordan. That's when they got the dogs. Alex told me that she even started sleeping with a baseball bat next to her bed."

Nick let out a sound that sounded strangely like a growl. The thought that someone had threatened that precious child filled him with fury. And when, he wondered, did I start to feel protective of Jordan? With a shake of his head, he realized that the feelings he felt for her so many years ago had never died. He had buried them behind walls of hurt and anger. He had argued with himself, trying to convince himself that he had always been wrong about her, that he couldn't trust her. But, despite his efforts, the love was still there.

"Go on, Luke, tell me the rest."

"I can't tell you much. We know that your father isn't involved in any of this. In fact, he doesn't really know much about it. I've been through all of his files, and most of the house...don't worry, he doesn't suspect a thing...and I've listened to his conversations with Marguerite. Your mother seems to trust me, and she tells me a lot of what's going on, too. She told me about the note Samuel got after Alex died. Your mother thought the note was preposterous, and she was furious with Samuel for paying attention to it. She said it was just some malicious person wanting to hurt them. But Samuel's grief has blinded him, and he's kept Jordan away from Joshua ever since. You didn't know that part, did you?" Luke asked, seeing the disbelief on Nick's face.

Nick shook his head and asked, "Why didn't Jordan fight him?"

"She was afraid for Joshua. She thought he'd be much safer here on the estate than in her house. And Samuel threatened to tell you the truth about Joshua."

"Tell me the truth about Joshua? What truth?"

Luke knew that Jordan would be furious for what he was about to do, but the time for truth had come, and he knew that Nick deserved to know. "Think, Nick. Count the months. When is Joshua's birthday?"

Nick sat in silence, then rested his forehead in his hands, his elbows resting on the table in front of him. "Is he mine?"

Luke, quietly, "Yes."

"I didn't know. I just assumed he was Alex's. They got married so quickly. How could I not have known?"

"Insecurity and jealousy often breed stupidity."

Nick, ignoring the insult, lifted his eyes to meet Luke's intense gaze. Surprise mingled with hurt as he asked, "Why didn't she tell me? Why did she marry Alex?"

"She tried to call you as soon as she found out she was pregnant. She wanted to fly over and tell you in person. But you weren't home, and your friend Lianna told her that you

219

had asked her to marry you." Now, accusing, "Just what was that woman doing answering your phone, telling people things like that? Was it true?"

"That's a long story, but I assure you it's an innocent one. I assume that Lianna did more than just intercept Jordan's phone call. Is she the one who took my mother's telegram when Paige died?" Luke nodded. "Yeah, I just found out about that. And the letter from Alex, when he wrote to give me my last chance or he would marry Jordan?" Now Luke looked confused.

"My mother told me that Jordan and Alex had both tried to be faithful to me. That they tried repeatedly to contact me, but that I returned their letters and even sent a rude telegram telling them to stay out of my life. I didn't believe it when my mother told me that. I figured that Alex and Jordan just told her that to pacify her. How could I have doubted my own brother?"

Luke had to push further. "How could you have doubted Jordan?"

"She'll never forgive me. I've treated her so horribly. And Lianna...I've allowed that woman to destroy my life, to turn me into some kind of cynical, self-doubting, angry monster. I almost stopped Alex and Paige's wedding because of her, I almost missed out on ever knowing Jordan, and now I find that she's kept me away from my own son and the woman I love. Yes," seeing Luke's questioning glance, "I do still love her. I think I always have, I just couldn't admit it. It hurt too much. But after today, after this," he waved at the table and at Luke, "I can't deny it any more. She'll never forgive me. I've been so cruel to her--I've hurt her so much."

"She'll forgive you. She loves you."

Nick's deep blue gaze met with Luke's brown. "Why are you telling me all this? You're in love with her."

Luke met his look securely and smiled. When he spoke, it was intentionally light. "That obvious, huh? Yeah, I'm beginning to think you're right. But what can I say? She's a one man woman."

Nick's jealousy returned. "How can you be sure that one man isn't you, or Alex?"

"Good grief, you are dense, aren't you? Alex said you were. Nick, Jordan and I are friends. That's all we'll ever be. Alex was very special to her. He was her friend, her best friend, and she loved him. But it wasn't the kind of love that starts fires. It was a love that came out of loyalty and loneliness and incredible pain. They saved each other, you know. Alex wanted to give up when Paige died. He wanted to die with her. He started drinking. He wouldn't eat. Jordan took him in and let him wallow in his self-pity for a while, but then she told him that enough was enough, and he had to come back to the land of the living.

"When he realized she was pregnant, he wanted to help her. He wanted to thank her for sticking by him through his worst moments. That's it, Nick. It was absolutely a marriage of love, love for a woman named Paige and a little boy named Joshua. They wanted, more than anything else, to give him a happy life."

"I know that. I guess, if I hadn't been such an idiot, I would have always known." Nick looked at his watch. Twenty minutes after midnight.

"Go," said Luke.

Nick nodded his head. "She's always been a night-owl. I'll just drive by her house. If the lights are on, I'll stop. If not..."

"You'd better stop anyway. Something tells me that she wouldn't mind waking up for what you have to tell her."

Nick stood up, rubbed his tired eyes with his hand, yet felt strangely rejuvenated. He held out his hand to shake Luke's. "Thank you, man. You're a good friend."

"I seem to be hearing that a lot lately. Hopefully, someday a lovely lady will think of me a bit differently."

Nick smiled, "No doubt about it, but if I have anything to say about it, it's not going to be Jordan."

CHAPTER FOURTEEN

And where two raging fires meet together,
They do consume the thing that feeds their fury.
-Taming of the Shrew

Jordan awoke to the sound of the dogs barking frantically in the back yard, and her neighbor pounding on her front door.

"Jordan, wake up. Fire, Jordan, fire." She could hear Phillip's voice growing more frantic as his pounding increased its intensity, and his yelling grew louder. "For God's sake, Jordan. Wake up. Get out."

She suddenly became aware of the smoke which rapidly filled her room. She grabbed the dressing gown which she had thrown on the foot of her bed and ran to the bathroom, got a washcloth, and wet it in her sink. Already beginning to cough, she put the cloth over her nose and mouth and ran to the door of her bedroom. She felt the wood and was relieved to find that it was not yet hot. She pulled the door open and found that the hallway was even more smoky than her room. With her eyes burning, Jordan made her way down the hall to the stairs. As she descended the stairway, she saw flames in her office and the kitchen, but she could reach the front door safely. She reached for the key, swiftly inserted it in the dead-bolt, and unlocked the door. She pulled it open with a jerk and felt Phillip grab her shoulders and pull her out. He took her to the edge of the lawn.

"Thank God! You're all right. I was so frightened when you didn't come. The fire fighters should be here any second. Pauline called them as soon as she saw the smoke."

As he was speaking, all Jordan could think about was Joshua. She was so grateful that he wasn't here. Joshua must be safe. Her mind raced. Joshua. Video tapes. Oh, no. I can't lose all of the videos.

She looked out toward the street, but still the fire department had not arrived. "The videos of Joshua - they can't burn."

Before Phillip or Pauline could stop her, she ran toward the house.

"Jordan, no, stop!" But she had already entered the burning building.

Jordan had forgotten her damp cloth and she felt the heat on her face, burning hotter as she ran toward the fire. Her mind raced as she pushed herself onward.

"I can't lose my negatives and videos. I could never replace all those wonderful memories of his life." She faltered as the heat intensified. "Too hot. Can't do it." But the realization that she had never made copies and put the originals in a safety deposit box kept her going. "I have to save them."

Jordan could barely breathe or see, but she managed to reach the cabinet where her videos and pictures were stored. The flames flew across the room as she emptied the contents of a nearby magazine rack and tossed all of the videos and negative packages into it. The fire was only inches away as she turned to flee, her treasures locked in her arms.

Outside a car pulled up. Nick threw himself out and tore across the lawn. "Jordan, Jordan," he screamed.

Pauline ran toward him, tears streaming down her face. "She went back in to get Joshua's baby pictures. She's been in there too long."

Nick barely heard her as he ran toward the house.

The oxygen was quickly consumed by the fire, leaving little for Jordan's struggling lungs. She could no longer keep her eyes open for any length of time, and she almost lost consciousness by the time she reached the front door. She automatically reached to pull it open, but this time she was unable to find the knob. The flames were chasing across the entryway, heading directly for her. Desperation revived her enough to get the door open. She stumbled through the door, holding the magazine basket out to Nick.

"Couldn't let 'em burn," her voice rasped.

As she fell, he caught her in his arms, not even noticing the contents of the basket as they spilled on the ground around them. He carried her to the waiting ambulance as the firefighters leapt off their truck and gathered their equipment. An emergency medical technician carefully placed an oxygen mask over Jordan's face as Nick lay her on the stretcher. He held her hand firmly in his own while the paramedic checked her over for possible burns. He pulled singed hair away from her face. "We could've made more videos, baby. We couldn't have replaced you." But Jordan couldn't hear his words.

The firefighters worked zealously, and finally succeeded in extinguishing the fire as Jordan regained consciousness. She turned to look at the hands grasping hers. Then she looked up at the face, hovering close to her own. "Nick."

Nick felt his heart leap in his chest and said a quick silent prayer, thanking God for the safety of this lady who had scared him to death only a short while ago. Oh, God, I've been such an idiot. I never want to lose her again, he prayed silently. He looked at Jordan, squeezed her hand and told her, "Don't talk. Just rest. Everything's under control."

Jordan wondered at the intensity of his gaze, and interpreted it as meaning that her house must have been completely destroyed. She struggled to sit up, looked at the house in despair and sank back onto the stretcher. The paramedic had just finished calling her vital statistics into the hospital and was preparing to take her to the emergency room.

Jordan's throat hurt and she found it very hard to talk, but she was insistent, "No. I don't like hospitals. I'm fine."

"You're not fine, and if this nice lady thinks that you should go to the hospital, then that's where you'll go." Nick's voice had a no-nonsense tone to it.

"Forget it." Jordan started to rise. "That's my house and I want to know what's going on."

"Miss, please. I'll lose my job."

"I'm not going."

Nick reassured the paramedic. "I'll take her myself, and don't worry about your job. I'll explain to your supervisor how stubborn she is. Ouch!" The "she" he was speaking of had just pinched his arm.

"Nick, help me up. I've got to talk to the fire chief."

Nick grinned at the paramedic, shrugged his shoulders and did as commanded.

The fire chief walked toward them. "Are you all right? Good," in response to her nod. "Lady, I've seen a lot of people run back into burning buildings for a lot of things--furs, jewels, paintings, pets--but I've never seen anyone run back in for baby pictures."

"Those are my most precious possessions," she coughed at him.

"I suppose my wife would agree with you, but having seen several charred bodies pulled out of various fires, I have to say that what you did was extremely foolish. I just thank God you weren't killed."

Jordan put her hand to her throat, wondering if it would ever stop burning. "I know. It's just that these mean everything to me." Then, looking around, "What happened to them? Didn't I get them out after all?"

Pauline, who had been hovering nearby, walked over and placed the recently refilled basket at Jordan's side. "You spilled them, dear, when you came out of the house. Phillip didn't want the firefighters to trample them, so he ran over and gathered them up quickly. I think he got all of them, but it was too hot for him to stay there for long."

"Oh, Pauline, bless both of you. If it hadn't been for you, I wouldn't have had a chance. I don't understand why the fire alarms didn't work." Jordan's speech was halted by her coughing, and she didn't see the grateful look that Nick bestowed upon Pauline. She turned back to the fire chief. "What can you tell me about this?"

"I can't tell you everything right now. We'll have to spend some time inside the house to determine all the facts. But, judging by what I've seen, my educated guess is this...it's definitely arson. You have any enemies?"

224

Jordan felt her heart stop beating. Am I the next target? she wondered. She took a few careful, painful deep breaths and tried to make light of the situation. "I suppose someone might not have liked the house I designed for them. Why do you ask?"

"I'd say this fire was probably meant to scare you, not kill you." Jordan shivered. Nick's jaw tightened as he put his arm around her shoulders. The fire chief continued, "They used some kind of fluid to start the fire, but it looks like they only sprayed it in your office. That's where the fire started, and since it's at the opposite end of the house from your bedroom, I don't think you were the target. Only three rooms burned, but you've got smoke damage throughout the rest of the house. I can't say for sure what ignitable fluid was used. Probably gas. If it were rare boat diesel or something, we'd have a good clue, but anyone can get gasoline. We won't know for sure, though, until the lab does its check on the draperies that didn't completely burn. Then we'll dust the floors and walls and everything else for fingerprints and footprints, to look for other clues."

"Footprints?" Nick asked.

"Yeah, it's a similar process to dusting for fingerprints. You'd be surprised what we can find on a floor when the naked eyes say nothing's been there. Then, if we find a clear print, we'll run a computer check on the make of the shoe. It's just one more way to help us identify whoever did this to you."

As he spoke, one of the firefighters walked toward them. "You're not going to believe this one. The batteries are all missing from her smoke alarms. Somebody sure doesn't like you, lady."

The fire chief turned back to Jordan questioningly. "Looks like I was wrong. These people meant business."

Jordan, her thoughts racing, said nothing. She started coughing again, and this time Nick insisted that it was time to go to the hospital.

"I was a fool to let you stay here so long. I should have let that paramedic haul you in right away." This time, Jordan didn't disagree.

*

As soon as Jordan had been checked over thoroughly by the emergency room doctor, she asked to be taken home. Nick, who hadn't left her side, said, "I have a better idea. Rather than return you to a dismal sight at home where your lungs will be bombarded by the remaining smoke, I'm taking you someplace safe, where I can keep an eye on you."

The nurse who had brought Jordan out of the

225

examining room handed her the final papers to sign, and released her into Nick's care. "Your throat and chest may hurt for a while, but you'll live." She patted Jordan's shoulder and told her to go get some much-needed rest.

Jordan promised that she would, repeating her request to be taken home. "Nick, I know that my house is in bad shape. But you heard what the fire chief said. Only three rooms burned. My bedroom is fine. And really, right now that's the only room I care about."

"Look, I know I didn't say anything when the chief asked you about your enemies, and you waved away the suggestion quite expertly, but I don't think you took his question as lightly as you seemed to. I want you safe. You're going home with me."

"Oh, no, I'm not. I want to be in my house, in my bed. I certainly don't want you mother-henning me, for whatever reason. And I don't want to deal with your father. Just take me home. I can take care of myself."

"Jordan, look, I'm only beginning to understand a great deal of what's been going on here in the past few years. I do know that two people I loved very much are dead, and I suspect that you're right in the middle of things. I don't want you to be the next victim. Please, just humor me. Come home with me. Joshua will be thrilled to have you there. Let me deal with my father."

At the mention of her son's name, Jordan closed her eyes and felt her heart spring into her aching throat. When she answered, she spoke quietly. "I miss him so much. Yes, it would be nice to be able to sleep without keeping one eye open. And it would be glorious to spend some time with Joshua." She turned to Nick and placed her hand on his. "All right, kind sir. Take me to your castle."

Nick drove slowly through the sleepy streets. Early commuters were beginning to emerge from their homes as the sun's tentacles reached into the sky. Jordan was quiet throughout the drive, and only spoke once as they were entering the Wyndham house. "Fire is such a beautiful thing. I think of all the evenings you and I sat in front of the fire, enjoying its glorious flames. But tonight the power of it was unleashed on me. It wasn't beautiful any more. Just frightening."

Nick took her into the house, sounds already beginning to emerge from the kitchen. He put his finger to his lips and whispered, "If we don't let anyone know we're here, we'll have a better chance of getting some sleep."

He took her into Alex's old room, gently steered her toward the bed, and sat her down on its edge. She sleepily lifted her feet up to untie the shoes that one of the firefighters had thoughtfully rescued for her. She was too tired to worry about changing out of the jeans and t-shirt that he had also provided for her several hours earlier. Nick watched her, and as she stopped mid-shoelace to yawn, he finished the task for her. She wondered at his kindness after the years of antagonism, but was too tired to ask questions. Maybe he just didn't want Joshua's mother to get barbecued, she thought.

Nick pushed her gently back onto the pillows, and pulled an afghan up to cover her. She was asleep before it reached her shoulders. She stirred about an hour later and thought that she saw Nick sleeping in the chair next to the bed, but decided that it must be wishful thinking, and she closed her eyes again.

*

A few hours later, Nick awoke, stretched out of the uncomfortable position the chair had inflicted on him, and stood up. He watched Jordan for a few moments, wondering how he could have misjudged her so completely. He wondered how he could ever explain the past pain-filled years to her, how he could let her know that he now knew the truth about their son. He wanted to lean over and kiss her, but was afraid to wake her. If he admitted the truth to himself, he really wanted to gather her into his arms and cry out all of his self-hate and remorse to her, but he knew this wasn't the time. He needed to tread carefully with her, to prove himself worthy, and "Please, God," he prayed, make her love him again.

*

Around noon, Nick revealed a few of the details of the previous evening's events to his parents. He found Noreen, who was in the garden watching Joshua play with Rasputin. He briefly explained everything to her, and went over to stand at his son's side.

Joshua looked up at the tall man next to him. His delight was evident as he put his hand in that of his father. "Hi, Uncle Nick," he said joyfully. "Did you see Raspy and me playing?"

Nick felt as if a knife were twisting in his heart. How could he have let the years of silence go on? He regretted the precious moments he'd missed in Joshua's life. I would have read to you and sung to you when you were still in the womb, Nick thought. I would have been there to greet you in the delivery room. I would have cherished you more than the earth's most precious jewels.

"Yes, Josh," he answered the smiling boy. "I saw you playing. And now, if you'll tell Raspy good-bye, I have a surprise waiting for you in your Daddy's old bedroom." It hurt to continue the charade, but the explanations could come later. For now, the relationship must be strengthened between

227

himself and this small, beautiful boy.

Joshua ran over and kissed Rasputin on the nose. "Bye, Raspy. Thanks for playin'." He returned to Nick, placed his hand in the larger one that was held out for him, and asked, "What's my surprise?"

"Let's go see. I promise that it's something you'll like. We have to go very quietly."

They tiptoed exaggeratedly up the stairs, down the hall, and into the doorway of the darkened room. It took Joshua a few moments to see the shape under the afghan, but as soon as he saw her, he raced forward.

"Mommy," he squealed and ran across the room, throwing himself on the sleeping form.

"Oh, Joshua," she said into his hair, her arms enfolding him. "My sweet baby."

"I'm not a baby," he said defensively, then snuggled in comfortably.

Mother and child said nothing else for the next few minutes. They were contented to hug and kiss one another. Nick, watching from the doorway, saw the tears stealing down Jordan's cheeks. He felt them burning in his own eyes and retreated.

Nick drove to Jordan's house, ostensibly to pick up extra clothes and items she might need over the next several days. In reality, he wanted to see for himself just what had been done to the once-beautiful house that she had built for Paige and Alex.

He found inspectors hard at work, doing precisely what the fire chief had explained the night before. They greeted him but continued with their work, more urgent things on their minds. Nick looked around, careful to stay out of their way and to keep out of any of the areas they warned him away from.

He walked up the stairs, the acrid odor of last night's fire lingering persistently in the air. He found his way to Jordan's bedroom, looking around at her old favorites which had once been in the beach condo. The dresser was an antique, the oak well preserved, but marred by years of use. Nick had asked her once why she didn't have it refinished, and she said that she would do it herself when she had the time. As he looked at it now, he smiled, realizing that she must have never found the necessary time.

Nick walked over to the closet, opened the door and pulled a small suitcase off the top shelf. He then returned to the dresser to pack some of her necessities. As his hand reached for the top drawer, his eyes scanned the contents of the top of the dresser and he reached, instead, for a picture of Alex and Jordan that had obviously been taken on their wedding day. Alex was dressed in a blue suit, which made his eyes seem darker.

228

"I miss you, brother," Nick whispered.

His eyes left his brother's face and traveled on to Jordan's. Though there was a smile on her face, her eyes looked sad as if she had faced all the sorrow she could possibly bear. Nick noticed the slight bulge at her tummy, and once again he felt his heartstrings being pulled. "My son," he said softly. "Jordan, you were probably beautiful even in your ninth month. I wish I had been there for you. Thank you, Alex, for being there for her when my stupidity kept me away."

He turned the frame in his hand, wondering if he should pack it in the suitcase for Jordan. As he turned it, he noticed words engraved on the back of the silver frame. "Jordan," the words read, "We *will* have joy again. All my love, Alex."

Nick placed the picture back on the dresser. "Now it's my turn to tell her that." He looked at the other pictures displayed next to the first one. There was a picture of a newborn Joshua, wearing a t-shirt that read, "If you think I'm cute, you should see my mommy."

There were other pictures that had probably been taken on each of his successive birthdays. There were also pictures of Jordan and Paige as children, as well as Alex and Nick when they were quite young.

Then Nick's eyes fell upon something that made them overflow with the tears that had been threatening to come since last night's fire. There, next to a beautiful picture of Joshua, was the small porcelain Lilliput English Cottage that he had given Jordan years earlier. He picked the cottage up in his hands, cradling it gently. As he looked at it, he turned it over and saw that his plaque was still attached to the bottom.

"Oh, Jordan. I can't believe you kept this. It may not be an English cottage, but I will keep this promise. We will have our own home."

Nick walked back and sat on the foot of the bed, deep in thought. He didn't stir until he heard the fire marshal's footsteps in the hallway. He answered the knock on the bedroom door and placed the cottage back in place.

"Excuse me, sir. I didn't mean to disturb you. I just wanted to let you know that we've finished downstairs. We'll be leaving now, but if you could tell us where to reach Ms. Blake, we'll need to talk with her."

"Yes, of course." Nick gave him the phone number of the Wyndham estate, packed up Jordan's clothes and left the house, still consumed by his thoughts.

*

Jordan was walking through the gardens with Joshua when she saw Marguerite and Samuel approaching her.

"Darling, why don't you go swing on Grandma's swing while I talk to them a little bit?"

Joshua ran towards the swing, stopping halfway there to turn and wave back at his mother. She blew him a kiss and turned to face her mother and father-in-law. Marguerite pulled her into an embrace.

"We heard what happened, Jordan. I'm so glad you weren't harmed. Thank God your neighbors saw the smoke."

"Yes," Jordan said, her eyes on Samuel. "I'll always be grateful for them, and for the dogs."

"Where are the dogs? Are they all right?"

"They're fine. Phillip and Pauline are keeping them until I get home."

"Jordan." Samuel finally spoke. He reached out his arm and touched her lightly on the shoulder. "This is very difficult for me. You know how much I loved my son, and Joshua. Please understand that I only kept you away from Joshua because I thought that note might be true."

"I know that, Samuel. And I don't blame you. In fact, I appreciated your protection of Joshua."

"I will always protect him, Jordan. But I'm sorry I treated you so badly. We're a family of stubborn men. I should never have believed an anonymous note over you. I guess the possibility that it might be true frightened me, and I couldn't take any risks."

Jordan reached out, grasping Samuel's hand in her own. "We've all been frightened. I just pray that this will all be over soon."

*

Jordan, Joshua and Nick spent a quiet day together. They explained to Joshua that there had been an accident at his house the night before, that part of it had been burned in a fire, and so they would all be staying at Grandpa and Grandma's for a while longer.

"Even Mommy?"

"Especially your Mommy."

At one point in the late afternoon, as Jordan and Nick sat on a bench near the pond, watching Joshua feed the ducks, Jordan ventured a question that had been plaguing her since she was in the emergency room the night before. "Nick, why were you at my house last night?"

Nick wasn't ready to tell her about his discussion with Luke. He wanted to have her all to himself, someplace quiet and free of any possible interruptions, and sometime when she wouldn't have any distraction. Sometime when she could face the future with him.

"Can I tell you about it another time? Let's just chalk

it up to pure luck and Luke's orders."

Jordan was not generally one to be put off, but before she could question him further she heard Joshua's laughter. "Mommy, Uncle Nick, did you see her? The mommy duck took the bread right out of my fingers and she didn't even bite me."

The two adults turned their attention away from one another and went to join the excited youngster. The talk would have to wait.

CHAPTER FIFTEEN

Thou speak'st like him's untutor'd to repeat;
Who makes the fairest show means most deceit.
-Pericles

Sometime in the night, Derek Frank's telephone rang. Reaching past the girl in his bed, he grabbed the receiver.

"Hello?"

"A fire? You idiot. You could have killed her. I told you to keep her occupied. To scare her. To try to find the notes. I told you specifically not to harm her."

"I know. But I couldn't find the notes, and she doesn't scare easy. She and that housekeeper of hers hardly ever leave the house. I couldn't get in to get a good look around. Besides, I thought she probably had the notes hidden in her office somewhere. I figured if we couldn't find them, we'd just burn them up."

"You could have killed her," the caller repeated.

"Not with those dogs of hers. They'd smell smoke a mile away."

"What about the fire alarms? Why did you take the batteries out?"

"Just wanted her to know you mean business, and she'd better not cause you any more problems. You said to scare her, and I think this did it."

"One more mistake, Derek, and you're dinner for the rats. Do you understand me?"

*

Early the next morning, as Jordan ate her breakfast with Joshua on one side of her and Nick on the other, Noreen came into the dining room, a portable telephone in her hand.

"You have a phone call, Ms. Blake. It's Nancy."

"Hello, Nancy. When did you get back? I wasn't expecting you for another week."

"I just got back this morning, Jordan. I'm calling you from the house. Pauline saw me drive up this morning, and she came in here with me. She told me what happened. Are you and Joshua all right?"

"Yes, I'm fine. Joshua's been staying here with his grandparents since the funeral, so he was in no danger. But, Nancy, I'd feel better if you didn't stay there yet. Someone's been looking for Alex's notes, and if they didn't find them last night, they may try again."

"Don't worry about me. Pauline invited me to stay

232

over at their place. She told me this place is jinxed, and I'm not to spend even one night here. But that's not why I called. Just after we came in here, you got a phone call from a man named Greg Whitby. He said that he's got a female Akita, and he wants to breed her with Tatsu. He said that he'd made all the arrangements with Alex."

"Why is he calling now?"

"Apparently he was waiting for his dog to reach two years before breeding her. He said he explained all that to Alex. Anyway, he wants to talk to you. I've got his number, if you'd like to call him."

Jordan thought for a moment. Alex had always been very careful in selecting possible mothers for Tatsu's puppies. Was this a reputable breeder? Would he care for the mother and the puppies? Did he have clean, well-cared-for facilities with all the necessities? Alex would have known what to look for. Jordan did not.

"I'll have to come home and look through Alex's records, Nancy. I'd like to see if he made any records of his agreement with this man, and if he didn't, I need to know what kinds of questions to ask.

"I'll be home in about an hour. Is that soon enough?"

Making her apologies to Joshua, she promised that she would be back as soon as possible. Noreen deftly diverted Joshua's attention, inviting him to the kitchen to help her make chocolate chip cookies.

Nick walked Jordan to the garage. Handing her the keys to his car, he said, "Are you sure you don't want me to come with you? You haven't been there since the fire. Maybe you could use some moral support."

"Nick, I don't want to seem ungrateful, but why exactly are you being so nice to me?"

Nick stopped walking, his hand on Jordan's arm, pulling her to a stop beside him. Grasping her shoulders in his hands, he turned her toward him.

"Just let me go with you. I promise I won't pick any fights. I won't even be rude to you. Not any more, okay?"

Unable to meet his gaze, Jordan looked past him toward the house. "Yes, you can come with me. I know that with the damage from the fire, smoke and water, it's not going to be a pleasant sight. Maybe you can help me figure out what to do about all of it."

They were halfway to Jordan's house when she started whispering to herself. "The dogs' files. That's it. I never looked in the dogs' files."

"What are you talking about?"

"Nick," suddenly excited, "that's it. Alex's notes that I've been looking for. They've got to be in the dogs' files. Did you know that Alex was playing detective? He tried to keep me from finding out most of what he was doing. But according to

Ed Colson and Luke," she stopped suddenly, looking guilty.

"It's all right, Jordan. Luke explained to me why he's working for my parents. Now, according to Ed Colson and Luke, what?"

"They said that Alex was keeping files on his own investigation. They were really angry with him for getting so involved, and they threatened to subpoena his records. But Alex was adamant. He told them that they'd have to wait until he was ready. Luke told me that Alex threatened to destroy everything if they tried to get the notes before he was ready." Jordan paused, "Your brother was a stubborn man sometimes."

"Sometimes? I think we first noticed that when he was a very sick newborn and he refused to die. And when he fought me tooth and nail over Lianna. And when he insisted that he play football in high school. And when he changed his name in med school. And when he married Paige. And, I suspect, when he married you. Yes, I'd say he was stubborn. Now, what about the dogs' files?"

"I started looking for Alex's notes just after he died. I couldn't find them in any of the places I looked. Not in any of the good hiding places around the house, not with his will, not in his clothes. I didn't have a clue where to look. But now it makes sense. If Alex wanted me to find them, he would have put them in a place I would only see if he were gone.

"Don't you see, Nick? When I wanted to get watchdogs, it was Alex who insisted on Akitas. He wanted purebreds that he could breed. It was very important to him that the dogs be of the highest quality. He kept immaculate records on them. I never thought to look in that file."

They pulled up in front of the house, Jordan barely waiting for the car to stop before she jumped out. Nick followed her up the steps. The front door was locked, so he waited while she dug in her purse for the keys, her impatience making her fingers clumsy.

He reached for her, holding her wrists in his firm grasp. "Relax, Jordan. We'll find the papers."

As they entered the house, Jordan looked around in despair. The damage to her home was worse than she had imagined. She called for Nancy. Receiving no response she explained, "She's probably already gone next door. She said she was going to stay with Phillip and Pauline."

Jordan led Nick up the stairs toward Alex's study. The room had originally been Alex's bedroom. Now it was furnished as an office, the walls lined with bookshelves. The shelves were filled with medical journals and a dozen years' worth of back issues of medical magazines. Two filing cabinets stood near the window, filled with his many years in school, as well as his personal documents.

Jordan was familiar with all of it. "When Ed and

234

Luke told me about the notes, I went through all of this. I checked behind and beneath each one of those books. I pulled them down one by one, holding them by the covers, upside down and shaking them. All that fell out were notes he'd written to himself; reminders to compare certain pages with those in other books, or to make notations in various patients' medical files. There were even occasional notes that had been passed back and forth in class between Paige and Alex. I saved them, if you'd like to look at them. I promise they'll put a smile on your face."

Nick looked at her wonderingly. A widow carefully saved love notes from her husband to his first wife? "Weren't you ever jealous of them?"

Jordan looked surprised. "Of course not. They were the most perfect couple in the world. I rejoiced over their love." She paused as her eyes misted. "When I read their notes, they take me back to happier times. Times when I still had them in my life.

"Come on," she changed the subject quickly, "let's find his notes." As she walked towards the filing cabinets, she explained. "I thought I'd find them in here, but I was on the wrong track. I thought he'd put them with his will. That way I'd find them immediately. But that's too obvious. If I thought of that, so would anyone else who looked for them. Alex must have known that.

"I've been through all of these drawers, rifling past each file. I read all the labels, looking for some clues to lead me to his notes. I finally realize that he'd never have put them in with his medical files. He'd know that if anything happened to him, many of those would be given to the hospital and to other medical students.

"The one file I'd have to keep would be this one." She smiled as she pulled it from the bottom drawer of the first filing cabinet. "When my house was searched, the intruders even went through this room. Books were on the floor, these drawers were left standing open. But who would ever think of looking in with pets' health records and Kennel Club papers?"

Jordan, holding the file in one hand, swiftly sifted through the papers with the other. "They're here," she said softly.

Relief washed over her and she sank into the chair by Alex's desk. Resting her elbow on the arm of the chair, she cupped her chin in her hand.

"I found them. After all this, I found them."

Nick knelt beside her chair, his fingers gently pulling the hair away from her face. "We need to take them to Luke, Jordan."

"I know, I just need a minute. Joshua and I were threatened for these notes. Our house was torn apart and then burned because of them. Please, let me read through them. I have to know what he knew. I have to know if this is why they killed him." Jordan looked calm, but she felt as if her stomach were turning flip-flops.

Nick pulled a chair across the room, stopping next to Jordan's. "All right. Luke's waited for them this long. A little bit longer won't hurt. I'll help you."

Jordan nodded, holding the file open so he could see the pages inside. Alex's notes began with Paige's sudden departure from Geneva, and his frantic search for her.

Jordan and Nick read through the notes, and Jordan felt herself growing nauseous as she read Suzanne's account of her abduction and molestation. Being reminded anew of the horrors the girl had experienced brought fresh grief.

Nick's face grew pale as he read his brother's carefully documented pages. "I didn't know about all of this," he explained.

"It still makes me sick, when I think about it. Here," Jordan said, handing Nick the page in her hand. "I can't read any more. I'm going to look further into the file."

They sat in silence, each locked in their thoughts and memories. Jordan began on the next page, coming to the end of Alex's account of Suzanne's narrative. She read of Suzanne's dream, near the end of her captivity, that a man had entered the room, caressed her hair, and spoke soothingly to her. When Jordan read the words, "Hush, little one," she exhaled quickly, a visible shiver racking her shoulders, the familiarity of the scene teasing at her subconscious.

"Jordan, what's wrong? What did you find?"

"Nothing, really. It's just something that Suzanne dreamed. It seems to be pulling at something in the back of my brain."

Jordan continued reading, growing angry as she read Alex's description of his day in the storefront in Pacoima. "I had no idea he was actually meeting with these people. I thought he was just following them and asking about them. How could he have been so foolish?"

She kept reading. She read of Alex's many conversations with Ed Colson and Luke Griffin. Alex described urging his parents to hire Luke, and subsequent meetings between himself and the F.B.I. agent posing as a chauffeur.

As Jordan neared the end of the file, her despair enveloped her. There's nothing in here, she thought. Nothing. As she turned to the last page, her heart began to beat faster, and then felt as if it had stopped altogether. "No," she whispered hoarsely, "it can't be." She grabbed the last page in her hand, abruptly standing, the remainder of the file falling to the floor at her feet.

"What is it?" Nick stood, ignoring the falling papers.

Jordan didn't answer, and she was out the door of the room before Nick began to follow her.

236

"Jordan," he called, racing down the stairs behind her. "Tell me what's going on."

"I have to go to Van Nuys."

"Why? What's on that page? Jordan, let me see it."

But Jordan was out the front door, clutching her car keys in her hand.

"Wait, Jordan, I'm coming with you."

"No, just wait for me here. I'll be back."

"I don't know what's written on that paper, but if it's taking you to Van Nuys, then I'm coming, too."

Jordan looked at him menacingly as she climbed into her Jeep. "Just stay here."

"I can be just as stubborn as you can. If you won't take me with you, I'll follow you."

Reluctantly, pensively, she said, "Get in."

Jordan drove quickly, oblivious to the angry drivers she passed. She still clutched the now wrinkled page in her left hand, wrapping it around the steering wheel.

Nick thought to ask for it, but her quiet agony stopped him.

As Jordan exited the freeway and drove toward the Blake and Kendell homes, Nick's patience ran out.

"Where are we going, Jordan?" he asked quietly.

"Home."

Nick knew there must be some logical explanation for her sudden flight home, but she didn't look like she would be willing to give it to him.

As Jordan pulled into her parents' driveway, slamming on the brakes to keep from hitting her father's car, her left hand was already reaching for the door handle.

Nick grabbed her right hand, pulling her back into the Jeep.

"Why are we here, Jordan? I think you should tell me."

"I can't." She choked on the words, tears slipping, unheeded down her cheeks.

Nick refused to let go of her hand. "Tell me," he demanded.

Jordan pulled her hand fiercely away from his, jumping to the pavement.

"Jordan." His voice was firm, insistent.

Unable to face him, straining to say the words, Jordan whispered, "It's my father," and she turned to flee into the house.

Jordan pushed passed a surprised Hendricks. "Where's my father?"

Shaken, Hendricks answered, "In his den, Jordan."

Jordan turned to look up at Nick, both hands pushing on his chest. "Please, let me do this alone. Please."

He nodded his assent, and Jordan ran into her

father's private haven. The beauty and glorious memories of this house, this room, this man filled her with misery and uncertainty.

As she looked at his familiar, beloved face, everything that she had planned to say got lost in her grief and her shock. She faced her father, her courage wavering as she looked at this man who meant everything to her world of reality.

This can't be true, she told herself. Dear God, please don't let it be true. But as she recalled the words written on the page in her hand, her rage took control.

Her father closed the book he had been reading and spoke as if everything were as it always had been. As if Paige and Alex were still here and in love. As if no one had ever tried to frame Samuel or tried to keep her away from her son. As if she herself had never been threatened, her house had never burned, and Mr. Smith's home hadn't been sabotaged.

"Hello, sweetheart. This is a wonderful surprise. Does your mother know you're coming today? She just left for the store."

In the battle between rage and sorrow, anger won out with the intensity of an impending hurricane. "How could you?"

The expression on her father's face barely changed. She thought, for a fleeting moment, that she saw fear, but it was gone as quickly as it had appeared. "You know. How did you find out?"

Jordan closed her eyes and sank into the chair behind her. She felt as if she'd been hit in the stomach. "Then it is true. I'd hoped you wouldn't know what I was talking about. I hoped it was all some horrible mistake."

"I suppose Suzi told you."

"Suzi?" Jordan was bewildered. Was it possible that the girl knew that Emerson Blake was involved with the pornography ring?

"Not Suzi? I thought that perhaps she'd heard me when I went to see her at the warehouse. I thought she was sleeping, but she stirred when I spoke to her."

Jordan clasped her hand over her mouth, realization finally coming to her. "'Hush, little one'. You were there with her. She didn't dream the words. You said them. It sounded familiar because that's what you used to say to me when I was little and had a nightmare. I heard you say it to Suzi one night when the Kendells were away and she stayed here with us. She was afraid, and you held her on your lap and soothed her. And when she was in that horrible place, you were right there in the room with her, and you left her there."

"I told them to let her go. She got home, didn't she? So, she's not the one who told you? Then I suppose it was Alex." Seeing the crumpled paper in her hand, Emerson wiped his handkerchief across his brow. "You found the notes.

Where were they? I had people search everywhere."

"Just how deeply are you involved in all of this, Dad?" Her hope was wavering. She knew, deep in her heart, that he had to be behind it all. That could be the only explanation for Alex's last entry in the file.

"Dear Jordan, I know now that you will have to read these notes. I am so sorry. I will keep it from you as long as I can. And I will stand beside you through what I know will be the most difficult thing you've ever faced.

"I'm so sorry, my darling, but you must know. I've been getting closer and closer to the pornography ring. I've followed them and even staked out their newest operation. I've seen many men enter and exit the building. But today, I saw someone new. Someone I'd never seen with them before.

"Suddenly it all makes sense. Someone recognized Suzanne, and she was released. The man who had kidnapped her was brutally murdered, as if someone wanted revenge. The pornographers always seemed to be ahead of us. Every time we knew something, they knew. When Suzanne and Paige wanted to work with the F.B.I., they knew, and even before she could really do anything, Paige was killed. They knew when you contacted Sandra Lee Chen, and they knew how to find her. And yet, Ed assured me that no one ever followed us around except his own people.

"They knew it all, and I could never figure out why. Now, at last, I understand. I am sorry, Jordan. I wish you would never have to know. I wish that I could make your world happy for you. That somehow you could have a perfect life. But it cannot be. It's inevitable that you will find out.

"Jordan, I sat outside their warehouse for days on end. You wondered why I didn't go to work, and why I came home late. I knew you were worried about me, so I couldn't tell you. But today, the wait paid off. At least, I guess it did. You see, I finally know who is the head of this whole organization. I'm sorry, love, but the man I saw at the warehouse today was your father.

"Please forgive me, Jordan. I would do anything to keep you from knowing this. But I know you would agree with me...the truth must be told now. He must be stopped."

The date on this final entry was the day Alex was murdered. The time written at the top of the page indicated that he had written it just prior to going to the park for his run.

Grasping the page firmly, Jordan waited for her father's answer.

"All the way, Jordan. I'm in as far as anyone can be. But you'll never be able to prove it. This conversation won't help you to pin anything on me. It would be your word against mine. And who would be believed, the upstanding, honest lawyer, or his hysterical, grieving daughter?"

Ignoring his question, Jordan had to know more.

She had to understand how her father, a loving, compassionate man, could be responsible for all of the atrocities that had been committed. "How did this happen?"

Emerson was silent for a moment, his head resting on the back of his chair, his eyes closed. When he opened them again, he spoke slowly.

"It started a long time ago, Jordan. I made some bad investments. My inheritance was almost gone. I had to salvage something for you and Mom. Your mother means everything to me, Jordan. I couldn't let her see how I'd failed. I needed some cash. I went to the bank to take out a loan, and the loan officer hinted that he knew of a business that was extremely lucrative. I was curious, so he explained. Cautiously at first. But when he saw that I was interested, we set up a private appointment and he told me the rest later that night.

"I was stunned when he explained it all to me. Child pornography was always something I'd abhorred. I refused to get involved with him.

"But, as time went by, my finances got worse. After a while, I had nothing left to use for collateral without dragging Celeste into it. My credit record was shot. So, I went back to the loan officer.

"He assured me that the children they used were willing participants. He said that most of them were runaways who had been prostituting themselves just to make a living, and what we offered them, a roof over their heads, three meals a day, and partners free of AIDS, was a welcome change for them.

"Believe me, Jordan, I had nothing to do with Suzi being kidnapped. That was beyond my control. I forbade them to kidnap any children. They were ordered to use only the young prostitutes. After the incident with Suzi, I found out that they were actually buying some of the kids from their own parents. I put an end to that, too. I do have some scruples, you know."

"Scruples? What about having that man murdered? The one who kidnapped Suzi?"

"He was a fool. He couldn't be trusted anymore. He had to be disposed of."

"Disposed of? Dear God, what about Paige? Did you have her 'disposed of,' too?"

Emerson covered his face with his hands. "It wasn't supposed to happen like that. I am truly sorry. It seems that I can't hire anyone reliable. They were supposed to shoot at the house, just as a warning to Suzanne and Paige to quit snooping around. I knew that Derek had seen Suzanne, and when Paige suddenly showed up, I knew they were up to something. But I never meant for her to die."

"Did you seriously think that having someone come and shoot at the Kendell house would stop the F.B.I. or the police?"

"No, but without Suzanne's cooperation they wouldn't get very far, would they?"

"What about Alex? He was murdered, Dad. Did you do that, too?"

"He'd found out about me. A couple of my men had encountered him several weeks earlier, hanging out around a storefront we were getting ready to use. Later on, he found the warehouse we were using. One of my men saw him, recognized him from their earlier encounter. He followed Alex, got his license plate number, had it checked, and told me as soon as he knew who Alex was. He saw me there, Jordan. I couldn't let him tell anyone.

"Don't you see," he looked at her pleadingly, "he would have told everyone. He would have told you. I couldn't let him do that.

"Jordan, I love you. You're my little girl. I would never let anyone hurt you. I had to keep Alex from telling you about this. I had to stop him."

"So, you killed him."

"I didn't kill anyone. I kept my hands clean of those messy details."

"Three lives taken and you call them messy details? I don't know you at all, do I?"

"Please try to understand, Jordan. I did it all for you and your mother. If anything happened to me, she would have been destitute. She was almost destroyed when your brother died. I promised her then that nothing bad would ever happen to her again. When you were born, I made the same promise to you. Part of that promise was to make sure that you would always have an inheritance you could fall back on, if you needed it."

"Do you think I'd want any money from this? Do you think Mom will when she finds out? And what about Samuel Wyndham? You tried to frame him for all of this, didn't you? Why?"

Emerson looked at his daughter, sorrow creasing his face. "It was the crib, Jordan. That damnable crib that killed my son. Wyndham's people designed and manufactured those deathtraps. He had to be punished. He'd hurt other children. It only seemed fitting that he be blamed for this. This is justice, Jordan. Your brother died because of Samuel Wyndham. Don't you want to see him suffer?"

"It was a terrible accident, Dad. They couldn't have known that would happen."

"He needs to be punished."

"What about my house? I could have been killed in that fire."

Emerson shrugged his shoulders, looking incongruously sheepish. "That wasn't supposed to happen,

241

either. My man was supposed to scare you and keep you out of the house so he could find Alex's notes. He wasn't supposed to harm you. Bill Mason was just supposed to keep you occupied, keep your mind on other things."

"Bill Mason was working for you? Why? Are you paying his children's college bills?"

"Jordan, please try to understand. I had to do this. You must keep quiet about it."

"You are a murderer and arsonist, and you abuse young children. No, Dad, I won't keep quiet. I'll make sure everyone knows. You will be stopped, just as Alex said in his notes." She held the paper in front of him as she stood to leave.

As she walked toward the door, she heard him opening the drawer of his desk. She heard him pull the gun from underneath the secret panel, the panel she had been forbidden to touch when she was little.

"Jordan, you forget that several people died trying to stop me."

She turned, facing the gun, looking directly down the dark, menacing barrel. "You're going to shoot me? I thought you didn't do these messy details yourself."

"Give me the paper, Jordan."

"No."

"I don't need to cock the gun, Jordan. No scary sounds like on television to frighten you into sudden obedience. All I have to do is pull the trigger. Now, give me the paper."

"How will you explain my death to Mom?"

Emerson's hand began to shake. "Please, Jordan, give me the paper. Don't bring me down. Don't you love me? Can't you understand why I did all of this?"

"I love who I thought you were, Dad. And, no, I can't possibly understand why you've done any of this."

Jordan turned back, walking towards the door. Her father, his hand trembling, the revolver held shakily in his hand, lowered his arm, letting the gun fall into his lap.

"No, Jordan," he said faintly, "I can't shoot you."

Jordan walked down the hall. She found Nick in the front room, pacing in front of the fireplace. Before she could speak, the doorbell rang. Hendricks answered it and led Ed Colson and three other agents into the room.

"I'm sorry, Jordan," Nick explained, "I had to call them."

Ed walked over to Jordan. "Where is he?"

"In his den. Please be careful. He has a gun."

Nick looked up, startled, walking swiftly towards Jordan. "I never should have let you go in there."

Jordan placed her hand on Nick's arm. "It's all right. He's done a lot of horrible things, but I knew he wouldn't hurt me."

Ed nodded to two of the agents and they went

outside, one positioning herself outside the window, the other standing outside the French doors. Ed and the other agent, weapons drawn, walked slowly, cautiously towards the den.

There was no need for their caution. Emerson still sat in the same position as when Jordan left the room, the revolver resting in his lap.

With all weapons aimed at Emerson, Ed spoke firmly. "Put the gun down, Mr. Blake."

As the agents led Emerson from the house, he turned for one final glance at his daughter.

"I'm sorry that everything turned out this way, Jordan. Please try to understand."

As Jordan sank onto the couch, Nick sat down beside her, gently placing his arm around her shoulders and pulling her firmly beside him. "Are you going to wait for your mother to come home?"

Silently, full of apprehension, Jordan nodded.

*

Celeste Blake walked down the steps of the courthouse, supported on one side by Judge Kendell, Liza holding her other arm. They had stayed at her side throughout the long and arduous trial. Their own shock and pain was checked as they sought to console their friend.

Jordan followed them slowly down the steps, her arm around Suzanne's waist, Nick and Blaine just a few paces behind them. None of them spoke. The nightmare was over, and yet the future still seemed clouded.

So much pain had been endured. So many brutalities had been committed. Celeste's emotions had run the gamut during the trial from disbelief and denial to slow acceptance and anguish. When her life's partner had broken down on the witness stand, confessing to all he was accused of, she felt too weak to go on. Only the love of her daughter and her friends sustained her.

Suzanne had watched the trial dispassionately, as if all emotions were foreign. Now, as she followed her parents to the car, she resolved to find life again. With all of its joys and sorrows, she thought, I want to feel again.

Blaine hugged Jordan and Suzanne. Then, pausing to shake hands with Celeste, "I'll have you in my prayers, Mrs. Blake. I'm always near a phone, if you need me."

Jordan and Celeste thanked Blaine for coming, and once the farewells had been made, Blaine walked to her car.

Celeste had ridden to the courthouse each day with the Kendells, and she now assured Jordan that she would like to return with them.

"I need some time to myself, honey. You need to go be with Joshua. It's over. We have to step forward into the future with faith and hope, even though that seems impossible right now."

She kissed her daughter once on each cheek, gave her a long, tearful embrace, and climbed into the car.

Jordan and Nick stood watching as the black Lincoln left the parking lot. Then Nick held out his hand, taking Jordan's in his own.

She squeezed his fingers lightly. "Thank you for being here for all of this, Nick. I'm sure it was difficult for you."

Nick gazed up at the blue sky, and the trees surrounding the parking lot. "Difficult? Yes, but I had to be here. For Suzi and Paige. For Alex. And," he paused, looking down into grateful, shining brown eyes, "for you. Now, come on. Before I take you back to the Estate, I have something to show you."

As he led her to his car, he began to explain. "Your mother was right, you know. It's time to step into the future."

Nick closed the door behind Jordan, and went around to let himself into the driver's side. Jordan reached across to unlock his door, and he grasped her hand again before she could pull it away. Gently kissing her fingertips, he continued, "Now, no questions, and when we get there I'll explain everything."

"Get where?" Jordan couldn't stop herself from asking.

Nick let go of her hand and waved his finger in her face. "No questions, remember? I know you're exhausted. You're white as Caspar the Friendly Ghost, you've lost too much weight lately, and you're about as lively looking as a piece of hamburger."

"Thanks a lot," she burst in.

"Don't interrupt me. You've been taking care of Joshua and the Kendells and your mother. Now, I'm going to take care of you. So sit back, close your eyes if you like," then very gently, his hand caressing her cheek, "and try to put the darkness behind you."

They drove in silence. Jordan was indeed tired. The emotional strain of the past three months, since the day of her father's arrest, had taken their toll. She knew that she was thin and pale, though she wasn't sure she appreciated Nick's noticing that fact. But she was grateful to have him with her.

All his animosity had disappeared the night of the fire. She'd questioned him about that fact on several occasions, but he always waved her questions aside, assuring her that the time wasn't right.

Jordan closed her eyes, enjoying the strains of Brahms' Lullaby as it played on Nick's compact disk player. "Are you trying to put me to sleep?" she asked, comfortably settling into her seat.

"Absolutely."

As she dozed, she felt the car surge forward, each turn rocking her into a deeper slumber.

"We're here, Jordan," his voice spoke softly as his lips grazed hers.

Jordan sat up as Nick unbuckled her seatbelt. As she took in the sight before her, he hurried around the car, opening her door, and holding his hand out for her.

Grasping his hand, Jordan climbed out, staring wonderingly at the house. "It's finished, isn't it?"

Jordan had turned all of her projects over to Quentin Galbraith on the day of her father's arrest. This house, the Smith house on what had once been Grant and Lauren Palmer's property, now greeted her with sunlight glinting off of the windows and a plush, newly-planted lawn beckoning at her feet.

"It's finished. Although, when you turned the project over to Quentin, we had to rely on Barbara to help with all of the finishing touches. Would you like to go in?"

"I'm sure Barbara did a wonderful job." Then, "What do you mean, 'we'?"

Nick reached into his back pocket and pulled a key out, a pink ribbon looped through the hole and tied carefully in a bow. "We, as in Mr. Smith and me. Well, would you like to go in?" he repeated.

Jordan walked toward the lawn, stopping to sniff the large, red Mr. Lincoln roses which now lined the front walk. "How do you know Mr. Smith?"

Nick standing next to Jordan, bent over and whispered in her ear, "I hired him to commission you to build this house."

Silence.

"Jordan, I built this house for you. I mean, you and I and Quentin and Barbara built this house for you."

Jordan felt too stunned to speak. She looked from Nick's adoring gaze to the house and back to Nick. "Why?"

Nick pulled her into his arms, holding her firmly with one strong arm as his free hand traced her jawline, the shape of her lips, and then slipped around her neck, resting at the base, his fingers softly massaging the muscles at the back.

"Because I love you, Jordan. Because you make me weak and foolish. Because even when I was trying to hate you, you had this incredible power to melt me, and I knew that you had to have this house. Besides, a long time ago I gave you a little cottage and made a promise to you. It's a promise I never forgot." As she stared at him mutely, he asked tenderly, "Can't you say anything?"

Jordan, her lips turning up into a slow smile, shook her head.

Nick bent to kiss her. "I love you, Jordan. Alex wasn't able to give you a happily ever after, but maybe you and I

245

can build one together, here, with our son, in this house."

"You know?" Jordan gasped breathlessly.

"Yes, beautiful, I know. But, I was too dense to figure it out for myself. And my ever lovin' mother was too faithful to you to say anything. So, Luke told me."

"You don't mind?"

"Mind?" he whooped in her ear as he planted several kisses on her face, her ear, and her neck. "The only thing I'll mind is if you tell me that you can never love me again, and that you don't want anything to do with this house, and that your happily ever after doesn't include me."

Jordan pulled on the back of his head, and standing on tiptoe, kissed him--softly at first, then with growing ardour as passion filled her soul.

When she stopped and tried to release him, he held her solidly against his chest. "Translation, please," he said quietly, urgently.

Jordan wriggled out of his grasp, pulling him by the arm toward the steps of the house. "Let me see what you've done to the inside of my house, first. Then I'll give you my answer."

- The End -

Tamalyn Nicholas

Tamalyn Nicholas lives in Long Beach, California, with her husband, Gary, and their two children, a son and a daughter. Now in the adventurous years of raising one full-fledged and one soon-to-be teenager, she finds that reading and writing offer many opportunities for escape! She believes wholeheartedly that her children are the true angels in her life, although they occasionally sprout devil's horns.

An ordained minister, Tamalyn's many interests include Feminist Theology, Christian Education, investigating her Irish and Scottish roots, and all things chocolate. She is also an enthusiastic camper, pet owner, and voracious reader of romance novels. If you need suggestions on good writers to investigate, she'll happily share her list of favorites with you. You may contact her at her e-mail address: RavensFthr@aol.com.

Tamalyn is currently working on two more novels, one contemporary, one historical. She's also completing her collection of story sermons and a book about women's roles within the church.

Petals of Life Order Form

Order Your Copy of *The Raven's Feather by Tamalyn Nicholas*!

We have two ordering options available:

1. Simply return to <http://www.petalsoflife.com> and click on the book cover to order as a download, electronic book, or print version. We accept virtual checks.

2. Please print and fill in the order form on this page to pay by regular check.

Mail Your Order To:

Petals of Life
231-C Oil Well Road
Jackson, TN 38305

Name:_____

Address:_____

City, State, Zip:_____

# of E-books (PDF) as downloads _____ @ $3.00 each _____

E-Mail address to send book to:_____

List additional addresses below if you are sending several copies:

# of E-Books on Disk (PDF) _____ @ $6.50 each = _____
ISBN 1-892745-15-1

# of Handcrafted Books _____ @ $20.00 each = _____
ISBN 1-892745-14-3

(above charges include shipping and handling)

Total = $ _____

Thank You For Your Order!